TESTIMONIALS

The title of this lovely book really says it all: but what it cannot convey is the sheer joy of learning so much about the beautiful vegan cuisine available to us, and how easy it is to make sensational dishes which will delight everyone eager to eat well and healthily. At once scholarly and entertaining, it is gloriously illustrated and the recipes are easy-peasy to follow. It's for everyone who wants the world to be a better place for animals, for plants and for us. Delicious in every way.

JOANNA LUMLEY

If you have a small plot, this is for you, if you have a balcony, this is for you, if you have a window box, this is for you, and if all you have is hope, this is for you. This book works at all levels, and it has compassion and love on every page.

Piers and Ella have created a very special book that is informative, and demystifies the art of being vegan and growing vegan. Their knowledge is vast, and the journey they take the reader on, from the soil to the plate, and to the kitchen, through the year, is original and insightful. That said, there is something else I get from these pages, and that is an overwhelming feeling that they both really care.

After reading this brilliant book something strange came over me, I just wanted to eat it. It's that good.

BENJAMIN ZEPHANIAH
poet, writer and musician

This is a particularly useful resource for those keen to grow then cook with their own food. Information is easy to access with chronological and alphabetical sections including what to sow, plant and harvest by month, with tips for growing each type of fruit and veg and vegan recipes using seasonal harvest. Punctuated by beautiful photographs, this is both a useful and inspirational book.

SAFFIA FARR
editor, JUNO Magazine

This is an exciting time to be part of the sustainable food movement and the vegan movement. They are both steadily gaining traction, and Piers and Ella invite us to make connections between the two movements – connections we cannot ignore. We must strive to create alternative food systems, and methods of growing food, that include both human and non-human animals into our community of compassion. Filled with great ideas for tasty recipes from the garden, this book will also introduce you to a more compassionate way of taking control of your own food.

LIZ ROSS
co-founder of Vegan Advocacy Initiative

Everyday I learn something new about veganism – despite being vegan for 20 years!

Reading *Vegan Cook and Gardener* is taking my plant based diet to the next level. With expert advice on growing your own vegetables, advice on sprouting, herbs and oils, this book also holds our hand with the best time to plant your veggies, when to sow and how to store. So, basically everything you need to know whether you feel supermarket foods don't taste like they used to, or perhaps you're fed up buying something that has travelled from overseas that could be grown on your doorstep – or like me you can't stand all of the unnecessary packaging ... whatever your reason, this is the must have book.

The seasonal recipes feature what you have grown and what shou[ld be ready] to each mon[th ... I have]n't seen a recipe that doesn't appeal to me. So watch this space on v[   ]u more about how I am getting on for the first time growing my own [   ]

RS
.tv

presenter, radio, vegan media and

I LOVE this book! As a nutritionist I'd been thinking for a while that I'd like to learn more about how food is produced. As a vegan I was pondering the conundrum of how, if I was to grow my own, I would keep pests at bay and also be in harmony with the planet? And then this landed in my inbox! A real treatise on the subject of permaculture.

Exhaustive, written in words that the layperson can understand and beautifully illustrated throughout (I would expect nothing less from a project that Piers was involved with). An amazing introduction to a philosophy which really resonates with me; becoming at one with the ecosystem. Truly fascinating and illuminating!

PAUL KERTON
YouTuber, Hench Herbivore

I'm really impressed by the attention to detail in this book. It is beautifully presented and an extensive tool to guide you towards a self-sustainable plant based diet starting from your gardening fork, ending with your table fork and everything in between. The recipes in the book look fantastic and I absolutely love the fact that the author lays out the benefits of a vegan diet being better for the planet, our health and for the animals. A truly invaluable horticultural resource.

EMMA PAGE
the Banana Warrior Princess (YouTube)

Current western expectations for meat and dairy to be available on the table three times a day, seven days a week, 52 weeks a year are globally unsustainable by any standards. In this beautiful book Piers and Ella show that another way is not only possible, but can provide opportunities to live abundantly and whilst doing the least harm to our fellow Earth Citizens, both human and non-human – Be well fed with not an animal dead!

GRAHAM BURNETT
permaculture teacher and author of
Vegan Book of Permaculture

The Vegan Cook and Gardener is a thorough guide into just how easy and rewarding following a plant based diet can be. Piers and Ella not only explain the huge health benefits for following a vegan diet, but they guide the reader carefully through how they can make minimal impact on the planet by growing and producing your own food.

To be plant based is one thing, but to be truly vegan, is to care about the world, the animals and the environment. To simply leave meat and dairy out of one's diet is not enough, if people are still purchasing supermarket products shrink wrapped in plastic that are being imported from all over the world with dire environmental consequences.

This book will show the reader how we can take the future of the planet into our own hands and be part of a revolution that will enlighten others into a reversal of today's adverse climatic changes and eventually see a return to not just a healthier body, void of preservatives and chemicals, but a healthier planet too.

ANNEKA SVENSKA
vegan and wildlife presenter

This is the book I have always wanted. It is gorgeous, and absolutely brimming with practical, hard-to-find information. It covers everything from organic gardening, permaculture and self-sufficiency, to detailed information about individual foods and gorgeous recipes. *The Vegan Cook and Gardener* is destined to become a cherished and trusted companion for vegans everywhere, and for all those wanting to make more conscious food choices.

BRENDA DAVIS
co-author of *Becoming Vegan: Comprehensive and Express Editions*

The Vegan
Cook & Gardener

Growing, storing and cooking delicious healthy food
all year round

PIERS WARREN & ELLA BEE GLENDINING

WITHDRAWN

Permanent Publications

Published by
Permanent Publications
Hyden House Ltd
The Sustainability Centre
East Meon
Hampshire GU32 1HR
United Kingdom
Tel: 0844 846 846 4824 (local rate UK only)
         or +44 (0)1730 823 311
Fax: 01730 823 322
Email: enquiries@permaculture.co.uk
Web: www.permanentpublications.co.uk

Distributed in the USA by
Chelsea Green Publishing Company, PO Box 428, White River Junction, VT 05001
www.chelseagreen.com

© 2019 Piers Warren and Ella Glendining
The right of Piers Warren and Ella Glendining to be identified as the author of this work has been asserted
by them in accordance with the Copyrights, Designs and Patents Act 1998

Photography by Piers Warren and Ella Glendining

Designed by Two Plus George Limited, www.TwoPlusGeorge.co.uk

Printed in the UK by Bell & Bain, Thornliebank, Glasgow

All paper from FSC certified mixed sources

The Forest Stewardship Council (FSC) is a non-profit international organisation
established to promote the responsible management of the world's forests.
Products carrying the FSC label are independently certified to assure
consumers that they come from forests that are managed to meet the social,
economic and ecological needs of present and future generations.

British Library Cataloguing-in-Publication Data
A catalogue record for this book is available from the British Library

ISBN 978 1 85623 318 7

All rights reserved. No part of this publication may be reproduced, stored in a retrieval system, rebound or
transmitted in any form or by any means, electronic, mechanical, photocopying, recording or otherwise,
without the prior permission of Hyden House Limited.

CONTENTS

About the Authors   viii
Foreword   ix

1. Introduction *page 1*

2. Why Vegan? *page 3*

3. Vegan Organic Growing *page 7*

Soil Fertility	8	Compost Teas	11	Dealing with Pests	12
Compost	8	Plant Teas	11	Barriers	14
Hot Composting	9	Other Vegan Organic		Relocation	14
Leaf Mould	9	Fertilisers	11	Companion Planting	15
Mulching	9	Crop Rotation	11		
Green Manures	10	Dealing with Weeds	12		

4. Permaculture *page 17*

The Ethics of		Forest Gardening	19
Permaculture	17	Courses	19

5. Self-sufficiency *page 21*

Choosing What to Grow	22	Successional Sowing	22	Crop Storage	24
Planning Quantities	22	Growing Under Cover	23	Seed Saving	27

6. Ingredients *page 29*

Sourcing Ingredients	29	Sweeteners	31	Nuts and Seeds	35
Improvising Recipes	30	Grains	33	Spices	37
Oils	30	Pulses	34	Other Ingredients	39

7. Herbs *page 41*

Basil	42	Fennel	42	Rosemary	44
Bay	42	Lavender	43	Sage	45
Chives	42	Lemon Balm	43	Savory	45
Coriander	42	Marjoram and Oregano	43	Tarragon	45
Cumin	42	Mint	44	Thyme	45
Dill	42	Parsley	44		

8. Salad Leaves *page* 47

Recommended Lettuce Varieties	48	Other Salad Plants	49

9. Sprouting *page* 51

Method	51	Sourcing Seeds	52
Equipment	51	Commonly Sprouted Seeds	52

10. Growing throughout the Year *page* 55

11. Fruits and Vegetables *page* 63

Apples	63	Cherries	75	Pears	87
Apricots	64	Chinese Cabbage	76	Peas	88
Artichoke – Globe	64	Courgettes	76	Pepper – Capsicum	88
Artichoke – Jerusalem	65	Cucumber	77	Pepper – Chilli	89
Asparagus	66	Currants – Black, Red,		Plums	90
Aubergine	66	White	78	Potatoes	91
Beans – Broad	67	Figs	78	Pumpkins and Squash	93
Beans – French	68	Florence Fennel	79	Radish	93
Beans – Runner	69	Garlic	79	Raspberries	94
Beetroot	70	Gooseberries	80	Rhubarb	95
Broccoli and Calabrese	71	Grapes	82	Spinach	95
Brussels Sprouts	71	Kale	82	Strawberries	96
Cabbage	72	Leeks	83	Swede	96
Carrots	73	Melon	84	Sweet Corn	97
Cauliflower	73	Onions	84	Tomatoes	98
Celeriac	74	Pak Choi	85	Turnips	99
Celery	74	Parsnips	86		
Chard	75	Peaches and Nectarines	86		

12. Challenging Crops *page* 101

Blueberries	101	Ginger	103	Quinoa	105
Chickpeas	102	Mushrooms	103	Soya Beans	107
Citrus	102	Nuts	104	Sweet Potatoes	107

13. Cooking throughout the Year *page* 109

JANUARY

Leek, Mushroom and Potato Pie   112
Lentil, Split Pea and Sun-dried Tomato
   Bolognese   114
Celeriac Mash   116
Carrot Cake with Macadamia and
   Cashew Icing   118

FEBRUARY

Sprouting Broccoli Gratin with
   Homemade Vegan Parmesan   122
Creamy Leek and Mushroom Pasta Sauce 124
Parsnip Hash Browns   126
Beetroot Brownies   128

MARCH

Purple Sprouting Broccoli Spring Salad   132
Crunchy Baked Kale   134
Cauliflower Steak with Tomato Sauce
   and Caper Relish   136
Apple and Blackberry Crumble   138

APRIL

Artichoke and Broccoli Pizza   142
Vegan Arancini   144
Aloo Gobi   146
Rhubarb and Orange Sorbet   148

MAY

Asparagus with Vegan Hollandaise Sauce 152
New Potato and Chickpea Stew   154
Lentil and Spinach Burger   156
Red Currant Shortbread   158

JUNE

Broad Bean Risotto   162
Asparagus Spanakopita   164
Walnut Pesto   166
Raspberry Truffles   168

JULY

Asparagus Quiche   172
Spinach and Pea Gnocchi   174
Arrabbiata Tomato Sauce   176
Chocolate and Strawberry Cake   178

AUGUST

Stuffed Aubergine   182
French Beans with Crispy Shallots and
   Toasted Almonds   184
Spitfire Sauce   186
Nectarine Delight   188

SEPTEMBER

Vegan Paella with Artichoke Hearts   192
Ratatouille   194
Green Houmous   196
Blueberry Flan   198

OCTOBER

Sweet Potato Shepherd's Pie   202
Homemade Vegan Gravy   204
Saint's Love Soup   206
Caponata   208
Fig and Dark Chocolate Tart   210

NOVEMBER

Pumpkin Soup   214
Homemade Baked Beans   216
Butternut Squash Pasta   218
Easy-Peasy Grape Ice Cream   220

DECEMBER

Swede, Sweet Potato and Bean Goulash   224
Cauliflower Couscous   226
Parsnip, Orange and Chestnut Winter
   Salad, with Homemade Tahini Sauce 228
Apple and Oat Cookie-cakes   230

Resources *page* 233

Index *page* 237

ABOUT THE AUTHORS

Piers Warren and Ella Bee Glendining are a father and daughter team who are both experienced vegan cooks.

Piers is a conservationist, author and keen grower of organic fruit and vegetables. He is the founder and Principal of Wildeye – The International School of Wildlife Film-making – and has written a dozen books, including the bestselling *How to Store Your Garden Produce*, plus hundreds of magazine articles. He has a long interest in self-sufficiency and permaculture and is convinced that growing your own food and following a vegan lifestyle are important contributions to lowering your carbon footprint and living more lightly on the Earth. He is on the council of GreenSpirit.

Ella Bee is a passionate advocate of animal rights, having been vegetarian since the age of five and making the transition to veganism several years ago. She's spent much time since experimenting with different ingredients and developing delicious new recipes. Ella is also a film-maker and physical theatre performer.

ACKNOWLEDGEMENTS

A huge thanks to Maddy and Tim Harland from Permanent Publications for publishing this book and working with us to produce it. Thanks also to the production team including Rozie Apps and Nicola Willmot.

Thanks to Matthew Nodwell for the cover photos of Piers and Ella (all other photos were taken by the authors).

Many thanks to all the following who helped and supported the production of this book in various ways: Graham Burnett, Nicole Vosper, Stella Hughes, Rose Titchiner, Mary Coates, Nina Ashton, Fiona Ballantine, Saint Ananda, John Winters and Karon O'Flanagan.

Finally, a big hello to our friends at Norwich Vegans: Penny Franiel, Lee Rose, Paul Kerton (aka Hench Herbivore), Gemma Nichols, James Green, Lisa and Emily Alaniz and the rest of the crew.

FOREWORD

At last, here we have a book that gives us up-to-date and comprehensive information on veganic gardening (gardening organically without using animal manures and other animal by-products such as blood, fish and bone) all in one place. Before this book, there was only *Veganic Gardening* by Kenneth Dalziel O'Brien, published in 1986. This was a good and innovative book in its time, but it's now very dated since it lacks newer fruit and veg varieties and recent innovations in gardening. *Growing Green – Organic Techniques for a Sustainable Future* by Jenny Hall and Iain Tolhurst is also a veganic book, but it is aimed at farmers, and gardening isn't farming – the techniques and the machinery can be very different.

There are plenty of people who say it can't be done, that animal manures are essential in organic farming and gardening. It's an easy thing for them to say since it's outside of what they know. Luckily, there's a growing number of farmers and gardeners who have grown veganically very successfully. Convincing the doubters is another matter, but this important book is going to help with this. A critic would also say that veganic gardening is undesirable and impossible since we are 'using' worms, beetles, etc., which are animals. But no, it's only farmed animals and their by-products that vegans are seeking to avoid. The worms and wildlife are there naturally, we haven't introduced them, and we're happy to have them helping us, there's no exploitation in that.

Many people, particularly scientific people, think that organic gardening means substituting synthetic pesticides for natural pesticides, and natural doesn't always mean benign. I'm pleased to see that this book doesn't fall for this substitution, and uses the stand aside approach, instead encouraging wildlife to keep problems at a low level. My belief is that we should look as 'pests' as creatures that are just as eager to feed themselves as we are, and to try to find kinder ways to deal with the problems that they cause. This is something that veganic gardening also tries to achieve; it's not just about avoiding animal manures and animal-based organic fertilisers. Both conventional and (non-vegan) organic gardeners rarely show any mercy to slugs, snails and pigeons.

To my mind, an ideal book on veganic gardening is in two parts. The first part discuses the techniques – composting, nutrients, whether to dig or not, etc. The second part moves on to a list of fruit, veg and herbs, how to grow them, when and how far apart to sow or plant them, how much sun and water they like, etc. We get both of these parts in this book, but we also get a third part – vegan recipes, incorporating ingredients from the garden, either fresh or stored. We get plenty of helpful photos too.

Do we need a book anymore? Why not use the internet? There is some information there on veganic gardening. The problem is that it's not all in one place, there are lots of gaps and contradictory advice, and the people who write it don't always make it clear what country and climate they are referring to, possibly making the information irrelevant to what we have in the UK and countries with similar climates. Being able to sit back at the end of the day with a real physical book has its attractions, no distractions by clicking here there and everywhere, going off on a tangent. Enjoy this book and enjoy your garden!

JOHN CURTIS
volunteer and garden adviser at
the Vegan Organic Network,
www.veganorganic.net

Pasta butternut squash, see page 218

1. INTRODUCTION

Welcome to the wonderful world of the most ethical, healthy and environmentally friendly diet possible, and also to the fun, self-reliance and planet-saving benefits of growing your own food. This book isn't just for those with large gardens or allotments; anyone can grow their own crops, even if it's just a few pots of herbs on a windowsill.

There is a current surge in interest in vegan food, as more people are starting to realise its beneficial impact on the future of planet earth as well as for improved personal health and animal welfare. As vegans for some years, our motivation to produce this book started when we discovered that many vegan cookbooks often contain long, complicated recipes with unusual ingredients that leave the readers unsure where they could obtain them (let alone what they would taste like), confirming the suspicion with some that vegan cooking is difficult. We aim to show that delicious vegan meals can be prepared with common everyday ingredients, which eases the path for those in the early stages of veganism, those who are busy, those who simply want a few new healthy recipes, and also for the many non-vegan relatives and friends who are frightened at the thought of adapting meals for vegans.

Furthermore, we meet many vegans who don't grow any of their food because they feel they don't have enough time, space or knowhow. We hope to show that anyone can grow something, will get enjoyment and exercise from doing so, and along the way will help in the fight against food miles, agrochemicals and climate change. As the future of the climate and global food production becomes more unpredictable, being able to grow your own food may be increasingly necessary as well as economical.

We start with an exploration of the benefits of veganism – for oneself, animals, other people and the planet. Then we look at the many reasons and methods for eating and growing organically, including how to deal with pests, weeds and soil fertility. An introduction to (vegan) permaculture shows how this applies holistically to how we live our lives, grow our food, and how various techniques can be used by someone growing a few crops at home.

We then take a look at self-sufficiency; what to grow and how much of it; whether you just want to grow a few favourites or aim for full food production. This is followed by a chapter on ingredients; where to obtain any vegan food items that you don't grow yourself, making sure they are as healthy as possible for you and the planet.

We then move on to the food production chapters, starting with a look at herbs, which can be grown on any scale; salad leaves, which can be produced all year round; and sprouting seeds, which can be done in the kitchen at any time.

We follow this by taking a closer look at growing throughout the seasons – when to sow or plant which crops, when to harvest them, and other jobs around the plot as we move through the months. This is followed by a more in-depth look at the most commonly grown fruits and vegetables, including recommended varieties, how to grow and harvest them, and storage techniques to keep you eating your home-grown produce throughout the year. We then look at further crops that you can have a go at growing at home which are more challenging or unusual.

Next is our main cooking chapter, which gives a selection of recipes month by month. Each one features at least one main ingredient that will be ready to harvest fresh from your plot that month, plus others that you may have in storage from earlier harvests.

Finally a section of resources that is packed with links and information about organisations, blogs/websites, YouTube channels, magazines, books, films, festivals, courses and suppliers, all of which are connected with veganism and growing your own food.

Happy growing and happy cooking!

2. WHY VEGAN?

Veganism is a way of living that seeks to exclude, as far as possible and practicable, all forms of exploitation of, and cruelty to, animals, whether that be for food, clothing or any other purpose.

Indeed, over the last few decades, the main reason people have turned to veganism has been through a desire to improve animal welfare. While some see the many health benefits as merely a bonus, increasing numbers of top athletes are now turning to a vegan diet as the optimum for fitness and strength. More recently, the realisation that the livestock industry worldwide is a huge contributor to climate change is causing many people to consume less meat and dairy in the fight against carbon emissions. Although the total number of vegans is still a small percentage of the population, the growth in numbers in the last 10 years (estimated at 350% in Britain alone) has caused veganism to be called the fastest growing social movement.

For many, veganism is the next step after becoming vegetarian, although there is perhaps more cruelty in the dairy and egg industries than in meat production, and the industries are closely linked. As cows, like humans, only produce milk having given birth, in order for humans to consume the milk, the calves are torn away from their mothers when only a few hours old, only to be shot or sent to veal crates overseas. Millions of day-old male chicks (useless for egg production) are tossed live into a grinder, suffocated or left to starve, not to mention the awful conditions most laying birds are kept in (free-range or not), and the list of horrors could go on and on. The animals we eat, from cattle to chickens to fish, are sentient beings with complex relationships with each other. Above all, they too want to avoid suffering and not die. Research shows that even lobsters and crabs feel pain – being boiled alive is not a good way to go.

The atrocities carried out in order to provide cheap animal protein are largely unknown to the general public. There is a reason for Linda McCartney's (now famous) phrase, "if slaughterhouses had glass walls the whole world would be vegetarian" and the same principle applies to the egg and dairy industries. Much of the hidden cruelty happens long before the abattoir however: piglets have teeth clipped and tails docked (without anaesthetic) before embarking on short lives, often in highly overcrowded concrete pens; chicks have beaks painfully clipped, then are reared in sheds housing tens of thousands of others; ducks are kept in similar conditions without access to water; goat kids are dehorned; most animals are artificially inseminated (in what even the industry call 'rape-racks') and deprived of space, daylight, fresh air and natural food. Furthermore, most animals are just babies when they are killed for meat: chickens at seven weeks old, pigs and turkeys at six months, beef cattle at 1-2 years; all these are animals with natural life spans of 10-25 years. Fish, which certainly feel pain, are vacuumed up in the billions by massive fishing trawlers and suffocate to death, while millions of turtles, dolphins, birds and other animals are killed as collateral damage in the process. However well this is hidden, all this horrendous activity is funded by those who eat meat and dairy.

As well as reducing this suffering, the personal health benefits of a cruelty-free diet are increasingly clear, backed up by science, and now recognised by leading organisations including the British Dietetic Association, American Dietetic Association, World Health Organization and more. Vegans are less likely to suffer from all the major diseases: cancer, heart problems, diabetes, obesity etc. and, on average, live longer than omnivores. Vegan diets have also been proven to be beneficial for sufferers of arthritis, asthma, cataracts, chronic obstructive pulmonary disease, fibromyalgia, kidney disease, depression, Alzheimer's, dementia, and many other conditions.

Our digestive systems and metabolism have evolved to thrive on plant-based diets as increasing amounts of scientific research prove – such as *The China Study* (see the Resources section at the end of this book). We have the same digestive systems and dentition as our close relatives, gorillas, who thrive almost entirely on shoots, leaves and fruits (the ants and termites they occasionally eat make up less than 0.1% of their diet). They clearly get enough protein and other dietary requirements from this plant-based diet to grow immensely strong. People eat so much meat and dairy worldwide simply because they like the taste – a shallow reason to fund cruelty and climate change at the expense of our own health, especially when vegan food can be extremely delicious.

Many people grew up eating meat and dairy not only because it was the norm, but also due to the massive power of marketing. For example, over several generations we have been led to believe that milk is essential for good bones and strong teeth whilst in fact osteoporosis (brittle bones caused by calcium deficiency) is more common in milk-drinkers than in vegans because animal proteins cause acidity in the body, which then leaches calcium from the bones to counteract it. Most of this calcium is then excreted in the urine, together with the acids, and therefore lost to the body. Numerous large-scale scientific studies have shown that diets high in animal protein cause bone loss, while diets high in vegetable protein actually increase bone density. Cow's milk was, after all, designed for calves not humans, and is only a recent addition to our diet in evolutionary terms.

You only have to question why we are the only species to drink another species' milk, and the only species to continue to consume milk long after weaning, to wonder if it is really necessary.

The same goes for the classic misconceptions that vegan diets are low in protein, iron, or omega 3 – all of which are plentiful in the right vegetables. Like any diet, there are good and bad ends of the spectrum; if all you ate were vegan burgers and chips, then you would get ill, as you would if you only ate beef burgers and chips. A balanced diet of a selection of fruits and vegetables is undeniably the healthiest around. Not only that, but switching to Whole Food Plant-Based diets (often known as WFPB diets), even late in life, has increasingly been shown to be able to reverse major life-threatening conditions such as cancers, heart disease and diabetes in a remarkably short space of time.

Here are just a few examples of sources of essential nutrients:

Protein (for building body tissues such as muscles)
Most vegetables include some protein but those with significant amounts include spinach, broccoli, avocados, sweet corn, peas, beans, lentils, mushrooms, nuts and seeds.

Carbohydrates (main fuel for energy)
Bread, oats, rice, pasta, potatoes, beans, peas, lentils.

Fats (carry vitamins and energy to cells)
Seeds, nuts, avocados, oils.

Fibre (keeps bowels healthy, reduces cholesterol)
All fruits, vegetables and whole grains.

Calcium (for healthy bones and teeth)
Almonds, broccoli, kale, beans.

Iron (essential for red blood cells to carry oxygen around the body)
Lentils, dried fruits, soya beans, spinach, sunflower seeds, chickpeas, dark green leafy vegetables, parsley.

Omega 3 fatty acids (important to reduce the likelihood of heart disease, arthritis, depression and dementia)
Walnuts, broccoli, spinach, soya beans, chia seeds, flax seeds.

Many of the vitamins and minerals we need for health are present in brightly coloured foods such as carrots, peppers, dark green leafy vegetables, tomatoes, aubergines and broccoli, which is why 'eating a rainbow' is recommended as a healthy way to approach meals.

B12 is one vitamin that you may need to supplement, but that is true for everyone, not just vegans. B12 is produced by bacteria in the soil, and is important in our bodies for the formation of red blood cells, replicating DNA and maintenance of the nervous system. We used to get our B12 from small amounts of soil residue left on vegetables, or via meat as a result of the animals ingesting some soil with their grazing. But modern pesticides kill B12-producing bacteria and so many farm animals are given B12 supplements themselves, some of which can be passed on to meat-eaters (but not enough, so all over-50s are recommended to supplement B12 regardless of their diets). As B12 is destroyed by heating, cooked meat is not a reliable source in any case. But these days it's easy to get enough B12, either through fortified foods such as nutritional yeast, breakfast cereals and plant milks, or in tablet form. The Vegan Society produce tablets called Veg1 which are designed specifically for vegans (though suitable for everyone) which contain recommended daily allowances of vitamins B2, B6, B12, D, folic acid, iodine and selenium.

If you would like to find out more about nutrition and health we recommend *The Incredible Vegan Health Report* (what science and experience say about vegan diets and human health), which refers to many of the latest findings with numerous scientific references. It can be downloaded free.* Another great resource is the website www.nutritionfacts.org – the latest in nutrition-related research delivered in easy to understand video segments brought to you by Dr. Michael Greger MD.

As mentioned, it has become increasingly clear that the meat and dairy industries are major contributors

* www.vivahealth.org.uk/veganhealth/report

to climate change (more than all the world's transport systems put together). It may feel easier to switch to a green energy supplier or use public transport more, but the greatest thing you can personally do to reduce climate change is to become vegan. There are many other ecological disasters associated with the drive for animal protein: for example, current projections are that by 2050 there will be no viable stocks of fish left in the world's oceans. The major cause of global deforestation (especially in vulnerable places like the Amazon) is to grow crops (such as soya) to feed livestock for meat production. However, replacing meat with soya in the human diet reduces the clearance of natural vegetation, per kilogramme of protein, by 96%.

Veganism can be summed up in three words: 'respect for life'. We are all connected. How can we feel at peace when we are causing so much cruelty every day? When more than a billion animals are slaughtered for food every year in the UK alone? There is nothing humane or ethical about slaughterhouses, no matter how modern they are. If you're not sure what truly happens in them, then we urge you to watch the documentary *Earthlings* (see Resources). It's a harrowing experience, but then if just watching a film is traumatising, imagine what it's like for the creatures for whom this life is a pitiful reality. There is nothing less valuable about the lives of pigs (who are more intelligent than dogs) than the pets we love and care for.

Respect for life extends to other humans too, of course. A billion people worldwide do not have enough to eat, yet the amount of grain fed to cattle to provide the West with burgers could alleviate all hunger in the world. The plant food needed to produce just one pound of meat could feed 10 people for an entire day. It is unjust in the extreme.

It is a myth that being a vegan is difficult. Once you get into the swing of which foods work for you (for example your favourite plant-based milks and cheeses), where you can eat out, and how to create simple but delicious meals at home, you'll wonder why it took you so long! In fact two of the most common things we hear from other vegans are, "I wish I'd started years ago", and "I know I'll never go back".

Nothing about being vegan needs to be arduous. Embracing a new diet goes hand in hand with creativity in the kitchen and opens you up to a whole new world of exciting prospects. It's perfect for those who like to improvise when cooking and come up with their own recipes or variants. For the gadget fan there are increasing numbers of food-tech gizmos available such as super-blenders, liquidisers, processors, juicers, smoothie-makers, steamers, dehydrators and spiralizers, and you may wish to explore other aspects of vegan diets such as eating more raw foods. Many of us do already eat a substantial amount of raw food with salads, fruits, smoothies and so on, but aiming for 50% raw or higher may lead to greater energy and many other health benefits, as well as making meal preparation quick and easy.

It's not all about eating though. Banishing animal suffering from your life will involve buying cruelty-free beauty and household products, clothing, footwear, medicines and so on. As the vegan market explodes, there are more and more options, and knowing you are following a lifestyle of reduced exploitation will make you feel great! Ethical Consumer (both a magazine and website) is a top source of information when comparing products and services to find the most ethical choice. The research takes into consideration which companies do more harm than others when it comes to animal rights, the environment, the workers producing the goods, etc., as well as many aspects which you may never even have considered. You don't have to do everything at once, and risk being overwhelmed by change: baby-step your way to a more ethical and healthy life!

Being vegan is all about caring for others, and so is intrinsically linked to other activities such as reducing your carbon footprint, supporting and/or volunteering for charities, engaging in political activism, spreading the word about how we can make the world a better place, and challenging fear and greed by spreading hope and compassion. Furthermore, numerous research studies have shown that the more we help and care for others, the happier we are ourselves.

If you feel isolated we recommend joining a local vegan society or club (most cities have them these days), which will organise regular meetings, meals out and other social activities. It's a great way to make new like-minded friends and support each other. There are also vegan festivals springing up all over, where thousands of people get together for a few days of workshops, talks, cookery demonstrations and so on, with hundreds of stalls where you can try different foods, find out about vegan-related organisations and activities, and buy vegan clothes and other merchandise. Facebook and YouTube are used by thousands of vegans to spread their news and views. There are also several vegan magazines available, packed full of recipes, news and tips, which can keep you motivated and inspired. Membership of organisations like VIVA! and The Vegan Society are great ways to get regular support and ideas. Details of all these and many more can be found in the Resources chapter.

There are already millions of vegans in the world, living healthy, cruelty-free lives, and more people are joining them every day as the horrors of the meat and dairy industries are further exposed. It's easier than ever to eat out as a vegan, and as more and more exciting alternatives and ingredients are becoming available, the easier it is to cook delicious food at home. This book, however, focuses on eating the very best kind of food – that which you have grown yourself.

Veganism has certainly boosted our enjoyment of growing and cooking food, and we hope you'll feel the same way too.

3. VEGAN ORGANIC GROWING

Growing your own food organically is the perfect partner to veganism for living more lightly on the earth, respecting life, and ensuring what you eat is healthy, fresh and delicious. It can be done at any level, from keeping potted herbs on a windowsill or growing vegetables in your back garden, to aiming for near self-sufficiency from a larger plot or allotment.

To grow organically means to use no chemical pesticides, herbicides, fungicides or artificial fertilisers. Furthermore, organic crops should not be genetically modified (GM), radiated or processed with chemicals in any way. Growing organically should go hand in hand with aims to lower our carbon footprints and care for the earth: using sustainable methods, reusing materials or using recycled products, improving biodiversity, using as little packaging as possible and as little fossil fuel energy as possible (ideally none).

An organic certification does, however, allow farmers to use animal products such as manure, blood, fish and bone to fertilise their soil. Some of these are purchased from slaughterhouses and can contain antibiotics, hormones, pesticides and other chemicals to which the animals have been exposed, as well as any pathogens they may have carried. Obviously this does not fit in well with vegan principles. The approach of growing without any animal input, focusing on plant-based soil fertility and using natural methods to reduce losses to pests, weeds and diseases has become known as vegan organic agriculture or stockfree organic growing (or veganic growing in certain countries like the US).

Initially there were sceptics who assumed it was impossible to create fertile soil without animal manures and remains, but there have now been a number of vegan organic enterprises that have been running extremely successfully for enough decades to prove that it is the ideal growing system for health and productivity without any exploitation. Another key aim of vegan organic growing is to create a closed loop of energy so that everything you need is produced on site. This is the ultimate in sustainability. Obviously the extent to which you are able to do this depends on the size of your plot, time available, resources and so on.

If enough people (and governments) embraced these methods of growing, it really could transform everything about food production worldwide. Over the last 70 years or so, intensive agriculture has depleted our soils, polluted our waterways, reduced biodiversity, decimated insect populations and reduced our wildlife by 50% or more, all to produce vast monocrops of chemical-soaked foods. To do this as cheaply as possible, farms have relied on government subsidies and reducing numbers of workers by using ever more technology; the result is huge farms and rural unemployment at the expense of our health and the environment. It is unsustainable, short-term thinking that cannot continue without the collapse of many natural systems and ultimately human civilisations. Those who talk about feeding the world only being possible with large farms and the use of chemicals are overlooking crucial long-term factors and are patently wrong according to the United Nation's *Trade and Environment Review 2013: Wake Up Before It's Too Late*, which advises "a rapid and significant shift from conventional, monoculture-based and high-external-input-dependent industrial production toward mosaics of sustainable, regenerative production systems that also considerably improve the productivity of small-scale farmers."

At the root of this is an urgent need to totally reform the agricultural system, away from a multinational corporate approach (highly dependent on fossil fuels and which is destroying our soils, climate and biodiversity) to a system incorporating permaculture methods (more on that later), which is community run, and has eco-literacy and education at its core. The health benefits of spending time outside in connection with the soil are innumerable.

All of this contributes hugely to why we should make sure that, as far as possible, the food we purchase is organic. Although it may cost a little more in a supermarket, it is the most important thing you will ever spend money on. Besides, there are plenty of ways to obtain organic produce more cheaply, such as from a local growers' group, buying in bulk from a mail-order supplier, direct from an organic farm shop, at a pick-your-own (PYO) facility or from neighbours or friends who grow organically.

To grow all crops with vegan organic methods would require a far larger number of smaller farms, producing healthier food, more sustainably, with more employment and vast improvements for biodiversity and our wildlife. All it needs is some courage and foresight from the government and landowners.

Meanwhile, as yet another sign of the corporate agro-chemical takeover, when you visit a garden centre you find shelves full of boxes and bottles with the word KILL emphasised. The chemical companies encourage us to exterminate everything that they can think of that might be undesirable for a gardener: slugs, snails, insects, weeds and so on, with no thought to the value of biodiversity and no respect for the life of other species. Millions of tons of chemicals that kill, chiefly pesticides and herbicides, are produced every year and sprayed on the food that we eat. It seems common sense that this constant use of substances created to end life cannot be good for us, let alone the health of the planet. Indeed

Soil Fertility

Other than carbon dioxide and oxygen from the atmosphere, and energy from the sun, plants get everything they need for growth from the soil, including water and nutrients. Organic methods involve ensuring the soil is healthy, water-retentive and replenished with nutrients naturally. Almost all soils, whether sand, loam or clay, will benefit from increased amounts of organic matter, and one of the main ways of producing this within a closed-loop system is making your own compost.

Compost

All gardens should have a compost heap or container, however small. To throw away your kitchen waste, weeds, grass-mowings and so on, is to throw away valuable fertility. There are numerous composting bins, cages, tumblers and containers available, many of which are suitable for small plots, but it's better to make your own if you can, using old pallets or other reused materials. If you have the space, the ideal is to create two or three bins or bays so that one is the freshest you are adding new material to, while the others are rotting down.

The speed at which compost becomes useable depends on the size of the heap, the type of materials added, how hot it becomes and how often it is turned. Small heaps may produce very little heat and will rely on the action of many creatures to break it down including worms, millipedes, woodlice and slugs, as well as many different types of bacteria and fungi. Obviously it's best if these heaps are built directly onto the soil so that the creatures can get access to the material.

Larger heaps with the right mixtures of materials can produce a significant amount of heat caused by the action of bacteria. These can rot down much more quickly and have the advantage of killing weed seeds and many pests and diseases if the temperature gets above 60°C. There are also specially insulated 'hot bins' available which create this ideal set-up with smaller amounts of compost. Even with a simple heap though, turning the compost with a garden fork will mix the contents and speed up the process. This can be done anything from weekly to every month or so. A heap that is regularly turned and reaches a good temperature can break down in as little as a couple of months, but in practice many heaps are left for longer, often a year, before being used in the garden.

One key aspect is the mix of materials added. Many garden heaps are made up largely of grass mowings, weeds and kitchen waste, all of which are rich in nitrogen and known as 'greens'. The ideal compost, however, will be produced from a mixture of roughly two-thirds greens and one-third browns. 'Browns' are carbon-rich and could be made up from straw, stems such as spent tomato vines, woodchips, sawdust, torn-up cardboard

the herbicide glyphosate, which is used in many brands of weedkiller, has been shown to be carcinogenic, yet is still marketed and sold in vast quantities worldwide. As a result, we ingest traces of glyphosate in many everyday food items such as bread (non-organic).

We've known for some time that the pesticides based on neonicotinoids have played a part in the decimation of bee populations across much of the world. But the latest research is even more alarming: it's thought that the accumulation and combination of many chemicals, including other pesticides and herbicides, have weakened the bees' resistance so that even an outright worldwide ban of neonicotinoids may not save the bees (and everyone who depends on them). The problem with a scientific analysis of the dangers of a chemical is that it is usually a highly reductionist approach. That chemical alone is tested (in high doses on lab rats, for example) to determine its safety in our food chain. But real life isn't like that – we all live surrounded by a cocktail of chemicals – so many that the possible effects of their myriad combinations could never be analysed. Increasingly we hear that these cocktails could be a contributory factor in the increasing rates of allergies, cancers and numerous other human health problems. Logic dictates that if the world is sprayed with deadly chemicals then they will be detrimental to our health.

Practically speaking, to garden organically with no animal inputs requires addressing three main aspects: soil fertility, dealing with pests, and dealing with weeds. Let's look at each of these in more detail.

and shredded paper. Add these in layers with your green material as you build the heap up, and if it is too dry, water with rainwater before covering the heap with something like a piece of old carpet to add some insulation and stop it drying out.

Once the compost has rotted down to a brown crumbly texture, it can be spread around the garden beds as a mulch (see below), used in trenches for crops like potatoes, to fill raised beds, or sieved and mixed with soil to make a growing medium for pots. Composting can be a complex process with many different schools of thought; there are plenty of books and articles on the subject should you wish to investigate in more detail.

Hot Composting

As already mentioned, the temperature of the compost heap will govern how long it takes to break down the material and make it useable. 'Hot Composting' is a technique that aims to produce enough heat to complete the decomposition in about four weeks. It does require a little more preparation and daily monitoring but pays back with the speed of the process.

Aim to create a heap of about one cubic metre in volume. This can be a pile covered by a tarp (to retain moisture) or in a suitably sized bin or enclosure. If you have the space, you could make the pile in your greenhouse, which will have the benefit of heating the building as it decomposes. The material needs to be half 'brown' and half 'green' and well shredded. For example, a mixture of grass clippings and dead leaves that have had a lawn mower pass over them several times to shred. Add a shovel of already-made compost to boost the microorganisms, spray with enough rainwater to make the material damp (but not wet), and mix thoroughly.

Over the next few weeks, check the temperature of the pile every day using a compost thermometer; after a few days the temperature will rise to between 49 and 77°C and then start to fall again. Four or five days later, once the temperature has fallen to 43°C, turn the whole heap thoroughly with a fork, adding a little more moisture if required, and it will then start to heat up again. Repeat this process until you have turned the heap at least four times.

After four weeks the heap should be a dark, crumbly compost and its temperature should have decreased to below 29°C. Then simply leave the heap for a couple of weeks, with no further turning, and it will be ready to use.

Leaf Mould

A small number of leaves can be added to the general compost heap and mixed in, but if you have a few deciduous trees, the large quantity of leaves will rot more slowly, so you will be better off building a leaf mould pile.

This needs to be open to the elements and can be as simple as a circle or cage of wire (reclaimed chicken wire, for example) which you fill up with the collected leaves. Depending on the type of leaves, they may take as much as three years to break down to a brown crumbly texture. This can then be used as a mulch or as part of your growing medium for pots and seeds trays.

Mulching

A mulch is any layer of material covering the soil. This could be organic, biodegradable material like compost, leaf mould, straw, cardboard, woodchips or seaweed, or inorganic material, like gravel, black plastic or landscape fabric.

The main benefits of all mulches are to help soil retain moisture and to suppress weeds, but there can be other good outcomes, including deterring pests, protecting plant roots and keeping certain crops off bare soil (strawberries or pumpkins, for example). Mulches of organic material like compost or leaf mould have the important extra benefit of improving soil fertility and texture. This is achieved as earthworms pull the material down into the soil and consume it, producing rich casts (worm poo), which add nutrients to the soil.

A healthy soil is one teeming with life: good for biodiversity and good for your plants. Unless soil is waterlogged or has been treated with chemicals, it should contain large numbers of bacteria and fungi, and numerous invertebrates including worms, nematodes, mites, centipedes, springtails and many more. All these create a rich ecosystem, which breaks down organic matter and makes it available to plants via their roots with the help of a network of fungal mycelium (known as a mycorrhizal association). To routinely dig soil is to damage its structure and disrupt these ecosystems, so many organic growers practice the no-dig method (easier on the back too!) whereby the soil is disturbed as little as possible. Mulching is the perfect accompaniment to the no-dig method – let the worms do the work for you.

Mulches are best laid in spring and/or autumn over a warm, moist soil, ideally between 5 and 10cm deep. They can be laid around established plants (but careful to leave some space around the stems) or on to bare soil and then the plants planted through the mulch when the time comes. Pots can be mulched as well as beds; you may just need to scrape a little away now and again to see whether the soil is dry and the pot needs watering.

If you have a large weedy area you can mulch with a layer of cardboard or black plastic. The weeds will gradually die off and you can plant crops through small holes cut in the covering. If cardboard is used it will gradually rot down, especially if covered with a layer of compost or leaf mould mulch.

Mulch

Green Manures

The aim should be to rarely have bare soil on your plot. If you do, nutrients will be washed away and it will gradually lose its texture and organic content. Green manures are fast-growing plants that are grown on bare soil to improve its quality. When the ground is needed for planting they can be lightly dug in, or cut down with a hoe and left on the surface as a mulch, and/or covered with a further mulch (garden compost, for example).

Green manures can be sown directly as seeds as soon as you have harvested a crop from an area, or even sown under larger crops that are spaced apart, such as tomatoes, pumpkins or sweet corn. The foliage of the green manures will also suppress weeds and provide cover for beneficial animals such as beetles, which will control pests. Some, like clovers, will also have the benefit of flowering and attracting bees and other pollinators. The green manures can be left until the area is needed again (although some may die off naturally over winter), or planted as a ley (an area of ground sown and left for a season or two to improve its fertility – see Crop Rotation below).

One of the most important nutrients for plants is nitrogen. It is a major component of chlorophyll, the compound by which plants use energy from sunlight to produce sugars from water and carbon dioxide during photosynthesis, and is also an important part of proteins. Green manures can help maintain or increase nitrogen in the soil either by nitrogen lifting (absorbing surplus nutrients so they are not washed away) or by nitrogen fixing (absorbing nitrogen from the air and storing it in the roots after it has been converted to non-gaseous nitrogen compounds by bacteria) which then improves nitrogen availability for future crops.

Common green manures are:

Nitrogen Fixing

- Crimson clover – sow April-September – weed-smothering foliage, flowers attractive to bees.
- Trefoil – sow March-August – tolerates shade, good for sowing under larger crops.
- Lucerne (Alfalfa) – sow April-July – deep rooting, can be left for years.

Nitrogen Lifting

- Mustard – sow March-September – quick growing for short-term use.
- Buckwheat – sow April-August – quick growing, regrows if cut.
- The organisation Garden Organic have produced a guide to green manures called Sort Out Your Soil (see Resources, page 235) if you want to study this subject in more depth.

Compost Teas

By steeping well-rotted garden compost in water, you can create compost tea which can be applied as a plant feed either direct to foliage or by watering the soil around plants. The steeping extracts beneficial microorganisms and nutrients from the compost, making them more immediately available to plants than by applying compost as a mulch or within a potting medium.

There are various methods for making compost teas: a simple one is to fill a bucket ¼ full of compost, top up with rainwater and leave for three or four days, stirring occasionally, then strain the mixture (putting the solids back on the compost heap) and dilute the liquid 1:10 before using immediately.

Other methods use an airstone and air pump (such as used in aquaria) to create aerobic conditions in the water so that the microorganisms multiply rapidly. To do this, place a handful of compost in a bucket of rainwater, add 4 tbsp of molasses (to feed the microorganisms) and aerate with the pump for one or two days. Strain and use immediately (certainly within four hours) on foliage or soil.

Plant Teas

Other homemade plant feeds can be made using foliage from other plants such as stinging nettles or comfrey. Their leaves are steeped in water and release nutrients as they decompose. Nettle provides nitrogen, potassium, magnesium, sulphur and iron and is good for feeding young vegetables and watering containers. Comfrey is particularly rich in nitrogen, but also provides potassium, iron, calcium and phosphorus and is good for feeding fruit crops such as aubergines and cucumbers.

To make a liquid nettle feed, harvest nettles (young ones in spring are highest in nutrients, but any will do) and pack them tightly into a bucket or barrel to within 15cm of the top. Pour in water until the nettles are just covered and leave for approximately two weeks. During this time a sort of fermentation will occur and the liquid may start to froth. It will also start to smell unpleasant, so place it away from the house and neighbours!

When the fermentation has died down, strain off the remaining stems and leaves – you can use a soil-sieve on top of a bucket and just tip the mixture in – and there you have it: a bucket of free, natural, concentrated plant food. Just throw the strained-out solids on the compost heap. To use this liquid, dilute 1:10 with rainwater and water pots and beds every week or two during the growing season.

To make a feed from comfrey, follow the same instructions but allow to ferment for four weeks.

Other Vegan Organic Fertilisers

If you are unable to make your own plant feeds, there are organic options available to buy, but you must make sure they haven't used any animal products. The most common is seaweed extract, which can increase yields of fruit and vegetables by producing healthier plants with a good root structure as well as extending cropping periods. It will come in concentrated form, so dilute as instructed before spraying onto foliage or direct onto soil with a watering can. It can also be used as an organic fertiliser for houseplants.

Crop Rotation

The aim of crop rotation is to increase long-term soil fertility by not always growing the same vegetables in the same place year after year, but instead growing different annual vegetables in different parts of the plot each year. The main benefits include: reducing the build-up of pests and diseases that are specific to certain plant families; reducing the chance of nutrient deficiencies developing in the soil as certain types of plants have different

Nettle tea

requirements; and aiding weed control as some crops with large leaves, like potatoes, suppress weed growth better than others.

Plan out which areas of the plot you will use for different groups. This will depend, of course, on how many of each type you wish to grow. Keep notes as it's quite easy to forget what was planted where two or three years down the line. Rotate the crops so that each is followed in sequence as suggested below for a classic four-year rotation:

1. Potatoes
2. Roots (carrots, parsnips, celeriac etc.) and alliums (onions, garlic, leeks)
3. Legumes (peas and beans)
4. Brassicas (cabbages, cauliflowers, kale, swede etc.)

If you have enough space, you could also include one or two further areas to grow green manure for a season or two (creating a 'ley') using red clover or lucerne for example. Some growers develop further rotations by separating roots and onions into two areas, and a further one for sweet corn and pumpkins, to the extent that it could be 9-10 years before an area is used by the same type of crop.

Crop rotation like this is easy to plan if you have a series of raised beds, or areas that can be clearly divided up, like on an allotment, but some gardens are more cottage- or forest-style, with vegetable plants dotted about here and there. This is known as polyculture with crops either fully interspersed, or grown in adjacent rows of different types (row intercropping). This has the advantage of getting further away from the monocropping style of growing, so plants are less likely to suffer from pest build-up or nutrient loss from a concentration of one type of plant.

Obviously with polyculture like this, it's not necessary to practise the same sort of rigorous crop rotation, but you can still bear in mind where certain annuals were grown the previous year, and try them somewhere else the year after.

Dealing with Weeds

A weed is any plant growing where you don't want it – whether it's an oak tree, a rose bush or a dandelion. There are a certain number of plants that we have been conditioned to think of as always being weeds: thistles, brambles, stinging nettles, and so on. However, all of these are hugely important to wildlife (and can be to us, too): thistles produce attractive flowers – good for butterflies and many other pollinating insects; brambles produce blackberries – good for us and many bird species; nettles can be used to make tea, ease arthritis, or be fermented to create a plant food (as detailed above); and dandelions have many health benefits as well as attracting numerous beneficial insects.

So before you pull up something that triggers your weeding reflex, ask yourself whether it is doing any damage where it is, or whether it is truly in the way. If not, maybe it can stay there a little longer and do some good (attracting insects and acting as a green manure, for example).

Sometimes weeds do have to be removed to make way for planting crops or to stop them smothering or taking nutrients from the plants you want to grow. Some methods that we've discussed already, like crop rotation and using mulches, can help suppress weeds in the first place, but when it comes to organic removal, your best friend is the humble hoe. There are many styles available, the most common being the Dutch hoe, although our favourite is the sharp-edged Swoe, which can be used in any direction and is easy to use in hard to reach places.

The best time to hoe is in the morning before a warm sunny day, so that the disturbed weeds will quickly desiccate and die. If you plant some of your crops in rows, make sure the gap between each row is wide enough for your hoe to run through without damaging any of the plants.

The weeds you can't reach with a hoe will have to be removed by hand. This can feel like a dreaded task at times, especially in the early summer when many weeds can be vigorous, but various techniques may ease your pain. Firstly, make sure you are comfortable and do not feel rushed. Use a kneeling pad and take your time. Do it mindfully and remind yourself of the good you are doing for your crops, thanking the weeds for adding fertility to your compost heap! Do it on a lovely day when it feels good to be outside doing something physical. Alternatively, some people prefer to be distracted from the task by listening to music or the radio; you could even spend the time learning a foreign language or listening to an audiobook using headphones.

Once weeds have been removed, this is the perfect time to add a mulch around the crops to prevent further ones getting a hold.

Dealing with Pests

A pest can be defined as an animal that is detrimental to humans or human concerns. In the vegetable garden, the most common ones are slugs and snails, aphids (blackfly and greenfly being the most prolific) and the caterpillars of large white and small white butterflies (often collectively called cabbage white butterflies). In the spring, in some areas, wood pigeons can also be a nuisance – eating young brassica plants in particular. Fruits can also be devoured by a number of different birds and some rodents.

The good news for vegans is that there is no need to kill any of these animals. We will look at barriers to keep pests away from your crops, and relocation (removing pests from your plot), but first, and by far the most important, is to create high biodiversity so that the pests are kept in check naturally.

The problem with chemical pesticides is that they kill the beneficial predators as well as the pests (upon which they prey). Classic examples include the larvae of ladybirds, hoverflies and lacewings, which devour aphids, yet are equally as susceptible to most pesticides as the aphids themselves. Without these predators in our landscape, pests like aphids, which breed very rapidly, can quickly get a hold and damage crops. With a healthy ecosystem there will always be a balance, however with predators keeping their prey under control.

It helps to start off with the notion that you will always share some of your crops with other animals, and that there's nothing wrong with that. Plant a few more than you need for yourself, knowing that some sharing will go on over the season. Enjoy the fact that your plot is an ecosystem and not just a production house and that you are playing a part in creating that.

So the most effective, environmentally friendly and least time-consuming method of pest control is simply to ensure your plot is as wildlife-rich as possible. Here are some examples of the types of predators you want to attract:

Bats

They eat flying insects and some caterpillars – attract them with bat boxes and flowering plants that night-flying insects visit, such as evening primrose, jasmine and honeysuckle.

Beetles and centipedes

Beetles eat slugs' eggs, and centipedes eat slugs and snails – attract both with moist shady areas such as compost heaps and mulches.

Birds

Small birds eat aphids and other pests – attract them with trees, shrubs, hedges and bird boxes.

Frogs and toads

They eat flies and aphids – attract them with ponds and damp logs or stone piles for hibernation.

Bird box

Hedgehogs

They eat slugs, millipedes, caterpillars – attract them with low shrubs, log piles and gaps under fences so they can come and go.

Ladybirds, hoverflies and lacewings

As mentioned, the larvae of all these eat aphids, as do adult ladybirds – attract them with insect hotels (hollow stems or straw packed in open-ended containers), and attract adult hoverflies with flowering plants.

Insect hotel

Newts

They eat slugs, snails and insects – attract them in the same way as for frogs and toads.

Slow worms

Legless lizards (not snakes) eat slugs – attract them with areas of long grass, stone piles and compost heaps.

It's easy and fun (for children too) to create gardens that attract wildlife. You'll see from the above list a clear number of additions to your garden, which will not only encourage beneficial animals, but also make your garden more attractive and interesting. Priorities would be:

- Pond(s) with easy access for small animals and shallow areas, marginal plants but no fish (which eat the eggs and young of amphibians and insects)
- A wild patch with long grasses and nettles
- A wildflower area
- Piles of logs, stones, leaves, hedge trimmings etc.
- Insect hotels, bird boxes and bat boxes.

Even small gardens can cater for many of these – they don't have to take up much room.

Another effective technique is to leave a small number of some crops in the ground to continue to grow (and maybe flower) after harvesting their neighbours. An example would be to leave one or two sprouting broccoli plants to fully flower, rather than pulling them all up once harvesting is finished in late spring. These will retain the population of beneficial predators visiting your patch, rather than moving on once their food source or homes have gone.

Barriers

In some cases you may need to create barriers to prevent other animals getting to your crops. Examples are:

- Fencing to keep rabbits off the allotment
- Fruit cages to keep birds off soft fruits like berries and currants
- Netting over cane or pipe structures to keep pigeons and butterflies off brassicas
- Horticultural fleece or mesh to prevent small pests like flea beetles or carrot root fly (as well as butterflies and larger pests)
- Barriers to deter snails and slugs such as soot, ash, human hair, or copper strips around raised beds and pots
- Cloches to protect crops – plastic bottles cut in half and placed over individual young brassicas or squashes, for example.

Relocation

Occasionally you may find you need to supplement your other protection methods by relocating a few repeat offenders! This is especially relevant for slugs and snails. In this case, relocating means gathering them up in a bucket or lidded container and taking them at least 100 metres away; snails are homing creatures so lobbing them over the garden fence certainly won't work!

The best time to collect molluscs is at dusk, after rain and during the spring. Ideally wear a head torch, hold the container in one hand and gently pick the snails off

Brassica cage

with the other as you move around your plot. You will find a large pair of tweezers or an old spoon will help with the slugs as their slime is particularly slippery (and difficult to wash off your fingers afterwards). You may be surprised at the large number you collect at first, but after a few days the numbers will decrease. Relocate them somewhere like a park, woodland edge or hedgerow, away from other people's gardens. You may find this nightly activity surprisingly addictive, and it's a great opportunity to experience other nightlife on your plot, such as bats, foxes and owls.

Another method is to collect them during the day by finding out where they hide away. Common places are under pots/tubs, around the rims of plant pots and under pieces of wood.

Companion Planting

Pest control can also be enhanced by using companion planting: using specific plants amongst your crops for their benefit. Examples include:

Nasturtium

- Sacrificial plants such as nasturtiums that are susceptible to blackfly attack. These will in turn attract the ladybirds, hoverflies and other predators which will control the aphids on your crops as well. They will also attract white butterflies away from your brassicas.
- Flowering plants that attract beneficial insects like hoverflies and other pollinators, such as lavender, thyme and poached egg plants.
- Mint which deters flea beetles.

- Onions and other alliums growing amongst carrots will deter carrot root fly.
- Strong smelling herbs like mint, chives, basil and thyme can deter aphids.
- French marigolds can deter whitefly.

4. PERMACULTURE

Permaculture (as described by the magazine of the same name) is "an innovative framework for creating sustainable ways of living; a practical method for developing ecologically harmonious, efficient and productive systems that can be used by anyone, anywhere".

Originally derived from the term 'permanent agriculture' (or 'permanent culture'), it is often associated with ways of growing crops that are more sustainable and environmentally friendly. However, as the description above suggests, it is much more holistic than that. Permaculture provides ethics and tools for creating and designing ways of life that are not only sustainable but regenerative, to repair and revitalise our damaged planet. It can apply to how we design our homes, livelihoods, communities, technologies and economies. Permaculture provides co-operative systems which support living ethically in symbiosis with, and in stewardship of, the earth.

These principles marry very well with those of veganism, encompassing many of the techniques for vegan organic growing that we have discussed already, such as no-dig methods, green manures, composting, mulching, companion planting and more. Permaculture has partly evolved from observing how nature functions and then developing strategies that work with nature, including systems that give maximum output for minimum input whilst producing no waste. It is increasingly clear that the livestock industry and intensive agriculture are damaging nature more than ever before, so permaculture ties in closely with our vegan ethics and vegan organic growing techniques. As nature has taken billions of years to evolve, we can learn a lot from observing and mimicking how it works with our growing strategies – such as the use of mulches, stacking plants vertically (see Forest Gardening later in this chapter) and stacking in time (growing a series of crops in the same space in the same year for maximum efficient use of space).

The Ethics of Permaculture

Earth care

Living/gardening in a way that leaves no waste or damage, but regenerates the earth (for example, by using the growing techniques discussed in the previous chapter such as no-dig methods, mulching, not using chemicals)

People care

Nurturing yourself and all other people (for example, by ensuring anything we buy does not involve slavery, child labour or other forms of exploitation).

Fair shares

Not consuming more than we need and redistributing surplus (for example, giving excess crops to neighbours or food banks).

There are numerous permaculture principles that can be applied to any design exercise. In the context of food growing and planning your garden, the concept of 'zoning' can greatly increase the energy efficiency and productivity of a plot, by carefully placing elements according to how frequently you may need to visit them. The zones can be categorised as follows:

Zone 00

Yourself.

Zone 0

Your house (pots on the windowsill, sprouting seeds).

Zone 1

The garden close to the house (herbs, salads, anything that needs daily attention, which could well include a small greenhouse).

Zone 2

Further down the garden (perennials, potatoes, sweet corn, fruit trees/bushes and so on) requiring several visits per week.

Zone 3

An allotment or area for commercial production requiring visiting once a week or so.

Zone 4

Managed woodland (logs for fuel or coppicing for poles) requiring several visits per year.

Zone 5

Wilderness (foraging for wild berries and mushrooms) requiring several visits per year.

The zoning system may seem obvious and simple, but it is so easy to place something in the wrong location, leading to inefficiency or it not being used at all. If some herb plants were at the bottom of the garden they may simply not be used in the kitchen, or if the greenhouse was too far away, you might not bother to check it was well ventilated each day. However long you've had your plot, you will benefit from drawing a plan of it on a piece of paper, mapping out the zones as described above, and gradually moving things around to increase efficiency and output and develop your own permaculture garden.

In our current situation we have a few herbs and sprouting seeds on the kitchen windowsill (Zone 0), further herbs, salads and a small greenhouse (for growing tomatoes, peppers, aubergines etc.) within a few metres of the back door (Zone 1) and raised beds for our main crops plus a few fruit trees and bushes at the bottom of the garden (Zone 2). We have a friend who manages a small woodland a short drive away (Zone 4), and various wild areas where we can collect berries and mushrooms slightly further afield (Zone 5), often combining visits to this zone with other activities.

One key aspect of permaculture is that of observation before action – taking time to observe the natural 'sectors' in your plot, recording how energy (sun, water, prevailing winds, frost, pollution, views and so on) flows through the area and might impact the optimum placement of various elements in your design (such as greenhouses, raised beds, compost heaps and ponds). It is often suggested that when you take on a new garden, plot or allotment, you spend the first year simply observing which plants appear, which grow well in certain positions, which areas get the most sun or frost and so on; to get a feel for how the rhythms of the year affect the plot, which areas have microclimates that might suit certain crops or styles of growing and how the sectors change with the seasons. In practice many of us are too eager to get on with sowing seeds and making the plot productive as soon as possible, but we must always stay in observational mode and adjust techniques and positioning of crops and facilities through the years as we learn how the plot works best – naturally. This way we can learn which plants thrive in our particular soil and climate and amend future crop-choice for the maximum output and efficiency.

We have found that growing certain crops in containers is useful in this regard in that we can easily move them to different zones or locations as we determine where they grow best or how easily/often they need to be accessed. They can also be moved over a period of time as these factors change. For example, we grow the tomato variety Tumbling Tom each year as it crops well outdoors and does well in large pots, producing masses of small cherry-sized fruits. We start them off in Zone 0 (kitchen windowsill) sowing the seeds in a heated propagator in March. Once the young plants are 10cm tall they go out to the greenhouse (Zone 1) for April and part of May, then into the large outdoor pots (Zone 2) at the end of the garden, for they will need very little attention as they grow throughout June and July. When they start fruiting in August we move them back to Zone 1 (near the back door) so that they can easily be picked daily for salads and pasta dishes (a quick meal simply made from wholewheat pasta, pesto and a handful of these cherry tomatoes (which burst with flavour in the mouth) is a delight!).

Modern agriculture has led to a decreasing number of crop varieties, chosen for their productivity and profit. Some major agro-corporations have even started taking out patents or trademarks for certain varieties so that it would be illegal for farmers to collect and use their own seeds (thus forcing them to buy new seeds each year). Along the way many old varieties have been lost. Those that have been developed over generations are known as heritage or heirloom varieties, and may have superior qualities such as flavour, colour, hardiness or suitability for particular climates and soils. The more of these varieties we lose, the more we lose biodiversity as well as the joy and health benefits that come from eating many different types of fruit and vegetables. For these reasons there is growing interest in the protection and growing of heritage varieties and the saving of seeds on small scales. The organisation Garden Organic runs a Heritage Seed Library* and we discuss seed saving in more detail in the next chapter.

Another useful permaculture tool for running your plot (as well as many other aspects of your life) is known by the acronym GoSADIMET (or SADIM for short) which is illustrated as follows:

Goal setting

Deciding what you want to achieve from your plot (including what you want to harvest, what are your favourite fruits and vegetables).

* www.gardenorganic.org.uk/hsl

Survey

Observing what is already there: plants, structures, climate, soil, water, wildlife, boundaries, access and utilities. Creating an initial base map. Finding out the wishes of other people sharing your plot (do they have uses in mind other than growing crops, what are their favourite fruits and vegetables).

Assess

Analysing your limiting factors (time and financial, for example) and resources (time, people, tools …).

Design

Creating maps of your ideal plot using zones and sectors (as above).

Implement

Building to your design in phases (this could be as simple as installing a few raised beds one year, adding a small greenhouse the next and so on).

Maintain

Managing the plot through the seasons.

Evaluate

Thinking about what went well, what didn't work, and what can be improved in the future. Keep evolving your ideas.

Tweak

Making practical adjustments as you learn how your plot works.

Forest Gardening

One of the most sustainable and stable ways of growing food, to be both productive and low maintenance, is to create a forest garden on part of your plot. This is a design to mimic a natural forest, using trees, shrubs and smaller plants, and can be produced even on a small scale in a back garden, replacing the lawn with an attractive, productive area, rich in wildlife and biodiversity.

A forest garden should have a diversity of species, including those that increase fertility (such as nitrogen fixers and lifters) and those that attract natural predators. Using the permaculture principle of stacking, a forest garden maximises the use of the available space by including plants that can flourish on as many different levels as possible.

Canopy trees

Depending on the size of your plot, these could include walnut, sweet chestnut, apples, plums and pears.

Small trees

Planted between the canopy trees, such as almonds, hazel and dwarfing fruit trees.

Sweet chestnut tree

Shrubs

Often shade tolerant, like berries and currants.

Perennials

These could be herbs such as sage, mint and thyme as well as plants to increase fertility, such as comfrey.

Ground cover

Creeping plants to create a living mulch, such as clovers and various herbs.

Climbers

Grape vines and kiwis, for example, which can climb up the larger trees.

Roots

Crops such as Jerusalem artichokes, potatoes, carrots and beetroot, as well as mushrooms.

A forest garden can be a long-term project, but will result in a beautiful area that is a joy for you and good for wildlife, much more environmentally friendly than a lawn, and requires very little work once established. There are some excellent books on forest gardening should you wish to explore this area in more depth (see Resources).

Courses

This is a very brief introduction to a powerful framework for living your life. To find out more we highly recommend taking the Permaculture Design Certificate course (PDC), which you can find out about via the Permaculture Association (see Resources). In particular there is an excellent Vegan PDC run by Graham Burnett (Spiralseed) and Nicole Vosper (Empty Cages Design).

5. SELF-SUFFICIENCY

Many of us dream of living off the land, being self-reliant, growing everything we need, living the good life and maybe even going off-grid. However, depending on how much land and time you have available, it needn't be a dream.

Diet also plays a factor; if you mainly eat fruit and vegetables then it is easier to grow all you need than if you also eat bread, rice, pasta and other grain-based foods. Of course it's possible to grow your own grains too, but this adds levels of complexity and needs more land. For many of us, the compromise is to be self-sufficient (or partly) in some of our favourite crops, whilst buying in some other essentials that are harder to grow or store or need complicated processing.

Storage is a key feature of self-sufficiency as many crops are only harvested at certain times of the year. There are various techniques that enable you to keep or preserve them to last throughout the year, some of which have been used by our ancestors for hundreds or even thousands of years. We will look at storage options in more detail below.

The question of how much land is needed for self-sufficiency is commonly asked. It is estimated that 0.07 hectares of land can feed one person on a plant-based diet. This is equivalent to 0.17 acres, 700 square metres or approximately three standard allotment plots – a lot less than many people expect. Bearing in mind the relatively low cost of renting allotments, it's easy to see how economical it can be to grow all your own food. Incidentally, it would take about 20 times this area to feed someone on a meat-based diet.

To put this in a nationwide context, the arable land in the UK is about six million hectares – enough to feed 88 million people on a plant-based diet (more than the current population of approximately 64 million), yet we currently only produce about half of what we eat. Furthermore, six million hectares is only the current arable land – much of the rest is grassland and grazing (not to mention all our back gardens which could also be used for crop-growing), so the total number of people who could be fed from the land is far more than the population. This further goes to show how wasteful the animal protein industry is.

On the home scale, the combination of a back garden and an allotment plot should be enough to provide half of all food needs for one person (or a quarter for two). Some rural gardens are large enough to feed a family of four. Currently this is rarely done, however, as few people

Mixed bed

have the time and skills, but hopefully more and more will realise the importance of growing their own in the future. Of course some people live in flats and have no garden, but they can still be self-sufficient in some plant foods, such as potted herbs on a windowsill. This alone can give a great feeling of satisfaction and self-reliance.

Choosing What to Grow

This will partly depend on the climate, whether you have a greenhouse or polytunnel and what other resources you have available. Most importantly, however, you should consider what you (and those you live with) like to eat! This might sound obvious, but it's amazing how many people grow too much of something they're not that keen on, or that produce a wasteful amount of something that's difficult to store.

Start with the simple task of listing all the foods you like to eat that could be grown with the space/climate available. If you provide food for others, get them to do the same. If you're not sure where to start, try a seed/plant catalogue (such as The Organic Gardening Catalogue – see Resources, page 236) to give you a number of options, or look at our list of commonly grown crops in the chapter, Fruits and Vegetables.

If you don't have much time to devote to caring for your crops, you might want to focus on a few that are easy to grow and need little maintenance, such as potatoes and onions. As these can be stored for long periods, they are easy crops to be self-sufficient in throughout the year. Conversely, if you have the time and want to be adventurous, you may prefer to grow a smaller amount of a large number of different crops, accepting that you will only be partly self-sufficient in them unless you have enough land.

If you only have a small area to grow in outdoors – maybe a balcony or patio – you may wish to choose a few plants that crop well in containers, such as courgettes, tomatoes and salad leaves. Alternatively you may prefer a few attractive perennial plants that provide fruits such as strawberries, blueberries, figs and apples on dwarfing rootstocks.

You may have inherited a garden/allotment with a large number of plants you don't like. If this is the case, don't just keep growing them for the sake of it; dig them up and give them to neighbours who do like them, freeing up space for crops you prefer.

Planning Quantities

When it comes to deciding how much of each crop to grow, keeping records from year to year is recommended. For each different produce, note down the varieties you grew, the size of the harvest and how long it lasted you. After a few years you will have a very good idea of how much is needed to be self-sufficient for particular crops.

It also helps to record or estimate how much you eat certain items. Take onions for example: if you are growing for two people and you consume an average of four onions per week between you, then a simple bit of maths (4 x 52 = 208) gives you an idea how many to grow to be fully self-sufficient. However, it's always a good idea to add a few extra for losses while growing and storing, for feeding guests, and maybe a small surplus for giving away, so, using the example described above, you may decide to grow 240 onions.

Successional Sowing

Some crops have a fairly long growing season and are usually sown at the same time of the year, then ripen over a short period. Peppers (capsicum and chilli), for example, tend to be sown in February/March and harvested in August/September, but other crops that grow faster can be sown in smaller batches throughout the warmer months of the year, giving you a much longer cropping season. This is known as successional sowing.

Salad leaves are a good example: They can be harvested as baby leaves after just a few weeks, so sowing a smaller amount every couple of weeks can keep you supplied throughout the whole year. This can be further supported by appropriate choice of varieties: Some are more suited to sowing/growing in the cooler autumn/winter months than others. There are more details on this in the chapter Salad Leaves, page 47.

Planting different varieties of potatoes at intervals is a form of successional sowing, but over a shorter period:

- First earlies – planted in March
- Second earlies – planted early to mid-April
- Early maincrop – planted late April to early May
- Late maincrop – planted in May

This routine should enable you to harvest potatoes from June through to October, and of course they will store

American cress

New potatoes

long after that, so this successional sowing approach is a great enhancement to self-sufficiency.

Other crops that are suited to successional sowing, many of which can be sown every couple of weeks once the soil has warmed up, include: spring onions, cauliflowers, cabbages, carrots, lettuces and other salad leaves, radishes, spinach and chard.

Growing Under Cover

Growing under cover entails the use of any of the following – a greenhouse, polytunnel, cold frame, cloche, conservatory or kitchen windowsill. The resulting faster germination and protection from frost is often said to add six weeks to the start and end of the growing season for any plant. Potting sheds with large glass windows can also be used for early seed sowing, and the use of horticultural materials such as fleeces and meshes can additionally provide protection and increase growing times.

A greenhouse or polytunnel will also enable you to grow tender plants that may not flourish outside, such as melons or aubergines, and will provide a space to overwinter non-hardy plants, such as lemons, that could be killed off by a harsh winter if left on the patio.

If you are lucky enough to have a large greenhouse, or want to build one using reclaimed materials, you can even practise forest gardening (as described in the chapter Permaculture), in which you create several layers of plants that benefit each other, whilst simultaneously creating a wonderful place to relax in. Advances in greenhouse technology are being developed all the time, but that doesn't mean it has to be expensive or high-tech. Climate batteries, for example, are based on large diameter pipes that are embedded about a metre deep in the soil under greenhouses and rise to open within the airspace of the structure. Low-powered electric fans at these openings slowly push air from the interior of the greenhouse through the underground pipes, and back into the airspace. During the day, this pushes warm air underground, which heats the soil (aiding plant growth), and during the night, when the ambient air temperature drops, it pushes warm air from underground back into the interior of the greenhouse. This provides a much more stable environment throughout the year and enables tropical plants to be grown even in regions which see snow for much of the winter.

Cold frames tend to be used for starting off seeds in trays or protecting or hardening off plants in pots before they are planted out in beds. Cloches are transparent covers used to protect plants in their early stages of growth when sown in open ground. These can be commercial plastic or glass domes, or tunnels made from plastic or fleece, stretched over hoops of pipe or wire. They can also be as simple as plastic drink bottles cut in half and placed over individual seedlings. They provide protection as well as warming the soil for early plantings. If you have planted a row of salad leaves, for example, cloches can be used to cover part of the row to stagger maturity times.

All types of cover also provide protection against animals that may want to feast on your crops, such as rabbits, birds and insects.

Crop Storage

For crops that are ready for harvest at only certain times of the year, the ability to store them for use throughout the rest of year is obviously key to self-sufficiency. Here are some general notes on storage techniques; more specific advice for each crop is detailed in the chapter, Fruits and Vegetables, see page 63.

Some crops, like leeks, can be left in the ground until required. Others, like potatoes and onions, benefit from being harvested and stored in cool but frost-free conditions. For most people the only option will be to use sheds and garages, which can be adequate at least until temperatures warm up in the spring. Low humidity is ideal for most stored produce, but fruit such as apples and pears prefer a more humid environment; if you have a slightly damp outbuilding, this will be better for them. Some roots, such as carrots, parsnips and beetroot, can be stored in boxes of slightly damp sand (or a peat substitute), making sure the roots don't touch each other. Keep the containers in a dry, frost-free place.

Drying

It is an ancient and effective method of preserving food and can also produce tasty snacks, such as dried apple rings and raisins. The easiest way to do this is with an electric food dehydrator. The produce is usually sliced and laid out on the trays before the unit is set for the required amount of time at the correct temperature. If you don't have a food dehydrator, however, you can use an oven set to about 50°C, but this may take a few hours or even a day to adequately dry the produce. Once dried, it must be stored in airtight jars.

Freezing

It is the best method to preserve vegetables that quickly lose their sweetness within minutes of being picked, like peas and sweet corn, but many fruits and vegetables will freeze successfully. It's also an easy method for storing extracted juices as they often start to ferment within just a few days, even in the fridge. Just remember to leave a space at the top of containers for expansion as liquids freeze.

Cold frame

Beans in pods

Pickled beetroot

Making chutney

Some produce, broccoli and raspberries for example, stick together in a lump when frozen, making it difficult to remove small portions later. To avoid this, lay the produce on a baking sheet so that the individual pieces are not touching, and place in the freezer. This method is known as 'open freezing' and some freezers have a pull-out tray in the top specifically for this purpose. When frozen, the food can be placed in a bag or container. Many vegetables benefit from blanching: the immersing of the fresh produce in boiling water before freezing. As a rule of thumb, blanch small pieces of vegetables, such as beans, for one minute, and larger pieces, such as cauliflower, for two minutes. After blanching, chill the produce in cold water immediately (to prevent further cooking) before placing in the freezer.

Bottling

It's not as common as it was and has the disadvantage that the produce in jars needs to be carefully heated for the right amount of time at the right temperature to prevent contamination from dangerous bacteria. High-acid foods, such as many fruits, tend to be safer in this regard. In general, hot syrup or water is added to the produce in sterilised jars (such as Mason or Kilner jars), which are heated in an oven or pan of boiling water before tightening the lid. Juices, purées and prepared stews (like ratatouille – see our recipe in the chapter, Cooking throughout the Year) can also be bottled in a similar way. Discard bottled produce if you are in any doubt as to its safety; in particular do not use the contents if the lid comes off too easily, as this may mean it has lost its suction and airtight seal. If you are new to bottling and want to give it a try, we recommend further research or

getting a specialist book on the subject, which will give you more detailed procedures and requirements.

Pickling

Basically storing produce in vinegar – malt, wine (sharp), cider (fruity) or clear distilled vinegar. Spices or herbs of your choice can be added to the vinegar. Chopped, or whole if small, vegetables are usually covered in salt or soaked in brine (100g of salt dissolved per litre of water) for a day before draining and jarring up with vinegar. Others, such as beetroot, may be cooked before pickling. Cover the produce with vinegar by at least 1cm and close the lid tightly.

Chutneys

These involve finely chopping all the fruit and vegetables and simmering in a pan (usually with salt, sugar, vinegar and spices of your choice). Onions, apples, raisins and tomatoes are common additions. Simmer the mixture until tender – 30 minutes to 3 hours depending on ingredients – then seal in sterilised jars (to sterilise jars and lids, boil in water in a large pan for 5-10 minutes, or place in an oven at 160°C for at least 10 minutes). See our recipe for gooseberry chutney in the chapter Fruits and Vegetables.

Jams

These are traditionally a favourite way of processing and preserving many fruits. Pectin and acid are both important in getting jam to set; some fruits high in both include apples, currants, gooseberries and plums. If your strawberry jam is too runny, then either combine the fruit with another that's rich in pectin and acid or add commercial

Harvested beans

Saved seeds

pectins and lemon juice. Generally, fruits, along with a little water, are simmered for 15-45 minutes until they have broken down to a pulp. Soft fruits like strawberries and raspberries will not need any extra water added and will only require 15 minutes, simmering. Sugar is then added (60% by weight), and the mixture brought back to the boil and boiled hard until setting point. To test for setting point, place a small blob of the mixture on a cold plate. After one minute it should have formed a skin that wrinkles when you touch it. Remove from the heat immediately, ladle the jam into sterilised jars and cover with a disc of greaseproof paper before putting the lid on.

Seed Saving

The ability to save your own seeds for sowing the next year can be part of your drive for self-sufficiency, and also helps towards creating your closed loop of energy. Other benefits of saving your own seeds on a small scale include:

- Saving money – commercial packets of seeds can be pricey
- Maintaining genetic diversity
- Choosing the crops that grow the best and/or taste the best with your particular soil/climate
- Sharing seeds with your neighbours
- Experimenting with creating new cultivars (note that you can only cross-breed from open-pollinated plants, not F1 hybrids).

Many plants go to seed a couple of months after they have flowered, so if the flower is the part you harvest (broccoli, for example), leave one or two plants to fully flower and produce seed in the autumn. Most seeds need to be dried properly, without being exposed to excessive heat, in order to be stored for long periods. Always collect seeds on a dry day and then leave them (or the flower heads) for a couple of weeks, spread out on paper in trays or open boxes, in a dry place indoors. Once they have fully dried, separate the seeds from the flower heads and any chaff (pieces of plant material that were collected inadvertently along with the seeds). Store the seeds in labelled paper envelopes or bags, somewhere cool and dry (a garage, for example) or in an airtight container in the fridge.

With fruiting plants such as tomatoes, apples, peppers, pumpkins and other squashes, the seeds will need to be separated from the flesh of the fruit and washed before being dried on kitchen paper. For those that produce pods, such as beans and peas, wait until the pods are dry and brittle on the plant before collecting them and removing the seeds for further drying indoors. If you grow plants that produce tubers such as potatoes, remember to save enough perfect specimens for planting the following year.

Bear in mind that if you grow a number of closely related varieties, such as pumpkins and marrows, they can produce unusual crosses ('mumpkins' in this case) which may or may not have desirable qualities. This is the process by which new varieties are created – you may be pleasantly surprised and will certainly have fun seeing what you come up with!

Purple sprouting broccoli spring salad; see page 132

6. INGREDIENTS

Although the ideal would be to grow all your own food, it is likely that there will be some ingredients that you haven't grown enough of, that are not suited to your climate or soil, or that are too complex or costly to process on a small scale. As interest in healthy food grows in popularity, the quantity of new ingredients available is growing exponentially. In this chapter we discuss where to get your extra ingredients from and how to choose which ones.

Sourcing Ingredients

The focus should be to obtain organic seasonal ingredients from the following sources, in order of priority.

1. Your own garden or allotment
2. From neighbours (bartered or purchased)
3. A local organic veg-box scheme or co-operative
4. A local organic farm shop or pick-your-own (PYO) enterprise
5. A national organic veg-box scheme
6. A mail-order organic wholesaler (you may need to buy in bulk or club together with neighbours to make this work)
7. Village greengrocers/health food stores (not all produce may be organic)
8. A supermarket.

Using seasonal ingredients grown locally helps the fight against food miles (how far a food item is transported from producer to consumer). It is nonsensical that we can buy asparagus imported from South America at the same time as our own local asparagus is available. Apples flown halfway round the world are on sale just as our local ones are in season. Every time we buy an imported foodstuff that grows in our own country, we are contributing to climate change unnecessarily. The priority list above also helps with reducing unnecessary packaging.

If you do have to resort to a supermarket for a certain item, note that some are more ethical and environmentally friendly than others. The magazine and website, Ethical Consumer (see Resources, page 233), often compares these and the products they sell in detail.

It goes without saying that it's important to read labels of foods that have been processed in any way. Labels like 'dairy-free', 'organic', or 'Fairtrade' don't necessarily mean they are free from ingredients that may not be vegan or conform to your ethics. A good example is vegan margarines or spreads. Some contain palm oil, which is responsible for mass deforestation in areas like Indonesia and Malaysia in order to grow palm trees. The result of the massive palm plantations is pollution, climate change, loss of biodiversity and the threat of extinction of many species including orangutans. Some products say they use 'sustainable palm oil', but this does not mean they cause no harm, and it is debatable how sustainable it is and exactly what their definition of 'sustainable' is. Many technically vegan products contain palm oil, from biscuits to margarines to toothpaste to cosmetics, but there are always alternatives available.

Organic veg-boxes are becoming increasingly popular, but these too can vary in their sources of produce and therefore contributions to climate change and pollution. Some of the larger ones often include items from overseas to give variety. Those that only sell local produce will also mean it is always seasonal. Perhaps vegetables like asparagus should be all the more enjoyable and special because we can look forward to eating them in late spring, rather than any old time of the year. Some veg-box schemes also sell meat and dairy products, so you may not wish to support them from a vegan standpoint.

Broad bean risotto, see page 162

Improvising Recipes

When it comes to following recipes, such as those in this book, it's important not to dismiss one because you don't have a particular ingredient. To be able to improvise around recipes and create your own is a very useful skill, which comes with practice and experience. One key aspect of this is to regularly taste what you are cooking, so you can tweak ingredients, especially seasonings such as salt, pepper, herbs and spices, as you go along. Professional kitchens always have pots of spoons available next to the cooking area.

Many of the ingredients in our recipes can be replaced and we have made various suggestions throughout, though most should be obvious. For example, our broad bean risotto works equally as well with peas, and many other vegetables too. Other ingredients may not be to your taste and can simply be omitted: not everyone likes olives, for example, but these are nearly always optional in our recipes. If you're making caponata but find you have run out of sultanas, don't worry; just leave them out!

Many herbs and spices can be substituted with others, depending on your taste and what you have available. The same goes for oils and sweeteners, all of which we discuss in more detail below. We may have listed agave nectar in a recipe for example, but if you don't have any, or don't like it, you can use a different sweetener, such as stevia, maple syrup or sugar.

Recipes involving baking cakes and breads tend to require more careful attention to ingredient quantities and oven timings. Start by following the guidelines, but be prepared to adjust as you go along as not all ovens are calibrated accurately.

Oils

There are many different edible oils to choose from and many factors as to why you might choose one rather than another. As you might expect, we recommend organic oils wherever possible, and to avoid those grown as large monocrops (such as non-organic rapeseed) that reduce biodiversity in our landscape and may be genetically modified. Palm oil is to be avoided as previously mentioned.

Flavour may be another factor: extra-virgin olive oil is often chosen for flavouring salad dressings and Mediterranean dishes, whereas nut oils can impart an extra flavour to stir-fries. Some are more nutritionally beneficial than others, like flaxseed and sesame oil. Cold-pressed oils are also favoured as they are less likely to have turned rancid or have had chemicals used in their extraction.

When using oils in cooking, it's important to understand 'smoke point'. This is the point at which oils start to burn, change chemically, and produce toxic compounds. Those with high smoke points, such as sunflower, are best for pan-frying and baking. Once oil has been heated, it actually lowers its smoke point, which is why it's not a good idea to reuse oil for deep-frying, for example.

There are also various dairy-free/vegan margarines and spreads available which can be used in frying, baking and for spreading. Check the ingredients as some that describe themselves as 'sunflower spread', for example, actually also contain a mix of other vegetable oils including palm. Many contain supplements such as vitamin B12, which can be a bonus.

Here's a guide to some of the more common cooking oils in order of decreasing smoke point.

Avocado oil

The highest smoke point – perfect for frying at high temperatures or roasting in the oven. Can also be used for salad dressings. High levels of vitamin E.

Sunflower oil

(Refined – note that unrefined oils tend to have a lower smoke point). A flavourless oil – good for baking and frying. High levels of vitamin E.

Corn oil

A general purpose oil with a relatively high smoke point which can be used for frying, baking and dressings. The downside, however, is that corn oil contains high levels of omega-6 with 98% of the fatty acids present. Excessive levels of omega-6 relative to omega-3 fatty acids may increase the probability of various diseases, including some cancers and depression.

Sesame oil

A nutty flavour, often available as toasted sesame oil, which has a stronger flavour, used with Asian dishes as a marinade or dressing. Light sesame oil can also be used for deep-frying.

Groundnut oil

Made from peanuts, can be used for frying and dressings.

Palm oil

Relatively high in saturated fats, so an unhealthy oil. Cause of deforestation and biodiversity loss as previously mentioned. Avoid if possible.

Almond oil

A nutty almond flavour. Good for baking and sauces.

Olive oil

Light olive oil is good for frying at a medium or low temperature, while extra virgin has a lower smoke point and a greater flavour and should be reserved for dressings and sauces.

Walnut oil

A delicate nutty flavour. Good for dressings.

Rapeseed oil

(Also known as canola – a variety produced in Canada with reduced bitterness and erucic acid, which may cause heart damage). Very low in saturated fats, good for frying, baking and dressings. Ideally only use when organic, however, as it is usually grown in vast mono-crops that are treated with pesticides and herbicides. Also note that about 90% of the world's canola crop is genetically modified.

Coconut oil

Increasingly popular as extra-virgin organic coconut oil (solidified) for cosmetic purposes as well as in cooking. Can be used for frying, baking and roasting. Imparts a slight coconut flavour. Unlike other plant oils, coconut oil has high levels of saturated fats, which has led to debate about healthy it is. However, as it also contains healthy fats that can reduce cholesterol, it is thought to be a good oil for heart health, though probably not as good as olive oil.

Hemp oil

Can be used in both cooking and dressings but not for frying at high temperatures. High nutritional values and good levels of health-giving omega-3 fatty acids.

Flaxseed oil

(also known as linseed oil): A very healthy oil but with the lowest smoke point, used in dressings. It has the highest levels of omega-3 fatty acids.

Sweeteners

There is much confusion over the pros and cons of the various sweeteners when it comes to health. Much of the sugar we consume (mostly unknowingly as it is added to many processed foods and drinks) comes from sugar cane or sugar beet. The extracted juices are refined by a series of boiling and crystallising procedures, which produces molasses/treacle as a by-product, to result in pure sucrose (white granulated sugar). When we eat sucrose it is broken down in the body into the simple carbohydrates glucose and fructose (50:50). Glucose is transported via blood to our cells where it is needed for energy; fructose is taken to the liver where it is metabolised directly into fat.

These carbohydrate sugars are essential for our bodies and occur naturally in most fruits and vegetables, but generally we consume far too many. Too much glucose causes unhealthy spikes in blood sugar. This is measured in foods as the glycemic index (GI). High GI foods contain a lot of glucose. Blood sugar spikes cause tiredness and can ultimately lead to heart disease. Too much fructose causes fat build-up and can cause obesity, insulin resistance (diabetes), heart disease and cancer. In general, fructose is considered unhealthier than glucose, but too much of any sugar is unhealthy and also bad for our teeth.

Note that a few sugar producers use animal bone charcoal (bonechar) in the refining process, in which case it's not vegan. This is more common in the US than in the UK. To make it even more confusing, the largest UK supplier states that their white sugar is vegan but they cannot guarantee their brown sugars are, as some bonechar may be used by their suppliers. You can research this online to get the latest information on which sugars are guaranteed to be vegan.

Artificial sweeteners have been chemically created to provide a taste of sweetness without the sugars and calories. The most well known are saccharin and aspartame, but there are many others. Both of these have been linked to cancer in the past, though a vast number of tests have suggested that they're actually safe for human consumption after all. However, the health scares and the unpleasant after taste have put many people off them (although they are in many processed drinks and low calorie foods). Further studies have shown that some artificial sweeteners may react with other food additives to produce toxic substances, and that frequent consumption may increase the risk of depression and other illnesses. One additional possible problem is that low calorie sweeteners can still lead the body to release too much insulin, which can lead to weight gain in the long term.

Honey is not considered vegan, partly because we are exploiting animals by taking their hard-earned, precious food reserves, which can affect their health, and partly because some of the bee-farming methods used are highly unethical. Many of the common blended honeys found on the supermarket shelves come from large farms where, in some cases, the hives, containing live bees, are burnt at the end of the season because this is cheaper than feeding the bees through the winter. Other unethical practices include artificial feeding regimes, artificial insemination, treatment with antibiotics and barbaric transportation conditions.

Below is a list of commonly used sweeteners, excluding honey and artificial sweeteners. Essentially all are ultimately unhealthy as our bodies receive all the carbohydrates they need from those naturally occurring in fruits and vegetables. Low GI may sound good, but may come at the expense of high fructose, which can be unhealthier, as explained above. Refined sugar is only a little worse from a health point of view, as the quantities of nutrients in unrefined sugar are tiny compared to the amount we get from plant-based whole foods. Some sweeteners, such as agave nectar, are hyped-up as being natural and healthy, but remember that regular white sugar comes from a plant too. A lot of this is just a marketing ploy. However, one advantage of some of the more recently popular sweeteners, like coconut sugar, is that they're more likely to be organic and better for the environment than vast monocrops of sugar cane and beet.

Stevia (see below) is certainly the healthiest option, but comes with its own disadvantages. Perhaps the bottom line is, apart from a few exceptions, don't get too hung up on which sweetener to use; concentrate on using less. An occasional treat is good for the soul!

Agave nectar

Extracted from the agave cactus. It's high in fructose (70-90%). As it's sweeter than sugar you can use less, resulting in fewer calories.

Apple juice concentrate

Can be used to add sweetness in baking and dressings. Contains some vitamin C but is essentially sugar.

Brown rice syrup

It produces almost 100% glucose in the body. It has a caramel flavour – used for dressings and cakes.

Brown sugar

Some is unrefined (technically less refined), but some is refined and then has a small amount of molasses added back to give the brown colour. High GI.

Coconut sugar

Extracted from the sap of the coconut plant, 35-45% fructose with

small amounts of fibre and nutrients, makes it healthier than white sugar.

Date nectar

Rich, dark extract from dates. Can be used as a replacement for honey in recipes. It is unrefined so contains some nutrients.

Golden syrup

(Also known as light treacle). Like treacle this is also a by-product of refining sugar cane or beet. A thick, amber-coloured syrup often used in baking and desserts or as a replacement for honey. It is a mixture of sucrose, glucose and fructose so has the same effect on the body as pure sugar.

High fructose corn syrup (HFCS)

Added to many processed foods in the US, a higher fructose content than sugar, banned for use in organic foods. To be avoided if possible.

Maple syrup

The sap of maple trees from North America and Canada. 100% pure maple syrup is the best, but expensive; cheaper ones are diluted with fruit syrups. Low GI.

Molasses/treacle

A by-product of refining sugar. Three successive boiling/crystallising procedures produce blackstrap molasses or black treacle. Retains some sugar and hence sweetness, plus various minerals including calcium and iron. Used in marinades, sauces and baking (gingerbread, for example).

Muscovado sugar

Dark and sticky due to the higher quantity of molasses – raw and unrefined. Used in baking. High GI.

Stevia

Extracted from the leaves of the stevia plant. Zero calories and zero GI but 300 times as sweet as sugar. It can have a bitter aniseed-like aftertaste but is probably the healthiest option. It is sold under various trade names; read the ingredients list as some contain lactose (from milk). It can be expensive but you can also buy a mixture of sugar and stevia, which is twice as sweet as regular sugar, enabling you to halve the amount you use in recipes, but  keep the taste. Stevia plants are tender perennials that can be grown at home from cuttings (the seeds are difficult to germinate). The dried leaves can then be used to sweeten teas.

White sugar

Refined, pure sucrose. High GI. Produces glucose and fructose 50/50.

We have used a variety of sweeteners in our recipes, but you can substitute them with any of your choice. Our conclusion is that if you get on with stevia then go with that, otherwise limit high fructose sweeteners and avoid, where possible, artificial ones.

Grains

In general, use organic whole grains where possible. White flour products and white rice have had the fibre, vitamins and minerals removed and can disrupt your blood sugar levels. Several servings of whole grains are recommended per day as part of a healthy diet. Store all grains in airtight jars and out of sunlight. Here are some of the most common grains.

Amaranth

Tiny gluten-free grains with a slight grassy flavour. Can be used as an alternative to rice or in soups and stews. High in protein.

Barley

Good source of fibre and selenium – can be used as a substitute for rice in risottos and also in soups and stews. Whole barley is better than pearl barley, which has been refined. Soak before use.

Buckwheat

A gluten-free seed often used as a flour. Higher protein content than other grains with all essential amino acids. Often made into wraps, pancakes and used as an ingredient in burgers.

Bulgur wheat

A cracked wheat product that has been parboiled. More nutritious than couscous, often served as part of a salad.

Couscous

Quick-cooking wheat berries originally from North Africa – goes well with salads or as an alternative to rice.

Corn/maize

Source of vitamins B1, B5 and C. It can be eaten as a side vegetable, mixed into stews, directly from the cob, or in salads. It can also be ground to make polenta (cornmeal), which is used in making cakes and breads as well as baked polenta. Gluten-free.

Millet

A nutritious seed with a slightly nutty flavour. Often toasted before cooking. Can be added to numerous dishes or made into a loaf.

Oats

Nutrient rich and lowers cholesterol. Technically gluten-free but can be contaminated, so check labelling if necessary. Excellent in breads and baking but can also be added to stews, smoothies and breakfast cereals.

Quinoa

A nutritious grain originating in high altitude areas of South America. It's unusual in that it contains all essential amino acids, and it has six times the protein level of rice. It can be grown in temperate regions but the processing can be time-consuming and fiddly on a small scale (see the chapter Challenging Crops, page 101). Imported quinoa has the associated problem of food miles and, as demand and prices rise, the Andean farmers cannot afford to eat their own crops. There are companies growing quinoa in the UK now, however. In general it is thought to be healthier and more environmentally friendly than rice.

Rice

A staple in many parts of the world. Grown in paddies (flooded fields) mainly in Asia, which brings the disadvantage of methane emissions from anaerobic bacterial action in the water. Methane is a more powerful greenhouse gas than carbon dioxide and as a result rice paddies worldwide are a sizeable cause of climate change. Imported rice has the additional issue of food miles.

Rye

It has an earthy, slightly sweet flavour. Delicious when used as a flour in bread-making, but can also be added to stews and salads.

Spelt

A wheat-based grain with a nutty flavour. Easier to digest than wheat. The flour makes tasty bread and the grains can be used to replace rice or in soups, stews and breakfast cereals.

Wheat

Most often used as a flour in bread-baking and for making pasta, but wheat berry grains can also be used in soups and stews. Note that most dried pastas are vegan as fresh pasta tends to be made with egg.

Pulses

Legumes are plants from the family Fabaceae that produce pods containing seeds known as pulses, such as peas, beans and lentils. They are a great source of protein, fibre, carbohydrates and minerals. Several servings per day are recommended as part of a healthy diet.

Pulses can be used fresh from the garden or purchased in dried or tinned form. Tinned pulses are pre-cooked and can be used immediately in recipes, but have less texture than dried, are more expensive and produce more waste in their manufacture. Dried pulses need soaking before cooking, often for eight hours or overnight, and then must be boiled for lengthy periods (45-90 minutes). Many pulses can be sprouted and eaten in that form as already detailed in the chapter Sprouting, page 51.

Note that when you are measuring dried pulses to use in a recipe, their volume increases by about three times during soaking/cooking. If you are short of time, a speedier way of soaking dried pulses is to place them in a pan with three times their volume of cold water, bring to the boil then turn off the heat, cover the pan and leave for at least one hour, ideally three or four. Then drain, rinse and proceed with cooking.

Some pulses, notably beans and lentils, contain toxins and anti-nutrients. These may be mild when young and fresh, which is why it's fine to eat a few French beans straight from the plant, but they concentrate as the seeds mature and dry. These toxins can be reduced by soaking and sprouting or by cooking. In particular, be careful with kidney beans, which can make you very ill if eaten raw.

There are many different pulses available worldwide, but the ones listed below are those we use most often.

Beans

Soya, haricot, kidney, black, black-eyed, aduki and mung. The latter two are often used for sprouting. Edamame beans are traditionally a preparation of immature soya beans cooked and served in the pod with salt. They originated in Japan hundreds of years ago but are now eaten all over the world. The word 'edamame' is now also used to describe young green soya beans and other immature pulses, whether served in the pod or not. At this young stage they are sweeter than when fully mature.

Lentils

Green, brown, red and Puy (which are grown in the Le Puy region of France and are known for their peppery flavour and for holding their shape during cooking).

Peas

Green peas, chickpeas, yellow split peas. Chickpeas are used to make houmous (also often spelt as 'hummus'). Yellow split peas can be used in stews and dhal, where they can be combined with red lentils. Chickpeas can also be made into 'gram flour', used in a variety of recipes including onion bhajis.

Shelled borlotti beans

Soya beans (also known as 'soybeans') can be eaten directly, but are most well known for being processed further (see below) to produce high protein foods.

Miso

A traditional Japanese seasoning made from fermented soya beans and grains, such as barley or rice. Very salty and rich in nutrients, it can be used to flavour soups, stews and sauces.

Seitan

Commonly used as 'mock duck'. Almost pure gluten; made from a flour called 'vital wheat gluten'. Used as a meat substitute and to add texture to burgers.

Soy sauce

Also made from fermented soya beans and grains, producing a liquid sauce used for flavouring dishes including tofu and stir-fries. The more traditional variety tamari is healthier and has a stronger flavour.

Tempeh

Made by fermenting soya beans and binding into a cake form. Often used as a meat-substitute.

Tofu

Compressed bean curd made by coagulating soya milk. Very versatile – soaks up other flavours and available in various forms including hard ('firm') and soft ('silken').

Soya beans have had a bad press in the last decade or so, as large areas of Amazon rainforest have been cleared to grow them in huge monocrops. However, the vast majority of this is to produce high protein feed for livestock, principally cattle grown for beef in America. Only a small percentage of soya is grown for human consumption, and that is produced by a variety of countries around the world. Bear in mind that virtually all US soya is GM contaminated.

Sweet chestnut

Nuts and Seeds

High in protein and nutrients, nuts and seeds make healthy snacks as well as having multiple uses in cooking. Various nuts can be soaked for a few hours to make them more easily digestible and to soften them before blending to make vegan milks, creams and cheeses. We have included several recipes in the chapter Cooking throughout the Year, page 109.

Nuts

A fruit with a hard shell containing a seed – not all the following are technically nuts, but have been included as they can be treated in the same way.

Almonds

An extremely healthy nut, packed with protein, vitamins and minerals, and especially high in calcium. Almonds can be soaked and made into a milk easily at home. They are also one of the few nuts that can be sprouted. Ground almonds, also known as almond meal, can be used in some cake baking as an alternative to wheat flour.

Brazils

Sizeable nuts from large trees that grow in the tropics, mainly in South America. High in selenium (an essential nutrient with antioxidant properties) as well as protein. Can be eaten whole or chopped and used in fruit cakes or on salads.

Cashews

Calorific, sweet and healthy nuts from a tropical evergreen tree that was originally from the Amazon but now grown all over the world. The nut most often used to soak and make into vegan milks, creams and cheeses at home as mentioned in several of our recipes.

Chestnuts

A versatile nut that can be foraged easily in the autumn and roasted, or puréed and added to sauces and deserts. High in starch. Store them in the fridge.

Coconuts

From the coconut palm grown in tropical countries. One coconut is said to provide all the essential minerals, vitamins and energy requirements for one person for one day. Available commercially as milks for cereals and drinking, full-fat milks and creams for use in desserts and curries, as coconut water for drinking and coconut flesh for cooking with.

Hazelnuts

(Also known as cobnuts or filberts which are cultivated varieties). Can be foraged or grown at home as a shrub or small tree. A very tasty nut that is often used in baking but can also be eaten as a snack or sprinkled on cereals and salads.

Macadamias

Expensive nuts originally from Australia but now grown in other countries too. Sweet tasting and rich in B vitamins. Excellent in desserts after soaking and creaming. Can also be used in pesto.

Peanuts

(Also known as groundnuts). Actually a legume from nitrogen-fixing plants that grow quickly in warm climates. A relatively cheap, protein-packed nut often eaten as a snack. Also used in Thai recipes and loved by many as peanut butter.

Pecans

From the hickory tree. Rich in vitamin E and minerals. Often used in desserts and can also be sprinkled on salads or eaten as snacks.

Pine nuts

Edible seeds from a variety of species of pine trees. A sweet, creamy taste that makes them useful when baking cakes or cookies. They can also be sprinkled on salads, in cereals and pasta dishes as well as being used as an ingredient in pesto. Often toasted before use.

Pistachios

High in vitamin E and minerals, especially iron and copper. The green-coloured nut is often used in baking and deserts, including ice cream, but is also delicious as a savoury snack.

Walnuts

From a large tree, which would be perfect as the canopy layer in a forest garden if you have the space and the time as it takes many years to mature. The only nut containing an omega-3 fatty acid. Toasting them can reduce their slight bitterness. Often used in baking, but can also be used in pesto (see our recipe in the chapter Cooking throughout the Year, page 166).

If you're eating nuts as snacks or sprinkled on cereals and salads, the general advice is to have a mixture of several different nuts to get a good combination of all the super vitamins and minerals they provide.

Seeds

All the grains, pulses and nuts are seeds, but some commonly used ones that we haven't mentioned so far include the following.

Chia

Known as one of the healthiest of seeds and often referred to as a superfood. Rich in protein, iron, calcium, vitamin C, antioxidants, omega-3 and fibre. Can be scattered on salads, breakfast cereals or used in desserts.

Flax

Rich in fibre and essential fatty acids – often used as a vegan source of omega-3. The ground seeds are more nutritious than when whole, and can be used in smoothies, breakfast cereals and in baking.

Hemp

The seeds contain all the essential amino acids and it is the highest botanical source of essential fatty acids. Commonly available as milk and oil.

Pomegranate

A rich source of antioxidants, vitamin C and potassium. Often sprinkled over salads and desserts.

Poppy

Tiny black seeds from the opium poppy. High levels of essential minerals including calcium and iron. Often used in and on breads, pastries, and cakes.

Pumpkin

Rich in protein and B vitamins. Said to be effective in treating depression and kidney stones. Can be eaten raw or lightly toasted, sprinkled over salads, cereals or as a snack. Try roasting them in tamari sauce.

Sesame

Often used as an oil, but the small seeds can also be used on salads and in baking. Rich in fibre and minerals.

Sunflower

Excellent source of vitamin E and magnesium. Makes a light oil for general frying and cooking purposes, or, as a seed, can be used in baking or scattered on salads and cereals.

Spices

Derived from part of a plant (seeds, fruits, roots, berries and so on, but not the leafy parts, otherwise they would be categorised as herbs), spices are used for colouring, flavouring and/or preserving foods. The spice trade has been important for humans for thousands of years. We have included some more seeds in the list below as they are used to add spice/heat to dishes.

Allspice

(Also known as Jamaican pepper or pimenta). A dried fruit from the pimenta tree native to Central America. Pungent and strongly flavoured, used in baking but also stews, curries and marinades. It's the largest component of Jamaican jerk seasoning. Not to be confused with 'mixed spice', which is a British blend of coriander, cinnamon, cloves, ginger and nutmeg – an excellent combination for spiced cakes and gingerbread.

Anise

A sweet aromatic spice with a strong liquorice/aniseed flavour. High in vitamins, good for coughs and colds. The seeds can be made into tea or used in baking.

Black Pepper

Originating in India and known as the 'king of spice'. Very commonly used as an everyday seasoning with a pungent and hot taste. Best obtained as whole peppercorns, which can be stored for years, and ground directly onto food just before consumption.

Caraway

A member of the parsley family producing anise-tasting seeds that can be added to breads, sauerkraut and salads.

Cardamom

A warm, aromatic spice often used in Indian cooking and in baking. It has many health benefits including aiding digestion and acting as an antiseptic.

Chilli

High levels of vitamin C, often included in dishes to add heat. Chillies can be easily grown at home as described in the chapter Fruits and Vegetables, page 89.

Cinnamon

Made from the outer bark of a *Cinnamomum* tree – a common spice in both sweet and savoury dishes. Very high in antioxidants.

Cloves

Dried flower buds from a tree from the Myrtaceae family – a sweet, warming spice used in baking and some curries. They have anaesthetic properties, which is why they were chewed to relieve toothache.

Coriander

The leaves are described in the next chapter Herbs, page 42, but the seeds are often used to spice curries, soups and stews. Delivering an earthy flavour, they can easily be grown at home – just let a few coriander plants run to seed then collect them when the seeds have turned brown.

Cumin

The seeds produce a strong, smoky, warm flavour often used in curries. Aids digestion and relieves colds. High in B vitamins.

Garam masala

Originating in India – a blend of coriander, cumin, turmeric, cinnamon, black pepper, cloves, ginger, dill seed and cardamom. It adds a wonderful flavour to curries but can be used in other dishes requiring a subtle spicy curry flavour. We sometimes add a little to tahini dressings, for example.

Ginger

A spicy, zesty flavour from the rhizome of a tropical plant originating in India. It can be used fresh and grated in many dishes, including stews, curries, cakes, desserts and drinks. Also available in dried powdered form, which is useful in baking. Used as a medicine to treat nausea.

Fennel

Packed with vitamins, fennel seeds have an aniseed flavour, but not as strong as anise itself.

Mustard

The seeds add heat and flavour to many dishes, including curries. They benefit from being fried in hot oil first until they crack/pop. Commonly used as a condiment in paste form in many countries.

Nutmeg

The ground kernel from the fruit of the nutmeg tree from Indonesia. Sometimes confused with mace, which has a more delicate flavour, and is made from the crimson threads that cover the dried fruit of the same tree. They both deliver a sweet, warm flavour used in sweet and savoury dishes.

Paprika

Made from dried red capsicum peppers, delivering a sweet, warm flavour and a bright red colour when added to stews. Also available in smoked form.

Saffron

A very expensive spice made from the dried stigmas of crocus flowers (*Crocus sativus*), giving a subtle, floral flavour, and often used to colour foods such as rice, an amber/yellow colour. Many health benefits: can fight stress, infection, cancer, and aid digestion amongst other things.

Tamarind

Made from the fruit pulp of the tamarind tree originating in tropical Africa. Often sold as a paste that adds a sweet and sour taste to dishes, both sweet and savoury.

Turmeric

A bright yellow spice made from the rhizome of a plant from the ginger family. Numerous culinary uses, including in curries and cakes. Sometimes used to colour foods yellow in place of the more expensive saffron. Known as one of the healthiest spices, it has been used to treat amongst many other ailments.

Vanilla

A strong aromatic flavour often used in baking and in ice cream. The flavour comes from the seeds inside the pod of a vanilla orchid originating in Central America. You can purchase the pods and scrape out the seeds yourself, or an extract in liquid form, or as a powder or flavoured sugar.

Herbs

As herbs are easy to grow we have dedicated a whole chapter to them – coming next!

Other Ingredients

Finally, we'd like to mention a couple of other ingredients that we use often and feature in some of our recipes. Both are available from health food shops and some supermarkets.

Bouillon

(Swiss vegetable). A powder that makes an excellent instant stock that is gluten and yeast free. It comes in several varieties including organic vegan. It also makes a quick and tasty hot drink – just stir a teaspoonful into a mug of hot, not boiling, water. Boiling water will reduce the vitamin and mineral content.

Nutritional yeast

(Engevita, also known as yeast flakes). Provides a cheesy, nutty taste when added to sauces, stews and soups, plus can be sprinkled on pasta dishes, salads and breakfast cereals. Made from a strain of yeast grown on sugar beet molasses then inactivated. Gluten-free and rich in B vitamins, folic acid and zinc. We usually buy the version with added vitamin B12.

7. HERBS

Even people with no garden at all can grow a selection of herbs in pots on the windowsill. They are easy to grow, generally hardy, and will make a fragrant and attractive display. Many can be grown and harvested throughout the year (especially those grown indoors) and as well as flavouring food they have many other uses: attracting and feeding wildlife (bees, butterflies, other beneficial insects and birds), repelling garden pests (used as companion plants), providing edible flowers as well as leaves, and making potpourris. Herbs also have many health-giving properties whether used directly as medicines or generally in food.

Most herbs are either annuals (completing their life cycle in one year, and therefore needing to be re-grown from seed each year, such as basil) or perennials (that live for more than two years, rosemary for example). While perennials will do well in a herb rockery or spiral, annuals are more often grown in pots or raised beds. All will also do well in hanging baskets, window boxes or other containers. In general they like good drainage, so mix some horticultural grit into the compost you use and make sure they don't sit in standing water. Many herbs are Mediterranean in origin and like warm, sunny positions. For annuals you will need to collect or buy seed, whereas some perennials can also be propagated by taking cuttings or dividing larger plants.

To take cuttings, choose a shoot about 10cm long and cut just below a leaf node. Remove leaves from the lower third of the stem and plant in a pot with free-draining compost. Cover the pot with a plastic bag, without it touching the leaves, and place in a sheltered spot. Check regularly and water lightly if the compost starts to dry. Once new growth is seen, remove the bag and place in a sunny position to grow on.

Ideally you should pick herbs on the morning of a dry day shortly before they flower. Choose the growing tips for the best flavour. Some herbs won't need storing as they can be grown all year round, but for those that are more tender there are various methods.

Freezing is a good way of keeping the flavour of herbs. One useful method is to chop them and freeze small amounts in water in ice cube trays. In each cube put as much as you like to use in your favourite recipes. You can either freeze each herb separately or make up your own mixtures. Once frozen, the cubes can be tipped into labelled plastic bags and placed back in the freezer so you don't run out of cube trays. Cooking with them is simple – just add a herby ice cube or two to your recipe as required.

Alternatively, sprigs of herbs such as parsley, coriander and mint can simply be washed, dried and frozen in plastic bags. They can then be crushed straight from frozen when required. Drying will concentrate the flavour of herbs and enable you to store them in jars for long periods (though they do gradually lose their flavour over time). A warm, dry place is needed for drying: an airing cupboard may do but will take a few days; a warm oven (at about 50°C) will take a few hours. Herbs can be hung in bunches or laid out on a baking sheet. When the leaves are dry, crumble them into glass jars, seal, label and store in a cool, dark place. Again, you can make up your own mixture of favourites to use as general 'mixed herbs' for many dishes. Our own general mix includes sage, thyme, oregano and parsley.

In some cases you may want to store the seeds instead of, or as well as, the leaves. Coriander is a good example: its aromatic seeds are often used in dishes such as curries. To collect and store the seeds, simply hang the whole plant, when the seeds have fully formed, to dry in a warm sunny room or outbuilding. Then shake the seeds off in a bag, and store in glass jars in a cool, dark place.

Many herbs can be added to vinegars to impart their flavour. These vinegars can then be used in salad dressings and to pickle other vegetables. To make a herb vinegar dressing, crush a few leaves of the herb (or herbs) and add to a jar of wine vinegar or cider vinegar. Keep in a warm place for a few weeks, shaking the jar every now and again. Then strain out the leaves and use or bottle the vinegar. Try it with thyme, rosemary, tarragon, basil, bay, dill or your own favourite herbs. The same technique can be used with oils like olive oil to give them a particular herby flavour. The resulting oils are great for cooking savoury dishes with, as well as for using in dressings.

There are hundreds of different herbs and their varieties available; here is a guide to the most commonly grown.

Chive flowers

Basil

Annual. Sweet Genovese is the most common variety with large, strong-flavoured leaves that have a sweet clove-like spiciness. Other varieties include Bush, Lemon, Cinnamon, Red Ruben, Greek and Lettuce Leaved. The leaves are the main ingredient in pesto (see our recipe in the Cooking throughout the Year chapter) but can also be torn up in salads, soups and sauces and to flavour vinegars and oils. Basil goes very well with tomato and garlic. Putting the whole plant on a windowsill can deter flies; a tea made from basil leaves can aid digestion. Sow from seed. They will do well in pots indoors as well as in the garden.

Bay

Also known as sweet bay – a perennial grown as a shrub or small tree, usually purchased as a potted young plant. Generally hardy but watch out for hard frosts. The leaves are often added to stews (but removed before serving as they are quite tough) and can also be used to flavour vinegar. Sweet bay is a type of laurel, but do not confuse this with other laurels, as they are poisonous. Cuttings can be taken in late summer to propagate further plants.

Chives

Perennial. It will die back in the winter if grown outdoors, and recover in spring, but grow new plants from seed

every few years as old plants lose their flavour. Both the leaves and flowers can be eaten. Finely chopped chives are a classic addition to a potato salad but will go with any dish that would benefit from a mild onion flavour. The flowers make an attractive topping for salads but leave plenty on the plants as they are a magnet for bees. Garlic chives have flatter leaves and a sweet garlic flavour. Chives can be used as a companion plant to deter aphids.

Coriander

Annual. Coriander (cilantro) is a variety suited for leaf production for use in salads and cooking. Collect the dried seeds in August and use in pickling, chutneys and cooking – grind with a pestle and mortar for adding to curries, for example. Save a few seeds for sowing next year.

Cumin

Annual. Produces spicy seeds, classically used to flavour curries, either ground or whole. When the seed heads turn brown, cut the plants and hang indoors to dry. The seeds can then be collected and stored in glass jars in a cool dark cupboard.

Dill

Annual. Both leaves and seeds can be used to flavour sauces, vinegars and pickles. The fine leaves can also be chopped and used to flavour soups and salads. In the garden, allow some flower heads to form and they should self-seed and grow new plants next year.

Fennel

Perennial. The leaves and seeds of common fennel have an anise flavour and can be used fresh or dried to flavour food such as bread, salads or soups. (See also Florence fennel in the Fruits and Vegetables chapter, page 79.) Plants can be divided in the autumn, but should also self-seed in situ.

Fennel

Lavender

Perennial. Usually grown as a small shrub in a border. The mauve flowers can be used sparingly to flavour sweet foods such as biscuits and jams. Lavender is a super plant in the garden for attracting bees and butterflies over the summer flowering period. A tea made from the flowers can relieve headaches; it has many other healing properties, as well as being said to promote good sleep. Once the flowers have faded, cut the stems back and, as plants become straggly, cut them back in the spring. Stem cuttings can be taken in spring or autumn.

Lemon Balm

Perennial. Produces lemon-flavoured leaves, perfect in salads, cooked dishes, drinks and fruit salads. Lemon balm tea is said to relieve headaches and feverish colds. The plants can be divided in the spring. They will also do well in pots indoors.

Marjoram and Oregano

Sweet marjoram is an annual, pot marjoram a perennial. Use fresh to flavour salads and vegetable dishes or dry

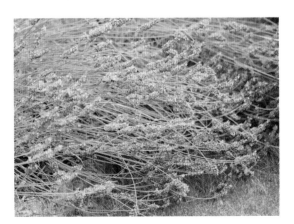

the leaves for winter use. Excellent for pizzas and most tomato-based dishes or sauces. Make tea from the flowering tops to relieve colds and headaches. There is often confusion between marjoram and oregano. Oregano is the name of the genus, within which are many species and varieties including the marjorams, which tend to be milder in flavour than other oreganos. All have similar uses. The plants can be divided in the spring.

Mint

Perennial. There are numerous varieties including peppermint, spearmint and apple mint. Each has a different flavour and strength. Use to make mint sauce and for flavouring dishes such as peas and/or potatoes. Mint tea is popular and is good for aiding digestion and relieving colds. It can be grown as a companion plant to deter aphids. The plant spreads vigorously so is best contained in a pot. They can be divided in spring to propagate new plants.

If you like mint sauce with roasted vegetables here's a quick and easy recipe to make your own:

Mint Sauce

1 handful of mint leaves
125g sugar
200ml malt vinegar

Wash the mint, chop it very finely and place in a glass jar. Heat the vinegar and sugar in a pan until the sugar has dissolved then allow the mixture to cool. Fill the jar with the vinegar mixture and seal immediately. Store in the refrigerator once opened.

Parsley

Hardy biennial (completes its life cycle in two years). Recommended varieties: Champion moss curled (classic tightly-curled leaves, crops over a long period), Italian giant (hardy and vigorous with large flat leaves). Rich in vitamins and iron, parsley is one of the most commonly grown and used herbs. Finely chopped parsley is often used as a garnish for many dishes but can also be used in salads, soups, sauces and in sandwiches. If used in a cooked dish, add the parsley towards the end of the cooking time. Use in generous amounts and include the stems too as they are more highly flavoured than the leaves. Sow parsley from seed but after two years they should self-seed in situ.

Rosemary

Perennial. An evergreen shrub with strongly-flavoured leaves that complement roasted vegetables. The small flowers can be used in salads. The plants can get quite large after a few years, but you can create new ones from cuttings.

Sage

Perennial. There are a number of different varieties available with different flavours and leaf colours. Purple-leaved varieties tend to have a stronger flavour, while those with variegated leaves are often milder. Use the leaves fresh or dried for flavouring stews and roasted vegetables. They can also be used to flavour vinegars, oils and breads. The leaves can be added to many dishes, and are also great fried until crispy in a little oil then crumbled over a pasta dish. After a few years the plants can get straggly, so grow new ones from seed or cuttings. Cut the plants back after flowering.

Savory

Winter savory is a perennial; summer savory is an annual. The winter variety has a peppery spiciness and does well in pots. Both can be used to flavour bean, potato and tomato recipes. A tea made from the flowering tops can ease digestion or be used as an antiseptic gargle.

Tarragon

Perennial. The flavour is a combination of sweet aniseed and vanilla. The leaves can be used in sauces and dressings and go well with avocados, tomatoes and various salads. Cut the plants back in the winter and they will grow back next year. To propagate tarragon you can either divide the roots in spring or take stem cuttings in the summer. They will also do well indoors in pots.

Thyme

Perennial. Low-growing evergreen plant with well flavoured leaves for cooking or tea-making. There are many different varieties available, all with small leaves and flowers, which are adored by bees. The leaves go well in sauces and soups and can also be used in jams and fruit salads. Use sparingly as the flavour of the fresh leaves is strong. Thyme is often a component of 'mixed herbs'. It has many medicinal properties and a tea made by infusing the leaves is good for digestion and to relieve hangovers, as well as to treat colds and sore throats. They can be propagated from stem cuttings or by dividing roots in the spring.

8. SALAD LEAVES

With the combination of successional sowing, growing under cover and choice of varieties, salad leaves can be cultivated and harvested throughout all seasons.

The days of simply sowing a few rows of lettuces in the spring and summer are long gone. There is a huge array of plants available now that produce leaves with many different shapes, sizes, colours, flavours and textures. Many can still be grown as individual plants and harvested as a whole, but increasingly more are grown as cut-and-come-again crops, or harvested as baby leaves (also known as micro leaves). If you are feeding just one or two people you may find yourself self-sufficient for salad leaves simply by sowing a seed tray or two of mixed leaves every couple of weeks throughout the year.

Salad leaves are quick and easy to grow and you can harvest as much as you need for your meal just minutes before eating, resulting in a far fresher and healthier (and more environmentally friendly) salad than you could possibly get buying leaves from a supermarket. If you cannot harvest immediately before preparing your meal, for example if you have an allotment which you visit only once or twice a week, pack the leaves in a plastic bag, keep out of the sun, and place in your fridge at home as soon as possible. If they look wilted, refresh in cold water.

In addition to the more traditional salad plants there are many others that can be harvested for their young leaves to add to salads, including carrots, cabbages, radish, beetroot, kale, peas, spinach, turnip and chard. If you have some old or excess seeds of vegetables like these, sowing a mixture in a tray for baby leaves is a great way of using them up. Never waste anything that could feed you!

As most salad plants are quick to grow they won't need special feeding as long as you start out with a good compost. Ideally use your own mix of garden compost with added grit for drainage, but be aware that if your compost has not heated up enough to kill weed seeds you may have trouble distinguishing them from the plants you have sown, especially when growing as baby leaves. You may have to buy in an organic peat-free multi-purpose compost especially for this.

If you wish to grow salad plants to full size you may need to space them 10-20cm apart, depending on the variety. Either raise them in modules then plant out at this spacing, or sow directly more thickly and thin out as they grow, using the thinnings in salads. You don't necessarily have to wait until the plant is mature before harvesting; with many varieties you can pick off the outer leaves as they grow. For baby leaves, sowing can be much more dense: sprinkling the seed on the compost surface so on average each mini plant is just 0.5cm or 1cm from its neighbour. Cover the seeds lightly with more compost and water.

Almost any container will do for salads, from raised beds to window boxes, troughs, pots, seed trays and so on. The plastic trays that you buy foods like mushrooms in will be fine for growing small amounts of baby leaves, especially with the smaller rapidly growing plants like cress, mustard, mizuna, rocket and radish. Ideally the containers will need drainage holes so the compost doesn't get waterlogged; if you are using old mushroom trays indoors you can make holes in the bottom of one and stand it in another, so excess water can drain through into the second one and then be tipped away.

Note that when you harvest baby leaves you can either cut them at stem level (easiest with a pair of scissors) or pick leaves off individually by hand, say one per plant each time. This is a little more time-consuming but the plants will produce further leaves for picking another day, whereas if you cut the leaves at stem level, they may not grow back. After a few weeks of harvesting in this way they will weaken and can then be composted before you re-sow the tray in fresh compost. After a while some plants may start to bolt (grow flower heads) even at a small size; these flower heads can also be eaten but it's a sign that the tray will be coming to its productive end.

Some herbs can also be grown for baby leaves for salads, but bear in mind they can be much more strongly flavoured than other salad leaves, so use sparingly. Those which can be used in salads include basil, coriander, chives, dill, fennel, lemon balm, marjoram, tarragon and parsley (see previous chapter, Herbs).

Growing under cover, whether it's in a greenhouse, polytunnel, cold frame, conservatory or on the kitchen windowsill, will mean faster germination, protection from frosts and less pest damage. Warmer areas such as the kitchen will be perfect for growing small trays of baby leaves through the winter, but there are also some hardy varieties that will survive in an unheated greenhouse or cold frame as detailed below.

Your sowing schedule will depend very much on what cover is available and what you want to grow. In general, outdoor sowings can be made from mid-March through to September. Cover, such as an unheated greenhouse, can extend the seasons at either end by about six weeks and be used over winter for some crops. Warmer cover, such as a heated greenhouse, conservatory or kitchen, will enable you to grow baby leaves for salads at any time, and will be especially useful over the winter months.

Time now to explore in more detail which plants to grow for salad leaves. We start with good old lettuces. There are five main types of lettuce: Batavia which have the crispness of an iceberg with the more open growth of a Butterhead; Butterhead (e.g. Tom Thumb) which are quick to mature and have a loose heart with soft leaves; Cos (e.g. Little Gem) which produce crisp oval heads and are claimed to have a higher nutritional value than other lettuces; Crisphead (Iceberg types – e.g. Webbs Wonderful) which produce large crisp heads with solid hearts and few outer leaves; and Loose Leaf (e.g. Lollo Rossa) which do not heart up and can be harvested a few leaves at a time as they grow.

Recommended Lettuce Varieties

There are many to choose from; the following is just a small selection of our favourites:

Batavia

Crisp heads like an iceberg, but more open-growing like a butterhead

BLONDE DE PARIS – sow spring and summer, crisp green leaves

RELAY – fast growing with red leaves

Butterhead

Mature in about six weeks

TOM THUMB – a superb dwarf variety which grows quickly and is slow to bolt; one lettuce is just the right size for a salad for two

ROXY – red with shiny blistered leaves

Cos

Slower to mature

LITTLE GEM – can be sown from spring to early autumn and, under cover, can be eaten into the winter

RUBENS RED – leaves of a deep red over dark green with good texture and flavour

Crisphead

Generally large-growing and slower to bolt when mature

SALADIN – classic iceberg type, large tight heads

RAPTOR – crunchy round heads, harvested spring, summer and autumn, resistant to bolting

Loose leaf

Harvest individual leaves as the lettuce develops, or entire plant when mature

SALAD BOWL – curly green leaves, crops over a long period

RED SALAD BOWL – attractive deep red-bronze leaves

Winter varieties

Sow late summer and autumn outdoors, and also under cover for extended cropping into spring

WINTER DENSITY – similar to Little Gem but with a larger head, slow to bolt

ROUGE D'HIVER – an old French variety with green leaves tinged with red. Upright with delicious leaves

In addition to packets of seeds of single varieties, there are now various seed mixes available which are especially suitable for sowing closer together for baby leaves. For example:

Mixed lettuce

RED SALAD BOWL, SUZAN, MARVEL OF FOUR SEASONS and **LITTLE LEPRECHAUN**

MultiSalad collection

MULTIBLOND, MULTIBABY and **MULTIRED**

Italian blend

ROCKET, BASIL, OAK LEAF LETTUCE, BROCCOLI RAAB, ITALIAN RED DANDELION

Spicy greens

ROCKET, MUSTARD GREEN WAVE, MUSTARD RED GIANT, MIZUNA

Asian leaves

Suitable for both salads and stir-fries:

BOK BHOY, MIZUNA, MUSTARD PURPLE and **GOLDEN FRILLS**

Other Salad Plants

Those that can be grown from seed include:

Chicory

Leaves have a bitter flavour which can be reduced by harvesting as baby leaves. Varieties: **ROSSA DI TREVISO** (radicchio type with long red leaves), **SUGAR LOAF** (hardy plants with sweet conical heads).

Cress

Perfect for growing on a windowsill throughout the year. Varieties: **CRESS** (line containers with kitchen paper and keep moist, ready to harvest in just a couple of weeks), **AMERICAN LAND CRESS** (easy to grow with a flavour like water cress), **WATER CRESS** (keep containers well watered).

Endive

Similar to lettuce but with slightly bitter leaves, can be grown year round (under cover in winter). Can be harvested as cut-and-come-again plants. To blanch the leaves and reduce the bitterness simply cover the plant with a pot, to exclude the light, a few days before harvest. Varieties: **BLONDE FULL HEART** (large green curly leaves), **EXTRA FINE DE LOUVIERS** (miniature plants that grow quickly to produce finely curved leaves).

Lambs lettuce also known as corn salad

Small plants, great for containers, high in vitamin C. Varieties: **VIT** (can be grown throughout the winter), **BARON** (fast growing).

Mustard

Spicy flavoured leaves, can be cut as baby leaves or grown on for larger plants. Varieties: **MUSTARD GIANT RED** (attractive red leaves), **ZLATA** (grow on a window-sill like cress), **MUSTARD PURPLE FRILLS** (fast growing producing delicate thin leaves).

Oriental Leaves

Fast-growing plants originating in China and the Far East. Varieties: **MIZUNA** (attractive narrow leaves with a slight mustard flavour), **MIBUNA** (long thin leaves with a stronger flavour than mizuna). Note that other oriental vegetables such as **CHINESE CABBAGE** and **PAK CHOI** (which are both covered in the Fruits and Vegetables chapter, page 63) can also be cut while young and used in salads.

Pea shoots

Quick and easy to grow; harvest the shoots while just a few centimetres tall and use raw in salads, sandwiches or as garnishes. There are many varieties of peas and all can be grown for their young shoots.

Rocket

Will grow outdoors for much of the year and under cover over winter. Varieties: **RUCOLA SALAD ROCKET** (rich spicy flavour, grows well in pots), **ROCKET ESMEE** (ready in just 30 days, slow to bolt, great flavour).

9. SPROUTING

By weight, sprouted seeds are more nutritious than any other food. High in protein, vitamins and minerals and easy to grow all year round, they are a gift to vegan home-growers! Because they can be grown in the kitchen they are also perfect for those without gardens, those with limited mobility, or elderly vegans, and, as results can be seen so quickly, are also great to enthuse children in the wonderful world of growing things to eat.

We're all familiar with the long bean sprouts common in Chinese cuisine, but a huge variety of other seeds can be sprouted including pulses, grains and even some nuts. As well as stir-fries most of them can be used in salads or sandwiches, and some are a delicious addition to juices or smoothies.

Sprouting is nothing new: there are records of them being used in Chinese medicine 5,000 years ago. Seeds are easier to digest once sprouting has started, so if you have trouble eating pulses or other seeds, try them in this form. We all know pulses, like lentils or beans, are a good source of protein for the vegan diet, but once sprouted these proteins are converted to simpler amino acids which are easier for the body to absorb.

Method

First the seeds are washed and then soaked in cold water, usually for 8-12 hours or overnight, then drained and left in a jar or dish to start sprouting. The soaking hydrates the seed and triggers the embryo to germinate. Emergence of the sprouts can happen quite fast – with some seeds you can see changes within the first day – and the sprouts can be ready to harvest between 1 and 7 days. Sprouts left to grow longer are suitable for stir-fries, whereas younger, shorter sprouts are favoured for salads. Some, such as wheat, can be transferred after a day to a couple of centimetres of compost in a tray for growing further (up to 12 days); the resulting wheatgrass making a highly nutritious juice.

An important part of the process is to regularly rinse the sprouts as they grow. At least twice a day partly fill the jar with cold water, swill round then strain out. As they are sprouting, make sure the seeds don't dry out. If the weather is hot you can cover the jar with a moist porous cloth, but they must not be completely sealed from the air as the seeds need oxygen to germinate and grow.

When they are ready for harvesting, simply rinse, drain and use. It's quite easy to accidentally grow far more sprouts than you need; any surplus can be transferred to the fridge, which will slow down their growth, but do keep up daily rinsing. Initially start with just one tablespoon of seeds, then adjust according to your needs as you discover the volume of sprouts this will grow.

You can either sprout individual types, or make up your own mixtures – such as mung beans, chickpeas and peas as shown here. Just be aware of the differing sprouting times of different seeds as detailed below; in this case the mung beans were started three days before the chickpeas and peas were soaked and added.

Equipment

Nothing fancy is necessary – you can easily sprout your own seeds in a glass jar, covered with a porous material like muslin or cheesecloth, in the kitchen. The twice daily rinsing will be easier with something more custom-made, however, like the bioSnacky® glass jar (pictured) with a lid that also functions as a sieve and stand.

Once you get into sprouting and want to grow several different seeds at the same time you may want to upgrade to a specialist sprouting set with several tiers. These are usually made in acrylic or fired clay.

Aduki beans

Dried chickpeas

Sourcing Seeds

Packets of seeds specifically for sprouting can be purchased from many suppliers, garden centres and online retailers including The Organic Gardening Catalogue (see the Resources chapter, page 233). In addition you may have saved and dried some of your own seed for this purpose, peas being an easy example. It's also possible to sprout from seeds that have been bought in larger quantities supplied for cooking (chickpeas, pumpkin or sunflower seeds, for example). This would probably be the cheapest method of obtaining seeds that aren't your own, but ideally buy organic varieties. You just need to make sure the seeds were sun-dried rather than oven-dried (which would kill the embryo and make sprouting impossible). Just try a few from a packet and if they sprout, you're good to go.

Commonly Sprouted Seeds

For each of the most commonly sprouted seeds listed below we give notes on flavour and nutrition, possible uses, and the recommended soaking time followed by sprouting time (to harvest).

Aduki beans

Good source of vitamin C and iron, nutty flavour. Salads, stir-fries, juices. Soak 12 hours, sprout 3-5 days.

Alfalfa

Tiny seeds that pack a delicious protein punch, high in vitamins A, B, C and E. Mainly used in salads. Soak 12 hours, sprout 3-5 days.

Almonds

Make sure they are raw and not baked dry. Nutty tasty sprouts. Soak 12 hours, sprout 2-3 days.

Broccoli

Tasty seeds that sprout quickly, mainly used in salads. Soak 8 hours, sprout 2-3 days.

Buckwheat

Good source of calcium and vitamins A and C. Juice or salads. Soak 8 hours, sprout 1-2 days. Can then be grown on in damp compost for a further 7 days for larger greens for salads if desired.

Chickpeas

Crunchy, nutty and fast growing. Salads or stir-fries. Soak 12 hours, sprout 3-5 days.

Green lentils

A sweet, earthy flavour. High in iron and vitamin C. Soak 12 hours, sprout 2-4 days.

entils

Mung beans

Fenugreek

High in protein, iron and vitamins A and C. Spicy flavour. Salads and stir-fries. Soak 12 hours, sprout 3-5 days.

Mung beans

The classic bean sprout for stir-fries and salads. High in protein and vitamins A, C and E. Soak 12 hours, sprout 2-7 days (depending on the length of sprout you wish to grow).

Peas

High in protein, can be sprouted for a few days as a sprout or longer in compost to produce pea shoots for salads. Soak 12 hours, sprout 3-5 days.

Pumpkin

Tasty, fast-growing sprouts for salads and stir-fries. Soak 12 hours, sprout 1-2 days.

Radish

Delicious in a salad with a hot tangy flavour. Soak 12 hours, sprout 2-5 days.

Red clover

Small seeds like alfalfa (try sprouting a mixture of the two together). High in minerals and vitamins A and C. Soak 12 hours, sprout 3-7 days.

Sunflower

Good source of calcium, magnesium, potassium and vitamin E. Soak 8 hours, sprout 1-2 days. Can then be grown on in damp compost for a further 7 days for larger greens for salads.

Wheat

Can be eaten as sprouts but often grown on as wheat-grass for making highly nutritious juices/smoothies. Soak 8 hours, sprout 1-2 days. Can then be grown on in damp compost for a further 9-12 days for wheatgrass.

Other possibilities include: amaranth, kamut, quinoa, oats, wild rice, sesame seeds, other bean varieties such as black, white or navy, and other types of lentils. Do NOT sprout red kidney beans, however, as they contain the toxin lectin.

All of the seeds above can be eaten raw once sprouted, but you may prefer to lightly steam sprouted beans and grains for just a couple of minutes. They can be sprinkled over salads (see our Spring Salad recipe in March in the Cooking throughout the Year chapter) or added to stir-fries in the last couple of minutes of cooking.

Additionally, as well as using the above to make juices and smoothies, try making houmous with sprouted chickpeas or peas instead of raw chickpeas. The result is just as delicious, yet lighter in consistency and easier to digest.

10. GROWING THROUGHOUT THE YEAR

In this section we look on a month-by-month basis at what you can sow, plant, harvest and store. Also included are lists of other jobs that may need doing on the plot for each month of the year. The months chosen for each activity are suggestions and flexible depending on many factors such as your location and climate, whether you are growing under cover, choice of varieties and so on. You can make adjustments as necessary. Some of the crops can be sown, planted and harvested over quite a long period – so we have chosen the months that have worked best for us in the past. The most commonly and easily grown crops are listed, with some more unusual ones covered in the chapter Challenging Crops, page 101.

Where sowing under cover is mentioned this could mean in the greenhouse, polytunnel, conservatory, under cloches or horticultural fleece. Some crops can also be started in pots or small trays on a sunny window-sill indoors. If it is early in the year and the temperature inside isn't warm enough (below about 15°C) then you can use a small heated propagator to initiate germination.

The sections headed 'What to plant' refer to planting tubers, sets, canes and so on, whereas the sections headed 'What to plant out' refer to crops that you have grown from seed in trays or pots that will need to be planted out into beds or larger containers.

When you have chosen which crops you wish to grow each month, refer to the next chapter Fruits and Vegetables, page 63, where you will find details on techniques and recommended varieties for each of those, including, where applicable, methods of storage.

January

What to sow

Carrots (under cover in a greenhouse bed for an early crop)

What to plant

January is a good month for planting soft fruit canes/bushes as long as the soil is not frozen or waterlogged, otherwise anytime between November and February will be fine. They can be purchased, either as bare-root plants or in pots, from garden centres or online by mail order.
Currants – black, red, white
Gooseberries
Grapes
Raspberries

Other jobs on the plot

This is a good time to plan your sowing for the year. List the crops you want to grow and when to sow batches of seeds, especially where successional sowing (as described in the chapter Self-sufficiency, page 21) will be key. Order any further seeds needed.

Check stored crops such as potatoes, apples and squash, and compost any that are starting to rot.

The practice of 'forcing' rhubarb is often used for an early crop of tender, pale stems. The easiest way of doing this is to cover one or two crowns in January with a large pot, upturned dustbin or a special forcing pot.

Place early seed potatoes out to chit (start growing sprouts). They can be laid in empty seed trays in a greenhouse or conservatory, somewhere light but frost-free. Stand them 'rose' end up (the end with most 'eyes' or dents).

Mature compost can be spread around the plot, leaving enough to make up your own potting compost.

Fresh from the plot

Artichoke – Jerusalem	Celeriac
Broccoli (early sprouting)	Chard
Brussels sprouts	Kale
Cabbage	Leeks
Carrots	Parsnips
Cauliflower	Spinach

February

What to sow

Broad beans
Cabbage (under cover)
Carrots
Cauliflower (under cover)
Peas (under cover)
Pepper – capsicum (under cover)
Pepper – chilli (under cover)
Radish (under cover)

What to plant

Garlic cloves
Potatoes – first early (under cover)

Other jobs on the plot

Prune autumn-fruiting raspberry canes down to ground level.

This is a good month for maintenance: check your greenhouse for any repairs needed, wash algae/mould from the panes of glass/polycarbonate; clean out your shed and organise seed trays and pots and make repairs to any raised beds and paths around the plot.

Fresh from the plot

Broccoli (early sprouting)   Kale
Brussels sprouts   Leeks
Carrots   Parsnips
Cauliflower   Spinach
Celeriac

March

What to sow

Aubergine (under cover)
Beetroot
Broccoli – calabrese (under cover)
Brussels sprouts (under cover)
Celeriac
Celery (under cover)
Chinese cabbage (under cover)
Courgettes (under cover)
Leeks (under cover)
Onion seeds (under cover)
Parsnips
Tomatoes (under cover)

What to plant

Artichoke, Jerusalem
Onion sets
Potatoes
Strawberries

Other jobs on the plot

Prune fig trees to remove weak or dead branches and improve the shape.

Prepare outdoor beds for sowing: dig in green manures, weed, mulch with compost, dig trenches for potatoes.

Fresh from the plot

Broccoli (early sprouting)   Leeks
Brussels sprouts   Lettuce
Carrots   Parsnips
Cauliflower   Rhubarb
Celeriac   Spinach, chard
Kale   Turnips

April

What to sow

Artichoke, globe
Courgettes
Cucumber (under cover)
Florence fennel
French and other beans
Kale
Melon
Peas
Radish
Rhubarb
Runner beans (under cover)
Spinach/chard
Swede
Sweet corn (under cover)
Turnips

What to plant

Asparagus
Figs
Potatoes

What to plant out

Cabbage
Cauliflower
Pumpkins/squash (under cover)

Other jobs on the plot

Prepare wigwams and structures of canes for peas and beans to grow up. Prepare netting cages to protect brassicas.

Collect nettles and comfrey leaves, fill a bucket tight with them and top up with rainwater. After a week or two they will have become a rich (but very smelly) liquid plant food. Dilute 1:10 with water.

Globe artichokes – remove rooted offsets that grow around the edges of the main plant and plant them separately for further years. Each plant will crop well for about three years and can then be composted.

Fresh from the plot

Broccoli – early sprouting   Rhubarb
Leeks   Spinach, chard
Lettuce   Turnips

May

What to sow

Beetroot
Broccoli – early sprouting
Cabbage
Cauliflower
Chinese cabbage

What to plant out

Aubergine
Broccoli – calabrese
Brussels sprouts
Celeriac
Courgettes
Chinese cabbage
Cucumber
French beans
Onions
Peas
Pepper – capsicum
Pepper – chilli
Pumpkins/squash
Runner beans
Sweet corn
Tomatoes

Other jobs on the plot

Start evening walks around the plot checking for slugs and snails. The best time is just as it's getting dark and after rain. Collect any you find in a lidded pot and release them at least 100 metres away in a wood or a park etc.

Liquid feed established crops fortnightly. Make further batches of nettle and comfrey liquid feed.

Regularly check greenhouse plants and pots for watering – on sunny days they may need daily watering, ideally in the evening or early morning.

Earth up potatoes as they grow.

As broad beans grow taller they may need supporting with canes and string.

Fresh from the plot

Asparagus   Pak choi
Broad beans   Potatoes
Cabbage   Radish
Cauliflower   Rhubarb
Chinese cabbage   Spinach, chard
Lettuce   Turnips
Onions

What to store or process

Asparagus   Rhubarb

June

What to sow
Carrots
Pak choi
Radish

What to plant out
Celery
Courgettes
Florence fennel
Kale
Leeks
Melon
Peas
Swede
Turnips

Other jobs on the plot
This is the time for formative pruning of young cherry trees, for example to train them in a fan shape against a wall. It's also the time of year for pruning plum trees.

Check apricot trees – if they have produced a large number of fruits then these can be thinned out to a few inches between each fruit.

Prune fig trees to remove the shoot tips from fresh growth.

Erect canes in the greenhouse for tomatoes, cucumbers and other climbers. Ventilate daily for the next three months unless there is a cold snap (an automated vent will help with this).

Pinch out side shoots from vine tomatoes.

Check crops sown in rows from seed and thin out where necessary.

Fresh from the plot
Artichoke, globe
Asparagus
Broad beans
Cabbage
Cauliflower
Chinese cabbage
Courgettes
Currants – red
Florence fennel
French beans
Gooseberries
Lettuce
Onions
Pak choi
Peas
Potatoes
Radish
Rhubarb
Spinach, chard
Strawberries
Turnips

What to store or process
Artichoke, globe

July

What to sow
Chinese cabbage
Spinach/chard
Turnips

What to plant out
Broccoli – early sprouting
Cabbage
Cauliflower
Chinese cabbage

Other jobs on the plot
Liquid feed plants in greenhouse and outdoor pots, especially those that start fruiting: increase to weekly. Also use seaweed extract as a foliar feed.

Cut down broad beans when they have finished cropping and mulch over the bed.

Check brassicas for the next few months for white butterfly eggs/caterpillars. Remove any found by hand and relocate (for example to a sacrificial bed of nasturtiums).

Check potatoes for signs of blight, browning/shrivelling of leaves – remove and burn any affected foliage.

Check potted greenhouse plants for greenfly, such as aubergines and peppers. If any are found, stand the pots outdoors for a few days for their predators to get to work.

Fresh from the plot
Apricots
Artichoke, globe
Aubergine
Broad beans
Cabbage
Carrots
Cauliflower
Cherries
Chinese cabbage
Courgettes
Currants
Florence fennel
French beans
Garlic
Gooseberries
Lettuce
Melon
Onions
Pak choi
Peaches
Peas
Pepper – chilli, capsicum
Potatoes
Radish
Raspberries
Rhubarb
Runner beans
Spinach, chard
Strawberries
Turnips

What to store or process
Broad beans
Cherries
Florence fennel
Gooseberries

August

What to sow

Cabbages – early spring varieties
Pak choi

What to plant out

Pak choi

Other jobs on the plot

Prune apricot, peach and nectarine trees in August, straight after fruiting, the main aim being to remove diseased or damaged branches/twigs, any that are crossing and rubbing each other, and to improve the shape of the tree. They can also be trained, by a combination of pruning and tying to canes/wires, to a fan shape against a wall.

This is also the month for the main pruning of cherry trees.

Summer-fruiting raspberry varieties should be pruned after all the fruits have been gathered. Cut canes that have fruited down to ground level but leave about six young canes per plant to grow on and fruit next year.

Check all winter squashes (pumpkins, butternuts etc.) and limit the number of developing fruits to 4-6 per plant.

Lift onions and dry them in the sun for a week or two before storage. The easiest method is to lay them in trays (clean seed trays will do), and leave them outdoors, bringing them inside if rain threatens.

Fresh from the plot

Apples	Lettuce
Apricots	Melon
Artichoke, globe	Onions
Aubergine	Pak choi
Beetroot	Peaches, nectarines
Broccoli – calabrese	Pears
Carrots	Peas
Cauliflower	Pepper – chilli, capsicum
Celery	Plums
Cherries	Potatoes
Chinese cabbage	Pumpkins/squashes
Courgettes	Radish
Cucumber	Raspberries
Currants – black	Runner beans
Figs	Spinach, chard
Florence fennel	Strawberries
French beans	Tomatoes
Garlic	Turnips
Grapes	

What to store or process

Apricots	Courgettes
Aubergine	French beans
Cauliflower (make	Garlic
piccalilli – see our recipe	Peaches, nectarines
in Fruits and Vegetables,	Peas
page 74)	Runner beans
Celery	Strawberries

September

What to sow

Spinach/chard

What to plant

Onion sets

What to plant out

Chinese cabbage
Turnips
Pak choi

Other jobs on the plot

Remove lower leaves from celeriac plants.

Sow green manures in areas where crops have now been harvested and cleared.

Remove any dying rhubarb stalks and compost.

Stake plants that may need it over winter such as purple sprouting broccoli, Brussels sprouts and kale.

Fresh from the plot

Apples	Pak choi
Aubergine	Peaches
Beetroot	Pears
Broccoli – calabrese	Peas
Brussels sprouts	Pepper – chilli, capsicum
Carrots	Plums
Cauliflower	Pumpkins/squashes
Celery	Raspberries
Chinese cabbage	Runner beans
Courgettes	Spinach, chard
Cucumber	Strawberries
Figs	Swede
French beans	Sweet corn
Grapes	Tomatoes
Leeks	Turnips
Melon	

What to store or process

Beetroot	Pepper – chilli, capsicum
Figs	Plums
Grapes	Potatoes
Melon	Raspberries
Onions	Sweet corn
Pears	Tomatoes

October

What to sow

Broad beans
Pea varieties that are winter hardy

What to plant

Rhubarb
Strawberries

Other jobs on the plot

Last year's leaf mould can be spread around the plot as a mulch. Clear this year's fallen leaves from around the garden and start a new leaf mould pile (a simple netting enclosure will be fine).

Harvest winter squashes such as pumpkins and butternuts before the first frost and leave in the sun to harden for a week or two before putting into frost-free storage.

Bring in, to the greenhouse or conservatory, pots of plants that will need winter protection, such as citrus trees.

Remove dead leaves from around parsnip plants.

Cut down asparagus ferns and compost. Weed the bed and mulch well with compost.

Fresh from the plot

Apples	Parsnips
Beetroot	Pears
Brussels sprouts	Pepper – chilli
Carrots	Plums
Cauliflower	Pumpkins/squashes
Celeriac	Raspberries
Celery	Spinach, chard
Chinese cabbage	Strawberries
Cucumber	Swede
Grapes	Tomatoes
Leeks	Turnips

What to store or process

Apples	Carrots

November

Jobs on the plot

Winter is the time for pruning currant bushes, removing old growth as the fruits form on young fresh shoots. Leave piles of prunings around the plot as wildlife habitats.

Prune grape vines to reduce the main stem and side shoots – see the next chapter for more details.

Clear out and clean the greenhouse.

Cut Jerusalem artichokes down to ground level and compost the stalks.

Cut down globe artichoke plants and mulch the crowns.

Fresh from the plot

Apples	Chinese cabbage
Artichoke, Jerusalem	Grapes
Beetroot	Kale
Brussels sprouts	Leeks
Cabbage	Parsnips
Carrots	Spinach, chard
Cauliflower	Swede
Celeriac	Turnips

What to store or process

Artichoke, Jerusalem	Parsnips
Celeriac	Swede

December

What to plant

Apples
Apricots
Cherries
Garlic cloves
Peaches, nectarines
Pears
Plums

Other jobs on the plot

Winter is the time for pruning apples and pears. The main aim being to remove diseased or damaged branches/twigs, including any that are crossing and/or rubbing each other, and to improve the shape of the tree. They can also be trained, by a combination of pruning and tying to canes/wires, into certain shapes, such as espaliers (a single stem with long side shoots) or cordons (with short side shoots), often against a wall.

Mulch around winter brassicas.

Keep checking stored produce, removing any that are rotting.

Fresh from the plot

Artichoke, Jerusalem	Kale
Brussels sprouts	Leeks
Cabbage	Parsnips
Carrots	Spinach, chard
Cauliflower	Swede
Celeriac	Turnips

What to store or process

Brussels sprouts

Artichoke flowers

11. FRUITS AND VEGETABLES

Arranged alphabetically, all the crops mentioned in the previous chapter are covered here in more detail with recommended varieties, notes on sowing, planting, harvesting, and methods for storing or processing the resulting produce. General notes on storage techniques are included in the chapter Self-sufficiency, page 21.

Apples

One of the most consistently popular fruit trees, apples can be grown in a wide variety of forms to suit any garden. When you buy an apple tree it will either be bare-rooted, which should be planted in the dormant season (late autumn to early spring) or as a potted plant, which can be planted at any time. Some varieties have been developed to stay in pots, which can fit in even the smallest garden.

When choosing apple trees take note of the rootstock, which will affect the eventual size the tree will grow to. A rootstock is the stump of a related species which already has an established root system, and to which a separate tree is joined by grafting or budding. Common ones for apples are:

- M27 is extremely dwarfing and good for pots or small gardens
- M9 is also dwarfing and suitable for small gardens
- M26 and MM106 are good rootstocks for small to medium-sized gardens/allotments
- MM111 and M25 are for standard trees, only for large gardens

There are numerous varieties available offering a wide range of flavours, textures and uses. Here are just a few well known ones:

> ### RECOMMENDED VARIETIES
>
> **Eating apples**
>
> **COX'S ORANGE PIPPIN:** A superb dessert apple that keeps particularly well
>
> **WORCESTER PEARMAIN:** Bright red fruits with a sweet flavour
>
> **EGREMONT RUSSET:** Crisp, sweet fruits with a nutty flavour
>
> **Cooking apples**
>
> **BRAMLEY:** Large fruits which keep particularly well
>
> **LORD DERBY:** Heavy crop of bright green fruits with a sweet flavour

If you plant bare-root specimens, they should be staked for their first two years. Do not put compost in the hole you dig to plant each tree in, as this can discourage the roots from spreading out into the surrounding soil. Mulch around the base of the tree regularly. Pruning should be carried out in winter, the main aim being to remove diseased or damaged branches/twigs, any that are crossing and rubbing each other and to improve the shape of the tree. They can also be trained, by a combination of pruning and tying to canes/wires, into certain shapes such as espaliers or cordons, often against a wall.

When to harvest apples will depend on which varieties are grown, as they ripen at different times, but generally it occurs between late summer to autumn.

Storage

Place apples in crates or on shelves in a cool, frost-free, but not too dry place. They should keep until spring. Check regularly and remove any showing signs of rot.

Other methods of storage include drying apple rings, adding them to jams and chutneys, freezing them as stewed apple or juice, and, of course, making them into cider. Windfalls and early maturing varieties do not store so well, so use these for jams and chutneys. Cooking apples are the best for jam-making because of their high acidity. Late maturing apple varieties will be sweeter, and therefore are the best for juice and making cider.

Apple tree

Apricot tree

Apricots

A ripe apricot eaten straight from the tree is a splendid thing! They can be grown in the garden, ideally against a south-facing wall, but you will have more success if you have space to grow them in a large greenhouse. In order to crop well they need a cold winter (ideally 30 days below 7°C) and a warm, dry summer.

They should be planted in the dormant season, winter to early spring. Mix compost into the soil around the plant and mulch well. If frost threatens when the tree is in flower in the spring, cover it with horticultural fleece overnight.

Prune in August, straight after fruiting, the main aim being to remove diseased or damaged branches/twigs, any that are crossing and rubbing each other, and to improve the shape of the tree. They can also be trained, by a combination of pruning and tying to canes/wires, to a fan shape against a wall. If they have produced a large number of fruits then these can be thinned out in June to about 10cm between each fruit.

Harvesting the fruit mainly occurs during August – eat the best specimens straight away as a snack or added to salads. If birds, such as pigeons, are eating the fruit or buds at any stage, cover the tree with netting, taking care that small birds can't get trapped in it.

Storage

Stoned fruits can be frozen in plastic bags, bottled, or dried in a dehydrator. They make a superb jam and can also be used as an ingredient in chutneys.

RECOMMENDED VARIETIES

MOORPARK: Large juicy fruits produced August to September

TOMCOT: Compact tree producing excellent juicy apricots. They bottle well, and any fruits too ripe for jam-making can be made into chutney

Apricot Jam

2kg apricots, 2kg sugar, 400ml water
Wash and halve the apricots and remove the stones. Most of the pectin is in the stones, so it helps to cook a few stones in the mixture and remove these as you jar up. Pectin is a polysaccharide found in parts of terrestrial plants which acts as a gelling agent, helping jams to set. Heat the apricots with the water and simmer until tender. Add the sugar, stir, boil, and keep boiling hard to setting point. Ladle into sterilised jars and seal.

Artichoke – Globe

These large attractive plants are perennials that produce large green thistle-like heads with edible pads at the base of the outer scales. It's always nice to leave one or two buds to flower, as the large mauve blooms are spectacular and loved by bees.

Seeds can be sown in April for transplanting the following year, or they can be purchased as potted plants in the spring. The latter is recommended if you only want one or two plants and don't want to wait a year for your first crop.

RECOMMENDED VARIETIES

GREEN GLOBE: Traditional green heads
PURPLE GLOBE ROMANESCO: Very attractive purple heads

The heads should be harvested while young and tender, before they flower in the early summer, and then will be followed by a further crop of smaller ones. They will keep fresh for a week in the fridge if the flower stalks are stood in water, which is refreshed daily. Small, young, globes can be trimmed to remove the stalk and outside leaves, then sliced into a salad or steamed or boiled whole. With larger globes you will also need to cut away the tough tops of the leaves and scrape out any hairy fibres (choke) from the centre. Cut into quarters, fry in olive oil with herbs and garlic then add some water and cover to steam until tender.

Tip: To stop cut surfaces quickly turning grey as they oxidise, immediately after cutting, submerge in cold water with added lemon juice.

Around April time you can remove rooted offsets that grow around the edges of the main plant and plant them separately for further years' cropping. Each plant will crop well for about three years and can then be composted. Alternatively the plants can be divided every two or three years, planting them 90cm apart.

Storage

They can be stored in the freezer after removing the outer leaves and stalks of small heads and blanching for 6 minutes before freezing in plastic bags. To cook from frozen, boil for about 10 minutes. They also make a great pickle: First cover the small heads, or removed scales of larger artichokes, in layers of salt and leave overnight. Rinse thoroughly in fresh water the next day, dry and pack into jars, covering with a vinegar of your choice before sealing.

Artichoke – Jerusalem

The knobbly tubers of Jerusalem artichokes have a distinctive taste and are an interesting alternative to potatoes. The plants are vigorous, the stems growing to 2 or 3 metres tall, so can also be used as an effective windbreak.

Around March plant the tubers 15cm deep and 60cm apart. As they can be quite invasive you may well have a neighbour who can spare a few tubers. Alternatively, you can buy them from a greengrocer or seed supplier.

Harvest the tubers from autumn onwards, saving a few tubers to replant for a crop the following year. Jerusalem artichokes can be roasted, baked, fried, boiled and so on, and can even be eaten raw, sliced into salads.

Occasionally Jerusalem artichokes can be affected by sclerotina – a fungal disease which rots the plants at the base and produces a fluffy white mould. If this occurs, remove any stems with signs of the disease and dispose of them (not on the compost heap).

Storage

Usually the tubers can simply be left in the ground until required. But if you are expecting very hard frosts, pack some tubers in damp sand in boxes. They should keep for a few months in a cool, frost-free building.

RECOMMENDED VARIETY

FUSEAU: Produces crunchy nutty tubers that are easy to peel

Globe artichokes

Jerusalem artichokes

Asparagus

These days you can buy asparagus all year round but there are associated air miles as it is usually imported from Peru. It's far better for the environment to treat this delicious vegetable as a treat for May and June, giving you something to look forward to!

The plants are perennial and may produce edible young shoots, known as spears, for up to 20 years or so. Although they can be sown as seeds, it will be four years before you can cut a full harvest. A quicker way to get started is to buy them as one, two or even three-year old crowns (buds with roots) and plant these in April. If two years old, you can harvest half the spears a year after planting, then a full crop the year after that.

The spears will appear in May and should be cut when they have reached about 15cm tall. Cut them 5cm below the soil surface with a long knife. Don't cut all the spears from each plant but leave a few to help it build strength year on year.

Asparagus beetle is a common pest; both the adult and larval stages eating stems and foliage. The adult

RECOMMENDED VARIETIES
CONNOVER'S COLLOSSAL: A favourite variety producing good-sized spears
CRIMSON PACIFIC: Produces purple spears

beetles are about 7mm long, mainly black with small yellow and red marks. A light infestation shouldn't affect the crop too badly, but control numbers by removing all stems at the end of the year, and removing the beetles by hand over the summer.

Steamed for just a few minutes, or charred lightly on the barbecue, the spears are delicious as a side vegetable and in quiches or on their own with a hollandaise sauce (see our recipe in the chapter Cooking throughout the Year). They can also be eaten raw, shaved or sliced into salads.

Storage

The quality of the cut spears declines rapidly after cutting. They will only keep for a few days in the fridge, but standing the spears upright in a mug of water will extend this a little (change the water daily). For longer storage, freezing is the best option: Immediately after cutting, wash well then blanch for 2 minutes. Pack in containers and freeze. To cook from frozen, steam for about 6 minutes.

Aubergine

Also known as eggplants, because of the ovoid shape of the fruits, aubergines are best grown in a greenhouse or polytunnel. Although most commonly seen as shiny purple fruits, they are available in a variety of different colours and shapes.

RECOMMENDED VARIETIES
LONG PURPLE: Deep violet fruits
ROSA BIANCA: Round pinkish-white fruits with a mild creamy flavour
BLACK BEAUTY: Dark glossy oval fruits that mature early

Aubergine flower

Sow the seeds in early March in pots on a windowsill or heated propagator. In early May the young plants can be potted on into larger containers in the greenhouse. As they grow, some plants may need to be tied to canes, especially when the fruits develop and become heavy. They will benefit a similar feed to tomatoes every couple of weeks; see page 98.

In the greenhouse the plants can be susceptible to red spider mite. As these thrive in hot, dry conditions, they can be deterred by spraying the foliage regularly.

Do not let the fruits grow too large, but cut them when no more than 15cm long, approximately, and before the skin loses its shine (normally July to September depending on the variety). Remove any fruits that start to form from late summer onwards; this will encourage the remaining crop to grow and ripen.

The fruits are usually fried or roasted in chunks or slices. Large fruits may need to be salted first to remove excess water and bitterness: sprinkle slices with salt on both sides, leave in a colander to drain for an hour, then rinse and pat dry with kitchen paper before cooking.

Storage

The fruits stay useable for several weeks in the fridge, or can be frozen or bottled as part of a ratatouille (see our recipe in the chapter Cooking throughout the Year, page 194). Aubergines are also a good ingredient in chutneys.

Beans – Broad

Broad beans, also known as field, horse or fava beans, are cool-season annual plants that are easy to grow and produce a highly nutritious seed packed with protein.

They can either be sown in autumn for spring/summer harvesting, or in early spring for a slightly later crop. Sow the beans 15cm apart and be prepared to stake the plants if they grow tall or are in a windy position. Once there are plenty of flower buds you can pinch out the growing tips; this prevents blackfly getting a hold, plus the tips are delicious in a salad or stir-fry.

A common pest for broad bean plants is the bean weevil, which eats the outside edges of the leaves, resulting in a wavy or scalloped appearance. This should not affect the harvest, however, and can be ignored. Alternatively, the weevils can be excluded by covering the plants with horticultural fleece.

The young pods can be harvested and cooked whole, or the immature seeds removed from larger pods.

> RECOMMENDED VARIETIES
>
> **EXPRESS ELEONORA**: Fast to mature if sown early spring, freezes well
>
> **RATIO**: Crops early with high yields – spring sowing only
>
> **SUPER AQUADULCE**: Sow in October/November for an early crop the following year

Broad bean flowers

Broad bean pods

Small young beans can be eaten raw or lightly steamed. They also make a delicious and simple risotto with spring onions and herbs (see our recipe in the chapter Cooking throughout the Year, page 162). Larger beans will develop tough skins but these can be removed by gently squeezing out the bean after steaming and cutting a small nick in the skin.

Leave a few pods to mature for beans to sow again next year.

Storage

To freeze, it's best to use young small beans before they get too tough: wash the shelled beans, blanch for 2 minutes; to freeze them spread out on a tray then bag up. To cook from frozen, boil for about 6 minutes. Broad beans can also be dried: Leave the pods on the plants until they have turned yellow, then cut the plant at ground level and hang indoors to dry completely. When the pods have become brittle, shell the beans and leave on trays for a few days. Then store in a cool dry place in airtight containers. Soak the beans before cooking.

Beans – French

There are numerous varieties of French beans available – dwarf, forming compact bushes, and climbing. All will fruit prolifically and routine harvesting of the young pods will keep you supplied for several months over the summer.

A few plants sown early in the greenhouse will provide beans from June onwards; those planted outside will crop later in the summer and autumn. In any case they can be started off in modules under cover then planted out when the risk of frost is over. Climbing varieties will need a framework of canes to grow up. They should wind themselves around the cane without the need for tying.

Beans on canes

Young plants can be destroyed by pigeons but are easily protected with netting or horticultural fleece. Once the plants start winding up supports this usually stops being a problem.

For fresh French beans, pick the pods while young and tender and eat as soon as possible after harvesting. Lightly steamed, they taste great in salads or as a side vegetable, or they can be added to stir-fries or curries. Let a number of plants grow on unharvested to provide beans for drying later in the year (and a few for sowing next spring).

Storage

To freeze French beans, trim the ends off the pods and blanch for 2 minutes before packing in plastic bags. To cook from frozen, boil for about 5 minutes.

To prepare beans for drying, leave the pods on the plants until they have turned yellow. Cut the plant at ground level and hang indoors to dry completely. When the pods have become brittle, shell the beans and leave on trays for a few days, then store in a cool dry place in airtight containers. They will keep for months and can be added to stews or made into casseroles or homemade baked beans (see our recipe in the chapter Cooking throughout the Year, page 184). Soak the beans overnight before cooking. Drain, rinse and boil vigorously for 10 minutes, then simmer until tender.

Beans – Runner

Runner beans are climbing plants that are actually perennials but are grown as annuals in cool (temperate) climates.

Sow the large seeds in modules under cover in April and plant out in May/June when the risk of frost is over. Alternatively, they can be planted outside in June, directly where they are to grow. They like a rich compost with plenty of organic matter and will need a framework of canes to grow up. If the young plants suffer from slug or snail damage, use some of the barrier techniques described in the chapter Vegan Organic Growing.

RECOMMENDED VARIETIES

SLENDERETTE: Maincrop, a dwarf variety, pods freeze well

ROYALTY: A dwarf variety that produces distinctive purple pods

COBRA: A climbing variety that produces long pale green pods

The following varieties are recommended for drying:

CZAR: Large white butter beans

PEA BEAN: Interestingly coloured white/brown beans that some say resemble tiny killer whales!

BARLOTTA LINGUA DI FUOCO: Purple and white beans in beautiful red pods

CANNELLINO: White beans, good for homemade baked beans (see recipe in the chapter Cooking Throughout the Year, page 216)

RECOMMENDED VARIETIES

SCARLET EMPEROR: Early maturing with excellent flavour

ENORMA ELITE: Crops over a long period

LADY DI: Long stringless pods with a great flavour

Runner beans

Harvested borlotti beans

Runner bean flowers

Harvest the flat pods of runner beans regularly, whilst young and tender, leaving some on the plants to mature for collecting the beans for drying and sowing the following year. The pods will be ready to pick from July to September.

After picking, cut the strings from the sides of the pods, top and tail, slice diagonally and steam for a few minutes.

Storage

To freeze runner beans, trim the ends off and string the pods (if necessary). Slice into short lengths and blanch for 2 minutes before packing in plastic bags. To cook from frozen, boil for about 5 minutes.

They can also be dried by leaving the pods on the plants until they have turned yellow, then cut the plant at ground level and hang indoors to dry completely. When the pods have become brittle, shell the beans and leave on trays for a few days, then store in a cool dry place in airtight containers. Soak the beans before cooking.

Beetroot

All parts of a beetroot plant are edible. Young leaves are tasty and attractive in salads, while the roots can be eaten raw, cooked or pickled.

Several sowings can be made between March and June. As the seedlings develop, thin them out, using the surplus in salads. Beetroot can be quick to bolt (grow seed heads) so harvest early roots while still small and slice or grate into salads. Bolting can be caused by dry soil, so keep the plants well watered. If it becomes a regular problem, choose varieties that are resistant to bolting such as Boltardy. Larger beetroot harvested later in the season (from August to November) can be boiled or roasted.

The juice can add an amazing colour and earthy taste to smoothies and drinks.

Storage

Pull beetroot for dry storage from July to October, before they get too large and woody. Gently remove the soil from undamaged beets and twist the foliage off (cutting causes bleeding). Pack in boxes with damp sand. They should keep until spring if stored in a cool, frost-free building.

To make pickled beetroot: First boil the beets for 1 or 2 hours (depending on the size) and rub the skin off. Then either slice, or if small, pickle whole by covering with vinegar in suitable jars. Pickled beetroot can be used after a week and will be at its best for 3 months.

R E C O M M E N D E D   V A R I E T I E S

EGYPTIAN TURNIP ROOTED: Early variety, quick growing with a great flavour, excellent for eating raw, large roots with a deep red colour

BOLTARDY: An early cropper, good resistance to bolting

CYLINDRA: Long cylindrical beets, perfect for slicing, stores well over winter

BARABIETOLA DI CHIOGGIA: This is an old traditional Italian beetroot, good for eating raw or cooked. Roots are a rosy-pink colour with the flesh having attractive concentric rings of white and pink.

Broccoli and Calabrese

The big green heads we all know as 'broccoli' are technically calabrese. Real broccoli varieties, such as purple sprouting, produce heads (or spears) that can be cut regularly. By careful choice of different varieties, early sprouting, late sprouting and calabrese, for example, you can have fresh broccoli available for much of the year.

For early sprouting varieties sow the seeds in modules in May, then plant out in their final positions after a couple of months. Calabrese types can be sown under cover in March then planted out in May. They will benefit from netting protection to keep the young plants safe from wood pigeons, and to keep butterflies from laying eggs on the leaves later in the season.

Regular cutting of the flowering heads of all types will encourage side shoots with new heads to form. This will prolong the cropping season considerably.

Storage

Broccoli can be frozen after blanching for 2 minutes but tend to go rather mushy, so it's better to rely on growing different varieties for fresh crops throughout much of the year.

RECOMMENDED VARIETIES

RUDOLF: A very early variety producing large purple spears from December

WHITE EYE: Delicately flavoured white spears ready from February

PURPLE SPROUTING EARLY: Ready to crop from March

BELSTAR (calabrese type): Ready from July

FIESTA (calabrese type): Cropping in late summer and autumn

ROMANESCO: Produces attractive pyramid-shaped yellow-green heads

Brussels Sprouts

Not everyone loves them but Christmas wouldn't be the same without them! Using two or three different varieties can keep you in fresh sprouts from October to February.

Sow seeds under cover in March and plant out a couple of months later. Like broccoli, they will benefit from netting protection to keep the young plants safe from wood pigeons and to keep butterflies from laying eggs on the leaves. In windy areas, tall plants may need staking. If plants wilt and die this may be caused by cabbage root fly, which eat the roots just below the surface of the soil. Covering the young plants with horticultural fleece can offer some protection.

Keep cutting Brussels sprouts whilst small, working up the stem of the plant. They often taste sweeter after the first frosts of the year. When all the sprouts are gone you can also use the top of the plant like a cabbage.

Young sprouts can be shredded into salads, halved and steamed for 4 minutes as a side vegetable, sliced into stir-fries or in bubble and squeak.

Storage

If you are expecting very hard frosts then you can pull up entire plants and hang in a cool frost-free building where the sprouts can be picked in good condition for a few weeks. To freeze sprouts for longer storage, pick while they are small and remove the outer leaves. Blanch for 2 minutes before cooling and storing in bags. To cook from frozen, boil for about 7 minutes.

RECOMMENDED VARIETIES

GRONINGER: Great flavour, harvest from October to December

DORIC: Harvest from December to February

RUBINE: Produces purple sprouts with a good flavour

Cabbage

This is another vegetable where use of a selection of varieties which mature at different times of the year will enable you to harvest fresh cabbages all year round.

Sowing times will depend on which varieties you choose. Early spring cabbages can be sown in August the year before. Summer cabbages are often sown under cover in modules during February and March, whilst autumn and winter cabbages are sown in May. In each case they will need planting out to their final growing positions a couple of months later. They will benefit from netting protection to keep the young plants safe from wood pigeons and to keep butterflies from laying eggs on the leaves later in the season.

If plants grow poorly, and/or wilt and die, they may have been attacked by cabbage root fly. The white larvae of the fly burrow down to eat the roots of the young plants. Practising crop rotation will help reduce the incidence of this; crops can also be protected with horticultural fleece. Otherwise, you can make collars for individual plants using a circle of cardboard, about 12cm across, placed at soil level around the stem of each plant. This prevents the fly laying eggs near enough to the cabbage.

Most cabbages can be left to grow and cut as required. The white cabbages are perfect for coleslaw and sauerkraut, green summer and pointed ones for salads or light steaming and Savoy varieties steamed as a vegetable dish. Red cabbages, apart from pickling or shredding into salads, can be braised slowly with red onions, cooking apples, brown sugar, spices and vinegar for a comforting winter treat.

Storage

Cut winter cabbages at the end of autumn, remove the outer leaves, and store nestled in straw or shredded paper in crates. They should be placed in a cool, dry building where the cabbages will stay in good condition until spring. Pickled red cabbage : Essential at Christmas in our household! Shred the cabbage, layer with salt and leave for 24 hours. Rinse the salt off, dry, pack into jars, and cover with vinegar. Pickled cabbage can be used after a week and should be consumed within 3 months or it loses its crunch.

Sauerkraut (fermented cabbage) has been a staple dish of Eastern Europe for centuries. There are many benefits of fermented foods such as increasing nutrients, making them more easily absorbed by the body, and promoting your friendly intestinal bacteria. To make your own sauerkraut: finely chop (or grate) 500g of cabbage hearts into a bowl, mix with 15g of salt and massage the mixture with your hands (or bash with a rolling pin or wooden spoon) to soften the cabbage. After a few minutes juices should form in the bottom of the bowl. Pack tightly into a large sterilised glass jar ensuring the juices are at a higher level than the cabbage (add a little water if necessary). Seal and leave for a few weeks in a warm place, checking daily and briefly unscrewing the cap to release any pressure. Taste it after a week. You can eat it at this time or let it ferment for a further week or two for a stronger flavour. Once you are happy, place the jar in the fridge to stop fermentation. It will keep for several months.

> ### RECOMMENDED VARIETIES
>
> **PYRAMID:** For spring greens or hearted cabbage, harvest from March to June
>
> **PREMIERE:** Round heads, harvest in July and August
>
> **MARNER LAGERROT:** Harvest from October to November, a red variety that stores well and is also suitable for pickling
>
> **ENKHUIZEN 2:** A Dutch white cabbage suitable for coleslaw, salads or cooking, harvest November to December
>
> **VERTUS:** A hardy Savoy variety, harvest from October to February

Carrots

These popular roots come in numerous different varieties, shapes and colours. With early sowings under cover followed by spring and summer sowings you could be eating fresh carrots from the plot for much of the year.

You can also buy packets of 'Rainbow Carrots' seeds that are a mixture of white, purple, red and yellow maincrop varieties.

RECOMMENDED VARIETIES

AMSTERDAM FORCING: An early variety with small cylindrical roots

PARISIAN: An early variety with spherical roots

CHANTENAY: Early maincrop, short wedge-shaped roots, rich colour, quick maturing and high yielding

COSMIC PURPLE: Early maincrop, tapered roots with a deep purple skin

AUTUMN KING: Large roots, good for storage, heavy cropper

First sowings of early varieties can be made as soon as January in a greenhouse bed. Further sowings can be made outside from February/March onwards. Maincrop carrots can be sown as late as June for autumn harvests. These are vegetables that work well with successional sowing: just a short row of seeds, sown every fortnight during the first half of the year, will keep a constant supply of young tender carrots for the kitchen. Ideally sow them in a soil that is free from stones (which would cause bent or split roots to form) – if this is a regular problem they can also be grown in tall pots containing sieved soil or compost mixed with sand.

A common pest is the carrot fly – a tiny insect that follows the smell of carrots (and some other roots like parsnips) and lays its eggs in the soil. The larvae burrow down and eat into the roots leaving blackened tunnels throughout. In a bad year they can ruin the majority of your carrots. There are various organic solutions: cover the crops with fleece/enviromesh so the flies can't get to them; interplant with onions as a companion crop as the strong smell confuses the flies; avoid thinning out, by sowing seeds further apart, as this releases the smell that attracts the flies; look for carrot fly-resistant varieties.

Pull the carrots as you need them. Grate into salads, steam, add to stir-fries or roast with other roots. The green carrot foliage is also edible – young leaves can be picked and added to salads, or excess seeds can be added to baby-leaf seed mixtures to harvest as cut-and-come-again salad plants.

Dry storage

Leave until October then pull up and gently remove the soil from undamaged carrots. Trim off the foliage and pack in damp sand in boxes – in a cool, frost-free building. They should keep until spring.

Cauliflower

There are summer, autumn and winter varieties of cauliflower available that mature at different times of the year. By sowing different varieties you can have fresh cauliflowers available most of the year. Most produce white or cream-coloured curds (heads), but there are also green and purple-headed varieties available.

Sow the seeds in modules according to the variety chosen. We often make at least an early sowing under cover in February, then a later one in May, but you may wish to practise successional sowing and do it more frequently. Plant out in the final growing position when the seedlings have reached a good size. Depending on the time of year the young plants may need protection from pigeons and white butterflies. They benefit from a rich soil, plenty of watering and a good layer of mulch, as stunted growth caused by the soil becoming too dry will result in small and deformed curds.

RECOMMENDED VARIETIES

MEDAILLON: Harvest from February to March

AALSMEER: Harvest from April to May

SNOWBALL: Harvest from July to September

BELOT: Harvest from October to December

Cut heads as required. Try a few shavings eaten raw in salads or steam or roast the florets. It also works well in curries.

Cauliflower rice

This is a recently popular alternative to rice and certainly more environmentally friendly and healthier for you. Simply pulse florets in a food processor until it resembles rice then roast on an oven tray with a little oil at 200°C for 10 minutes, stirring halfway through. Alternatively it can be microwaved for 3 minutes. Season lightly before serving. Excess cauliflower rice can be frozen before or after cooking.

Storage

Cut into florets and blanch for 2 minutes before freezing. Adding a little lemon juice to the blanching water will help the cauliflower keep its white colour. To cook from frozen, boil the florets for about 6 minutes.

They are also a main ingredient in the popular chutney piccalilli.

For 3 or 4 jars, you'll need about 1kg of mixed vegetables (cauliflower, marrow, small onions and gherkins for example), 10g salt, 10g turmeric, 10g ground ginger, 10g mustard, 10g cornflour, 100g sugar and 750ml vinegar.

Break the cauliflower into tiny florets, and cube the marrow and gherkins. Peel the onions. Soak all the vegetables in brine (100g of salt dissolved per litre of water) for 24 hours. Put the sugar and spices in a pan and stir in the vinegar. Add the drained vegetables, stir and heat to boiling. Simmer until the vegetables are tender but not pulped. Add the cornflour (mixed in a little vinegar), stir and boil for a further 3 minutes before jarring up in sterilised jars and sealing. Once opened, keep refrigerated.

Celeriac

You can eat the leaves and roots of celeriac; both taste like celery. It is also known as 'turnip-rooted celery'.

Sow the seeds in March in modules then plant out in May about 30cm apart. They will need watering well through the growing season and will be ready to harvest after 6 months.

If the leaves show brown blisters, this is most likely caused by the burrowing activity of the larvae of a small fly called the celery leaf miner. Remove affected leaves and cover the crops with horticultural fleece.

The young leaves can be used in salads or finely chopped as a garnish. The roots can be peeled then roasted, boiled, steamed or grated raw for use in salads.

> RECOMMENDED VARIETIES
>
> **PRINZ:** Will tolerate light shade
>
> **BRILLIANT:** Superb flavour, the roots store well

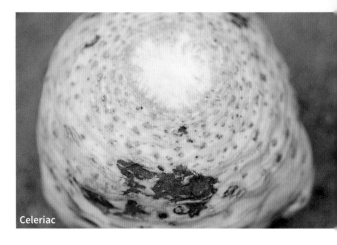
Celeriac

One of our favourite ways of eating the roots is as celeriac mash – see our recipe in the chapter Cooking throughout the Year, page 116.

Storage

They can be left in the ground until required, but if hard frosts are expected, you can store a few by pulling up in November and removing the soil from the roots. Trim off the foliage and pack in damp sand in boxes. In a cool, frost-free building, they should keep until spring.

Celery

Super in salads and stews. The stalks are perfect for scooping houmous or other dips!

Sow seeds under cover in modules in March then plant out in May or June. They grow best with a rich soil with plenty of organic matter, and regular watering. Note that some varieties are known as 'self-blanching' and can simply be planted at ground level 20cm apart. The 'blanching' refers to shading of the stems which helps them stay pale and not too coarse and fibrous. Other varieties, such as Solid Pink, will need help with blanching by planting them in a trench and earthing up (mounding soil around) the stems gradually as they grow.

If you have excess celery seeds, they can be added to baby-leaf seed mixtures to harvest as cut-and-come-again salad plants.

Celery can be left in the ground until it is needed. Frost protection is rarely required, in fact there are some who say that the flavour improves after the first frost. They should be ready to harvest from August, but young leaves can be picked for salads at any time. Harvested

> RECOMMENDED VARIETIES
>
> **DAYBREAK:** Early maturing for summer cropping
>
> **GOLDEN SELF BLANCHING:** Cream-coloured flavoursome stalks, ready from August
>
> **SOLID PINK:** Produces large pink stems ready from November

celery

Chard

sticks will keep fresh in the fridge for some days, especially if stood upright in water.

Storage

To freeze celery, wash well then cut into small chunks or slices. Blanch for 2 minutes, then cool and bag up before placing in the freezer. Add frozen to stews.

Chard

A type of leaf beet often known as Swiss chard, though this is just one variety. Attractive plants, prolific and easy to grow.

RECOMMENDED VARIETIES

RAINBOW CHARD: A mixture of red, orange, yellow and white stems. Long growing season.

SWISS CHARD: Broad white stems and mid-ribs

RHUBARB CHARD: Tasty variety with bright red stems

Sow the seeds from April through to August in trays or modules then plant out 45cm apart in their final positions. With successional sowing and protection in the winter (cloches or similar will do) they can be harvested fresh from the garden all year round. They can also be sown more thickly in trays or other containers as cut-and-come-again baby leaves for salads.

If the leaves or other parts of the plant become covered by grey mould or downy mildew, this can be because the planting is too dense. Remove any affected foliage and thin the plants out so air can move freely between them.

The brightly coloured stems are attractive both in the garden and in salads. The leaves can also be eaten cooked in the same way as spinach. When large, the stems should be cut away and cooked separately for a little longer than the leaves.

Cherries

If you are planning on growing cherries you need to be clear on the differences between sweet cherries and acid cherries. Sweet varieties (of *Prunus avium*) are larger, suitable for eating raw, and are often self-sterile (so two different cultivars are required to produce a crop). Acid varieties (of *Prunus cerasus*) are smaller, used for cooking and making jams, and most cultivars are self-fertile.

Cherry trees should be planted in the dormant season. Acid cherries tolerate shade and can even be planted against a north-facing wall. Sweet cherries require a sunnier position. If you plant bare-root specimens, they should be staked for their first two years. Mulch around the base of the tree regularly. If frost threatens while the tree is in flower in spring, cover it with horticultural fleece overnight. Bullfinches love the flower buds of cherries, so, if they are a problem, cover with tree with netting, taking care that small birds can't get trapped.

Pruning should be carried out in August – the main aim being to remove diseased or damaged branches/twigs, any that are crossing and rubbing each other, and to improve the shape of the tree. This summer pruning also reduces the chance of the tree getting silver leaf

RECOMMENDED VARIETIES

EARLY RIVERS: An early, sweet cherry

MERTON GLORY: Mid-season, sweet variety

STELLA: A late, sweet cherry with large black fruits, self-fertile

MORELLO: An acid variety with small fruits suitable for cooking or jam making

disease, which is caused by fungal spores produced in the autumn and winter. Cherries can also be trained, by a combination of pruning (in spring) and tying to canes/wires, to certain shapes such as fans, often against a wall.

Pick the fruits when they are ripe and of good colour, but not too soft. Sweet cherries can be eaten straight away, frozen, dried or bottled; acid varieties can be cooked (in pies for example) or made into jams.

Storage

To freeze cherries, remove the stone then pack the fruits in plastic bags or containers in the freezer. To dry cherries, cut the fruit and remove the stones before drying them in a food dehydrator. Once the fruit feels dry and squeezing produces no juice, it can be jarred up and sealed. The product can be eaten dry as a snack or soaked for a day in water before adding to recipes.

Chinese Cabbage

A fast-growing oriental cabbage that can be cropped 6 weeks after sowing.

Early varieties like Kaboko can be sown from March, others from July through to September. Plant out into their final positions 30cm apart for full heads. Alternatively they can be sown closer together in containers and used as a cut-and-come-again crop for salads.

Chinese cabbage plants can come under attack from various insects including the cabbage root fly and flea beetles. If this becomes a problem, remove damaged plants and grow new ones under horticultural fleece.

The plants like a rich soil and regular watering. If they bolt you can cut the flower heads and use as you would broccoli. Leaves can be shredded into salads, stir-fried or cooked like regular cabbage.

Storage

Later in the year, as frosts approach, remaining heads can be cut and stored in the fridge or a frost-free outbuilding for a few weeks.

RECOMMENDED VARIETIES

KABOKO: Early cropping, sow from March

ATSUKO: Firm, barrel-shaped heads with a sweet flavour

Courgettes

Courgettes, or zucchinis as they are also known, are 'summer' squashes, which in general, are those that are harvested and used straight away in the summer, as opposed to other squashes like pumpkins that are grown and stored for winter use.

Sow the large seeds under cover in March and April in pots or trays. A heated propagator will get them off to a swift start. Plant outside, 1m apart, when the risk of frosts has passed. They can be planted in a bed or in large pots. Water well.

Powdery mildew, where the leaves become covered with a grey/white deposit, is very common with courgette plants. It is usually a sign of conditions being too dry and/or hot. In light cases this shouldn't affect fruit production but if the leaves start to curl and dry up this will certainly weaken the plants. Water the plants often and, if it becomes a regular problem, try growing the plants in cooler parts of your plot.

The key to summer squashes is to pick regularly while the fruits are small to ensure a constant supply. If you

RECOMMENDED VARIETIES

BLACK BEAUTY: A classic dark green courgette

YELLOW ZUCCHINI: A yellow courgette variety with more of a buttery texture and a slightly different flavour from green varieties

BIANCA DI TRIESTE: Pale green slightly bulbous fruits

TIGER CROSS: Stripey green fruits ideal for leaving to grow as marrows

'Patty Pan' type squashes:

CUSTARD WHITE: Flat, creamy white fruits

SCALLOPINI YELLOW: Bright yellow, very tasty fruits

like marrows you can leave one or two fruits to grow large (per plant) or grow a variety like Tiger Cross which produces excellent marrows that will store well after harvesting in the autumn.

Courgettes and other summer squashes can be grated or sliced raw into salads, stir-fried, roasted or made into fritters or cakes (see our recipes in the chapter Cooking throughout the Year, page 109).

Storage

Courgettes and other squashes can be frozen after washing, slicing thickly, and blanching for 1 minute. To cook from frozen, boil for about 2 minutes or add frozen to stir-fries. They can lose their texture and become rather mushy after freezing. They can also be pickled in much the same way as gherkins: slice larger fruits or leave small ones whole according to your preference. Then cover with salt for a day before rinsing, drying, packing in sterilised jars and topping up with vinegar.

Cucumber

Summer wouldn't be the same without sliced cucumbers! For centuries they have been eaten both fresh in salads and also pickled. Gherkins are merely varieties of cucumber that are harvested when small (7-10cm long) and pickled whole.

Commercial greenhouse varieties need higher temperatures and humidity, but traditional 'ridge' cucumbers crop well in an unheated greenhouse or outside.

Sow the seeds under cover in April in pots and then pot on to larger containers or plant out in May or June when the plants have several leaves each. Feed and water well as the fruits develop. Pinch out the growing tips when seven or eight leaves have formed to encourage side shoots to grow.

Keep harvesting the fruits before they grow too large – more will come!

Although cucumber seeds are soft, some people find them hard to digest, hence the production of 'burpless' varieties, which have very tiny seeds (sometimes incorrectly called 'seedless'). If you do prefer to remove the seeds of your cucumbers, simply slice the fruit in half and scoop out the seeds with a teaspoon.

Storage

Small cucumbers or gherkins pickle well. First, scrub gently with a scouring pad (which will also remove the tiny prickles) and dry. Slice larger fruits or leave small ones whole according to your preference. Then cover with salt for a day before rinsing, drying, packing in sterilised jars and topping up with vinegar. Seal and store in a dark place.

RECOMMENDED VARIETIES

All the following can be grown outside, although will do better in a frame, unheated greenhouse or polytunnel.

MARKETMORE: Dark green fruits up to 20cm long, high yields

TENDERGREEN BURPLESS: Non-bitter fruits, smooth skins, tie the plant to canes as it grows

CRYSTAL LEMON: Round yellowish fruits

If you want to grow a gherkin variety specifically for pickling, then try:

VERT PETIT DE PARIS: Small, prolific and can be sown up to the middle of June

Currants – Black, Red, White

Packed with vitamin C, currants are great for pies, jams, jellies, smoothies and juices.

They can be obtained either as potted plants or bare-rooted and planted out in the winter, either in the ground or in large pots. Winter is also the time for pruning established bushes – removing old growth as the fruits form on young fresh shoots. If frost threatens when the bushes are in flower, cover them with horticultural fleece overnight.

They will be ready for harvesting in the summer. Cut strings of ripe fruits and then top and tail – a fiddly business! If birds are stripping the bushes of fruits you may need to cover them in netting or grow them in fruit cages.

Storage

They can be frozen as they are, after removing stalks, or the fruits can be frozen as a purée after stewing and sieving. They can also be bottled or made into jams or jellies.

Freshly squeezed black currant juice has to be tasted to be believed! The juice can be extracted using a fruit press or electric juicer. Freshly-pressed juice will keep

RECOMMENDED VARIETIES

BEN CONNAN: High-yielding black currant with large berries
BEN HOPE: Great tasting black currant with high yields
JONKHEER VAN TETS: A red currant with large, juicy berries
WHITE VERSAILLES: A white currant with large, sweet fruit

only for a day or two in the fridge before fermenting but can also be frozen in plastic containers (leave a 5cm space for expansion as the juice freezes). You may wish to dilute the juice for drinking, or try mixing with other juices – black currant and apple juice make a good combination.

Figs

A warm fig, eaten straight from the tree in late summer, is a luscious experience.

April is a good time to purchase a young plant and pot it up. Fig trees can be vigorous so it's often a good idea to restrict the roots by planting in a barrel for example. They like good drainage so add some grit to the potting mixture. Place in a sunny position.

Once the fruits appear, feed the plant every two weeks. Tiny fruitlets produced in late summer will over-winter and ripen the next summer. Those produced in the spring are unlikely to ripen. Remove any large fruits that have not ripened in the late autumn.

Pruning can be done in March to remove weak branches and shape the tree, and again in June to remove the shoot tips from new growth. Fig trees grown in a greenhouse may be susceptible to red spider mite; as these mites thrive in hot, dry conditions, mist the leaves daily.

The fruits will be ready for harvesting around September time, when the skin is soft and the figs split if squeezed gently. Ripe figs do not store well, so eat or process as soon as harvested or keep in the fridge for just a few days.

Storage

To dry figs, cut them in half and sprinkle with a little sugar before drying them in a food dehydrator. Once the fruit feels dry and squeezing produces no juice, it can be jarred up and sealed. The product can be eaten dry as a snack or soaked for a day in water before adding to recipes. The fruits can also be bottled or made into jam.

RECOMMENDED VARIETIES

BROWN TURKEY: A hardy variety but for the best fruits grow in a greenhouse or conservatory or against a warm wall
BRUNSWICK: Hardy with large, sweet fruit

Florence Fennel

Florence fennel produces feathery leaves that taste of aniseed and can be treated in the same way as the herb common fennel. But in addition, Florence fennel produces edible bulbs (swollen stem bases) also tasting of aniseed that are a good source of vitamins A and C as well as potassium and calcium.

Sow the seeds depending on the variety as above, then plant out a couple of months later. They benefit from regular watering and mulching to keep the soil moist.

As the bulbs swell, earth them up (mound soil around the base of the stems) to blanch the bulbs and protect them from early frosts. If the plants set seed too early, rather than growing decent-sized bulbs, choose bolt-resistant varieties like Finale in the future. The bulbs should be harvested when the size of a tennis ball in late summer. If they are cut just above ground level, the base will grow new feathery leaves that can be used like a herb.

The bulbs can be sliced horizontally and used raw in salads, or can be roasted, fried or added to stews after quartering.

Storage

The cut bulbs of Florence fennel will keep for several weeks in a cool, dry place. To freeze, trim and cut into slices before blanching for 3 minutes. Pack into plastic bags and place in the freezer. To cook from frozen, boil for about 8 minutes or add frozen to stews.

RECOMMENDED VARIETIES

FINALE: Excellent resistance to bolting so can be sown from March for an early crop June onwards

ROMANESCO: Sow from May to July for large bulbs

Garlic

An easy crop to be self-sufficient in all year round, taking little space and effort to grow and storing well. Choose varieties developed for cultivation in your region (rather than supermarket-bought ones) and save a few bulbs each year for future sowing. Varieties are described as either 'hardneck' or 'softneck': the softneck ones are recommended for longer storage but they produce smaller bulbs with a milder flavour, so you may wish to grow a mix.

RECOMMENDED VARIETIES

PICARDY WIGHT (softneck): Suits a cool, wet climate, good flavour

VALLELADO (softneck): Large bulbs for planting early winter

FLAVOUR (hardneck): Medium-sized bulbs for planting late winter

ELEPHANT GARLIC: Not a true garlic but actually closely related to the leek. Produces large bulbs and big fat cloves. The flavour is sweeter and milder than traditional garlic.

Garlic plants

Red gooseberry

Depending on the variety, the cloves are often planted in winter, around November/December time, but a second planting can also be made in February. Plant individual cloves 30cm apart, just below the soil surface.

Garlic can suffer from onion white rot – a fungal disease that lives in the soil and causes the foliage to wilt. If this happens, check the bulbs for signs of rot or a white fluffy fungus. Remove affected plants as soon as possible and in future years grow garlic (and other alliums such as onions) in a different part of the plot as the fungus will remain in the soil for some time.

Cut off any flower heads that form – they can be used in salads. After the tops have died down in mid-summer, the garlic bulbs should be carefully lifted on a sunny day and left on the ground or on a wire rack to dry. Excess soil can then be brushed off the bulbs and they can be used immediately or put into storage.

Storage

When the skin on the bulbs is dry and papery, they can be stored in a cool, dry, frost-free place (not in the kitchen, or they will soon start to sprout). The dried stems can be plaited together to hang them like onions. If the conditions are right they will stay in good condition for months – although some will start to sprout as the weather warms up again next spring. Either use these straight away or plant them for a late crop later in the year.

Gooseberries

Gooseberries are easy to grow in a sunny position in the garden/allotment or in a container.

Bare-root plants should be planted in winter, while potted ones can be planted out at any time. Mulch well and, if in a container, make sure the soil doesn't dry out.

In July, bushes can be pruned to reduce the new growth and shape the plant. This will not remove the developing fruits as they grow on old wood. Then in winter, a further pruning can remove dead branches or those growing close to the ground, and shorten other branches.

The berries will be ready for harvesting from June/July. If birds are stripping the bushes of fruits you may need to cover them in netting or grow them in fruit cages.

Storage

To freeze gooseberries, top and tail before bagging up and placing in the freezer. They can also be frozen as a purée after stewing and sieving. Gooseberries can also be bottled, made into jams, jellies, chutneys (see our recipe on the next page) and wine. Berries that are young and hard have a higher acid and pectin content so are better for jam-making. Use older, softer ones for chutneys or wine.

RECOMMENDED VARIETY

INVICTA: High yields of large, pale green berries

Gooseberry Chutney

Makes 2 jars – approximately 400g each – adjust amounts throughout if you wish to make more in one go. This lovely chutney goes well with crackers and vegan cheese, salads, quiches, vegan sausages – you name it!

500g gooseberries
100g onions
100g raisins
10g salt
125g sugar
50ml water
125ml vinegar
Spices of your choice (e.g. ginger, pepper, chillies)

1. Finely chop the gooseberries and onions and simmer in the water until very soft (about 20 minutes).

2. Add the raisins, vinegar, sugar, salt and spices then stir and simmer until a pulpy consistency is achieved (about another 20 minutes).

3. Ladle into sterilised jars and seal. This will keep for several months but once opened store in the fridge and use within a couple of weeks.

Grapes

Under the right conditions one or two mature grape vines can provide many bunches of grapes – for eating fresh, juicing, wine-making or even drying your own raisins.

There are many varieties available, some for outdoor growing, some more suitable for greenhouses; some for wine-making, some for eating as a dessert. Here are just a few examples.

> ## RECOMMENDED VARIETIES
>
> **BOSKOOP GLORY**: An outdoor variety producing black dessert grapes
>
> **BLACK HAMBURGH**: For the greenhouse, producing large bunches of black grapes
>
> **BLACK CORINTH**: Small black grapes, sweet, juicy and seedless
>
> **SUFFOLK PINK**: Best in the greenhouse, producing attractive pink grapes that are seedless and well flavoured
>
> **MADELAINE SYLVANER**: Early-ripening green grape for wine-making

Grape vines can be planted in the dormant season in soil with plenty of compost added. They will need support, so can be planted against a wall and trained along wires, or up any sort of trellis, pergola or frame. Mulch in the spring, water well and feed every few weeks. Grape vines grown in a greenhouse may be susceptible to red spider mite; as these mites thrive in hot, dry conditions, mist the leaves daily.

For the first two years, remove all flowers to let the vines grow strongly; in years three and four allow about four bunches of grapes to grow, then in future years you can let them flower unlimited.

In the first winter (one year after planting) prune the main stem back two-thirds and all side shoots to one bud. A year later prune the main stem back by a half and reduce side shoots to two buds. In subsequent years the winter pruning will also reduce side shoots. There are many different techniques and schools of thought when it comes to pruning grape vines, so to get it right you may wish to research this topic in more detail.

Harvest the bunches by cutting them off with scissors when the grapes are ripe (sweet tasting). To keep cut bunches of grapes, cut them with a piece of branch attached – stick this in a jar of water and store in a cool dark cupboard or fridge where they will stay fresh for a few weeks.

Storage

The juice can be extracted with a fruit press or extractor and used fresh, frozen in containers, or used for wine-making. If you have seedless varieties you can try making your own raisins: dip the grapes into boiling water in a bowl for a few seconds to break the skin then dry in a food dehydrator. Once the fruit feels dry and squeezing produces no juice, the raisins can be jarred up and sealed.

Kale

Kale (also known as borecole) is well known for being very good for you: the dark green colour is a clue that the leaves are full of iron and vitamins A, C and E. It is frost-hardy and you can be harvesting the crop right through winter with no need for protection.

Grape leaves

Young grapes

Kale cage

Seeds can be sown in modules in April then planted out into their final growing positions in June, 45cm apart. Young plants may need netting protection from pigeons.

Old leaves can be bitter, so regularly harvest the young tender shoots. Once the plants have gone through the first frosts the bitterness will be reduced. Freezing the tender shoots ensures you have a year-round supply at your fingertips.

It can also be grown as a cut-and-come-again crop. Young leaves can be shredded into a winter salad, otherwise kale can be steamed, added to soups and stews, or made into nutritious smoothies.

Storage

To freeze kale, blanch the young shoots for 1 minute before chopping and bagging up for the freezer. To cook from frozen, boil for about 5 minutes.

RECOMMENDED VARIETIES

DWARF GREEN CURLED: Harvest from November to April, tightly curled leaves

PENTLAND BRIG: Harvest from November, plus you can eat the broccoli-like flower spears that grow in the spring

RED CURLED: Harvest from November to February, an attractive variety with purple stems

NERO DI TOSCANA: Long dark green blistered leaves with a peppery flavour

Leeks

Leeks are extremely hardy, easy to grow, and you should be harvesting them for 6-8 months of the year: September to April.

Sow seeds in trays in March and plant out in June. If grown as mini-leeks in containers they can grow just a few centimetres apart. For large leeks space them 20cm apart. Make 15cm deep holes with a dibber, separate the seedlings and drop one in each hole. You may find that trimming the roots with scissors helps getting them in. There is no need to fill the holes will soil, but water well immediately after planting out.

Leeks can suffer from onion white rot – a fungal disease that lives in the soil and causes the foliage to turn yellow and wilt. If this happens, check the stem base for signs of rot or a white fluffy fungus. Remove affected plants as soon as possible and in future years grow leeks (and other alliums such as onions and garlic) in a different part of the plot as the fungus will remain in the soil for some time.

They can be harvested at any size, the smaller ones having the greater flavour. You can also pull baby leeks in the early summer for use in salads. Mature leeks can be baked, stir-fried or added to soups and stews.

RECOMMENDED VARIETIES

PANDORA: An early variety for harvesting from September, long uniform stems

LANCIA: An early variety with long white shanks that can also be grown close together and harvested young as mini-leeks

BANDIT: A late variety for lifting in winter through to spring, high-yielding white stems

Storage

Leeks can be left in the ground until they are required. Otherwise freezing is the main storage method. Top and tail and wash carefully to make sure there is no soil left between the layers of skin. Slice thickly and blanch for 3 minutes before bagging up and freezing. To cook from frozen, boil for 8 minutes, or add the frozen slices to stews.

Onions

Used in so many savoury recipes, onions are an essential crop for the kitchen gardener, and to store for self-sufficiency throughout the year. They can be sown as seeds or planted as sets (immature onions that have been dried) in the spring. Some varieties can be planted as sets in the autumn for an early harvest the following spring. As sets have had an early start they can produce larger onions.

Seeds can be sown direct in the ground where they are to grow and then thinned out, or in a seed tray and then planted out about 6 weeks later. Those intended as spring onions won't need thinning. Sets can be planted 10-15cm apart with just the tips of the small bulbs visible. If birds pull them out you may need to net the crop temporarily while the roots grow. By all means mulch around the crop as it is growing, but not deeply around the bulbs themselves – they need to be exposed to the sun as they swell.

Melon

Melons are climbing annuals that are usually grown in the greenhouse or coldframe, but can be planted outside in early summer in a sunny sheltered spot in warmer climates.

Sow the seeds under cover in April and pot on as required.

String or canes can be used to support the plants, and when the fruits start to reach a certain size they will need to be supported in nets. They like a humid atmosphere so on hot sunny days leave a bucket of water in the greenhouse, or soak the path every morning. Melon plants grown in a greenhouse may be susceptible to red spider mite; as these mites thrive in hot, dry conditions, mist the leaves daily in addition to creating a humid atmosphere as described above.

As the fruits form, allow four to grow per plant, removing others and any further side shoots. Harvest the fruits when they smell sweet and the skin cracks near the stem.

Storage

Once harvested, the fruits will keep fresh for several weeks if stored at temperatures between 10-15°C.

RECOMMENDED VARIETIES

AMBROSIA: Sweet orange flesh

HONEYDEW GREEN FLESH: Pale skinned with light green flesh

RUGOSA DI CASENZA GIALLO: A yellow skinned cantaloupe variety with sweet flesh

RECOMMENDED VARIETIES

WHITE LISBON: Grown as spring onions, can be sown as seeds in autumn and spring

RED BARON: Sow as seeds or sets in spring, attractive red onions, popular in salads

STURON: Sow as seeds or sets in spring, large globe shaped bulbs, store well

RADAR: A Japanese variety, sow as sets in autumn to harvest June/July and eat fresh

SHALLOT LONGOR: A traditional French shallot with a mild flavour, plant sets in February/March to harvest in July/August

Onions can suffer from onion white rot – a fungal disease that lives in the soil and causes the foliage to wilt. If this happens, check the bulbs for signs of rot or a white fluffy fungus. Remove affected plants as soon as possible and in future years grow onions (and other alliums such as garlic and leeks) in a different part of the plot as the fungus will remain in the soil for some time.

Onions can be harvested and eaten fresh at any stage.

Storage

After the tops have fully died down at the end of summer, onions should be lifted on a sunny day and left on the ground. They then need a week or two to dry. The easiest method is to lay them in trays (clean seed trays will do) that are left in the sun, but brought indoors if rain threatens. When dry, the best specimens can be hung in nets or strung together. They will store well in a cool dry place until the end of spring. There are various methods for stringing – plaiting works well, or you can take four onions and tie the stalks together, then tie the knotted stalks to a piece of string. Hang this from the roof of your store and then add further onions, one at a time, by tying their stalks around the string and sliding them down to meet the others.

Onions are an ingredient in most chutneys and you can also have a go at making your own pickled onions. Peel small and medium-sized onions and soak in brine (100g salt per litre of water) for a day, before drying on kitchen paper and covering in vinegar in sterilised jars. To avoid overly sour pickled onions, add a couple of tablespoons of sugar to each jar and mix well. You can also add a variety of spices or a few fresh chilli peppers. Ideally leave the onions a month or more to mature before eating.

Pak Choi

A versatile and fast-growing oriental brassica that can be eaten in salads or stir-fries. They can be grown for cut-and-come-again baby leaves, or grown on to produce large plants with thick succulent stems.

Seeds should be sown between June and August, either in trays for baby leaves or in modules and then planted out 20cm apart for growing larger.

Flea beetles are a common problem, rapidly covering the succulent leaves with tiny holes. Protect crops with horticultural fleece.

Water the plants well to avoid bolting. Harvest mature heads about 60 days after sowing.

RECOMMENDED VARIETIES

CHINA CHOI: Dark green leaves, thick stems

BABY CHOI: Smaller plants – good for container growing

Parsnips

Roasted parsnips are a Christmas classic, but they can also be made into mashes (try mixing with different combinations of potatoes, sweet potatoes, carrots and celeriac) or added to soups and stews. Parsnip wine is a favourite amongst those who enjoy home-brewing country wines!

Sow the seeds in February or March in the ground where they are to grow. Thin to 20cm apart. They are slow to germinate and grow but you can sow small fast-growing crops, like radishes, in between them.

Parsnips can also suffer from carrot fly – a tiny insect that follows the smell of the plants and lays its eggs in the soil. The larvae burrow down and eat into the roots leaving blackened tunnels throughout. There are various organic solutions: cover the crops with fleece/enviromesh so the flies can't get to them; interplant with onions as a companion crop as the strong smell confuses the flies; avoid thinning out, by sowing seeds further apart, as this releases the smell that attracts the flies.

Parsnips can be left in the ground until they are needed. If there are still some left in the ground at the end of winter they can be lifted then for storage

Storage

Lift the parsnips and gently remove the soil from undamaged roots. Trim off the foliage and pack the roots in damp sand in boxes. Store in a cool, frost-free building. They can also be frozen: trim, peel, and cut into chunks before blanching for 3 minutes. Place in plastic bags in the freezer. To cook from frozen, boil for about 10 minutes or add frozen chunks direct to soups or stews.

RECOMMENDED VARIETIES

HALF LONG GUERNSEY: An heirloom variety with a smooth skin and a sweet flavour that produces medium length tapered roots

TENDER AND TRUE: Superb flavour and large, long roots

Peaches and Nectarines

Peach and nectarine trees all have a chilling requirement (ideally about 30 days below 7°C in a year) in order to fruit. They require a fairly dry sunny summer in order to crop well and in some areas more success will be had if they are grown under cover – fan-trained against a south-facing wall in a large glasshouse for example.

They should be planted in the dormant season – winter to early spring – unless purchased as a pot-grown plant. Mix compost into the soil around the plant and mulch well. Prune in August, straight after fruiting, the main aim being to remove diseased or damaged branches and twigs, any that are crossing and rubbing each other, and to improve the shape of the tree. They can also be trained, by a combination of pruning and tying to canes/wires, to a fan shape against a wall. If they have produced a large number of fruits then these can be thinned out in June to 15cm between each fruit.

Peach leaf curl is a common fungal disease affecting peaches, nectarines, almonds and apricots, causing the leaves to become red and blistered before dropping off. Eventually this will reduce the vigour of the plant. As the spores are spread by rain-splash during the first few months of the year, cover susceptible plants with

Parsnip plants

Nectarines

RECOMMENDED VARIETIES

PEACH – PEREGRINE: A good cropper of large well-flavoured fruits. Can be grown under glass or against a warm wall.

NECTARINE – LORD NAPIER: Produces large juicy smooth-skinned fruits. Can be grown under glass or against a warm wall but needs a warmer position than peaches to grow good quality fruit.

a rain-proof material (such as polythene sheeting) until May when it can be removed.

Harvesting the fruit mainly occurs during August – eat the best specimens straight away as a dessert or snack. They will not all ripen together so check regularly.

Storage

Peaches and nectarines are best eaten fresh but can be dried, frozen, bottled or used in jams and chutneys. To dry them, cut the fruit in half and remove the stones before drying them in a food dehydrator. Once the fruit feels dry and squeezing produces no juice, it can be jarred up and sealed. The product can be eaten as it is or soaked for a day in water before adding to recipes. They can be frozen either fresh after peeling and removing stones, or after stewing.

Pear flowers

Pears

Pears do not store as well as apples, but in addition to eating them fresh they can be bottled, juiced or made into perry – the pear equivalent of cider.

If you plant bare-root specimens in the dormant season they should be staked for their first two years. Mulch around the base of the tree regularly. Pruning should be carried out in winter – the main aim being to remove diseased or damaged branches and twigs, any that are crossing and rubbing each other, and to improve the shape of the tree. They can also be trained, by a combination of pruning and tying to canes/wires, to certain shapes such as espaliers or cordons, often against a wall.

During wet summers pears can be attacked by a fungal disease called brown rot, which causes fruits to turn brown with white pustules on the surface. To prevent this from spreading, remove affected fruits as soon as you see the signs.

RECOMMENDED VARIETIES

BETH: Medium-sized, well-flavoured fruit that turns yellow when ripe

CONCORDE: Heavy cropper, sweet, juicy fruits

CONFERENCE: Heavy cropper, firm, sweet fruits

SENSATION: An attractive tree with red foliage producing red fruits with juicy flesh

MERRYLEGS: A variety particularly suitable for making perry

Peas

Peas are so good for you and tasty too! Packed with vitamins, minerals, fibre and protein, every vegan should try growing them. Peas eaten straight from the pod immediately after harvesting are so sweet they can be eaten as a snack or added to salads raw. They have a multitude of uses in other dishes from stir-fries to stews and soups. The young pea shoots can be eaten in salads, the pods made into peapod wine, and dried peas can be sprouted and used in salads and stir-fries after just a few days.

Sow according to the variety: autumn for an early harvest; early spring under cover. Later successional sowings every two or three weeks should give you fresh peas from June to September. Some varieties can grow tall and will need pea-sticks or canes for support.

Pea moth is a common problem – the adults laying eggs on flowering peas in June and July. Once the creamy-white larvae have hatched they burrow into the pods and eat the developing peas inside. They may well not be noticed until the peas are shelled. If this becomes a problem, in future years you can either cover the plants with horticultural fleece over the flowering period (as peas are self-pollinating this won't reduce the crop), or make early and late sowings (March and July, for example) which will flower outside the moth's peak laying season.

Peas lose their sweetness rapidly after picking – the sugar is converted to starch within minutes of harvesting, so only pick the pods when you are going to use them, or freeze the peas straight away. When harvesting, hold the plant stem with one hand while you pull the pods off with the other – otherwise you may break the stem.

Storage

To freeze peas, pick while tender, shell and blanch for 1 minute before bagging up and freezing. To cook from frozen, boil for about 5 minutes. Varieties where you eat

RECOMMENDED VARIETIES

FIRST EARLY MAY: Can be sown in October/November for an early June harvest

GREENSHAFT: Sow in early spring, matures quickly

RAPIDO: Hardy, good for early sowings, a small Petit Pois type, perfect for freezing

SUGAR PEA NORLI: A classic mange-tout variety

SUGAR SNAP: Pick young and eat the plump pods whole, or leave to mature and shell

the pod too – such as mange-tout and sugar snap – can be frozen whole or sliced, after blanching for 2 minutes.

To dry them, leave the pods on the plants until they turn yellow, then cut the plant at ground level and hang indoors to dry completely. When the pods have become brittle, shell the peas and leave on trays for a few days. Then store in a cool dry place in airtight containers. Soak dried peas overnight before cooking.

Pepper – Capsicum

These are best grown in the greenhouse or polytunnel but can fruit well outside in a hot summer. Most peppers grow green fruits that gradually turn red if left on the plant in the sun – they can be harvested as desired. In general, the longer you leave the pods on the plant the sweeter capsicums become.

They need quite a long growing season so sow seeds under cover in February, or ideally in a heated propagator. Plant out into larger pots in April/May. Fruits will be ready for harvesting in August/September.

Red spider mite can become a problem for greenhouse crops – causing leaves to become mottled and pale before dropping off. As the mites need dry conditions, mist the leaves regularly. Dark patches at the bottom of

Red Pepper Relish

8 red peppers
8 green peppers
8 onions
500ml vinegar
200g sugar
50g salt

Finely chop the onions and peppers and discard the seeds. Simmer in the vinegar with the other ingredients until soft. Jar up and seal as you would for chutney.

capsicum fruits are a sign of blossom end rot. This is actually caused by neither a pest nor disease, but by calcium deficiency as a result of inadequate watering. Remove rotted peppers and maintain a regular watering regime.

Storage

Capsicums will stay fresh for several weeks in the fridge. For longer-term use they can be pickled, frozen or made into delicious sauces. All peppers can be pickled and make attractive and unusual gifts in glass jars: Slice the peppers and remove the seeds then cover in vinegar and seal. Large juicy capsicums should be covered in salt for a day before pickling or can be roasted first for 30 minutes in a hot oven (220°C) – remove the charred skins before covering in vinegar. If you use a mixture of different coloured peppers they can be packed in attractive layers or patterns in the jars. They will keep for up to a year.

To freeze them, first remove the stalks, then cut in half and scrape out the seeds and white pith. If you plan on cooking them in the future, then blanch for 3 minutes before bagging up when cool and freezing. This helps them to cook more evenly. Otherwise they don't need to be blanched.

Pepper – Chilli

Chilli peppers are best grown in the greenhouse or polytunnel but can fruit well on a windowsill or outside in a hot summer. The longer you leave the pods on the plant the hotter chillies become. When handling hot chilli peppers, take care not to touch your face as the juice will sting if the tiniest amount gets in your eyes.

They need quite a long growing season so sow seeds under cover in February, or ideally in a heated propagator. Plant out into larger pots in April/May. Fruits will be ready for harvesting in August/September.

Storage

Chilli peppers will stay fresh for several weeks in the fridge. For longer-term use they can be dried, pickled, frozen or made into fabulous sauces. Drying is an effective way to store chillies for up to a year. Pods can be dried on a rack in a food dehydrator or simply hang the chilli pods on strings (tie clusters of three or four pods by the stems every few inches along a piece of string) in a dry

RECOMMENDED VARIETIES

BENDIGO: Small fruits ready from August

MARCONI ROSSA: Large elongated fruits, deep red when mature

LUNCHBOX ORANGE: Tall plants producing small orange fruits

RECOMMENDED VARIETIES

RING OF FIRE: Long tapered peppers that turn bright red

HABANERO: Small fruits, very hot

HUNGARIAN HOT WAX: Sweet, milder fruits on small plants

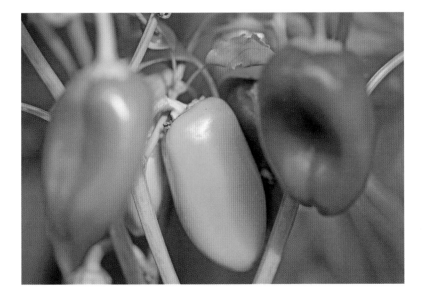

airy place until the pods snap when you bend them. Once fully dry, chillies can be stored in glass jars in a dry dark place.

Chillies can be pickled and, like capsicums, make attractive and unusual gifts in glass jars. Slice the pods open and remove the seeds then cover in vinegar and seal. If you use a mixture of different coloured peppers they can be packed in attractive layers or patterns in the jars. They will keep for up to a year.

To freeze them, first remove the stalks, then cut in half and scrape out the seeds. Blanch for 1 minute – bag up when cool and freeze.

See the chapter Cooking throughout the Year for our hot chilli Spitfire Sauce recipe!

Plums

Plum trees, including damsons and greengages, require plenty of sun and prefer good drainage. There is a wide range of cultivars and rootstocks available: some, such as Victoria plums, can form quite large trees, while others will be more suited to fan-training against a south-facing wall.

RECOMMENDED VARIETIES

VICTORIA PLUM: Popular variety with large juicy fruits, heavy cropper

EARLY PROLIFIC: Small purple plums that can be eaten fresh or made into delicious jam

MARJORIE'S SEEDLING: A good cropper of large juicy blue-black plums

MERRYWEATHER DAMSON: Blue-black fruits with a strong flavour, good early cropper

OLD GREENGAGE: Fruit has translucent flesh and excellent flavour

Plum Chutney

For about 4 jars you'll need:

> 500g stoned plums
> 250g apples
> 250g onions
> 250g raisins
> 25g salt
> 100g sugar
> 300ml vinegar
> spices of your choice
> (e.g. ginger, allspice, nutmeg, cloves)

Finely chop the apples and onions and add to the plums in a large pan. Add the other ingredients, stir and simmer until a pulpy consistency is achieved. Jar up into sterilised jars and seal.

Plum trees should be planted in the dormant season. If you plant bare-root specimens, they should be staked for their first two years. Mulch around the base of the tree regularly.

Pruning should be carried out in spring or summer – the main aim being to remove diseased or damaged branches/twigs, any that are crossing and rubbing each other, and to improve the shape of the tree. They can also be trained, by a combination of pruning (in spring) and tying to canes/wires against a wall. Do not prune in the dormant season as there is risk of infection from silver leaf disease and bacterial canker.

Harvest plums when they feel slightly soft when squeezed gently. If wasps become a problem, keep harvesting as soon as the fruits are ready, and regularly clear up any that have fallen on the ground.

Storage

Plums can be frozen, dried, bottled or made into jams or chutneys. Freeze fresh after removing stones – or after stewing. You can skin them first, or they can be easily skinned after freezing by immersing the frozen plums in hot water for a minute or two, after which the skins will slide off when the fruit is squeezed.

Try making your own prunes: cut the plums and remove the stones before drying them in a food dehydrator. Once the fruit feels dry and squeezing produces no juice, it can be jarred up and sealed. The product can be eaten dry as a snack or soaked for a day in water before adding to recipes.

Most plums make good jam; purple plums are best for freezing and chutneys. Pick when ripe but still hard. Damsons set well as jams but greengages will need lemon juice adding.

Potatoes

Potatoes are easy to grow and easy to store. Even if you only have a small garden you can still grow your own small crop in a bucket, large pot or bag on the patio. There's nothing like your own new potatoes, straight from soil to pan.

RECOMMENDED VARIETIES

First earlies

Fast growing, eat as new potatoes rather than for storage.

RED DUKE OF YORK: Deep red skinned with yellow flesh, less susceptible to disease than the old and well-known Duke of York, but retaining texture and flavour

MARIS BARD: Smooth skin, scrapes well

Second earlies

Can be eaten as new potatoes or left to grow bigger.

BRITISH QUEEN: Great flavour, good for roasting

Orla: Smooth white skin, some resistance to scab and blight

Early maincrop

Ready for harvest around September.

SANTE: The most commonly grown variety on organic farms, resistant to eelworm and blight, yellow flesh

DESIREE: Great for roasting, red skin and yellow flesh

Late maincrop

Take the longest time to grow, good for storage over winter.

LINDA: Great tasting and stores well

ARRAN VICTORY: Eye-catching purple/blue skin and white floury flesh, good yield and blight resistance

Early varieties can be sown as soon as February under cover – in a large pot in the greenhouse for example. Later varieties in a trench in the garden in March and April. They benefit from a good layer of moisture-retaining compost at the bottom of the trench. Water well during dry periods. As the leaves show, gradually earth up the shoots to create a mound along the row – the leaves will keep pushing through – this will enable more tubers to form and reduces the chances of any turning green through exposure to the sun.

Blight, a disease spread by a fungus, can be a common problem, especially during warm and wet summers. Leaves and stems will turn brown and collapse and eventually the rot will spread to the tubers underground. Remove affected foliage as soon as you notice blight damage and harvest the tubers early. If blight is a common occurrence in your area, grow early varieties and practise crop rotation.

New potatoes can be harvested in May and June as required. For the maincrops, once the foliage has died down at the end of summer, cut the stems off at ground level and remove them, but leave the tubers in the ground for a further week or two. Then carefully dig up the potatoes on a sunny day and leave on the surface to dry for a few hours. Throw away any green potatoes as these are poisonous.

Storage

Once dry, the tubers can be stored in boxes or paper sacks in a dry building in the dark. They should keep in good condition until spring, but check regularly and remove any that are rotting.

Pumpkins and Squash

Pumpkins and other squashes are good sources of potassium and vitamin A with a sweet nutritious flesh. The seeds can be roasted as a tasty snack or used in baking breads and cakes. The flowers can also be used like others of the squash family, for example batter-dipping and frying them.

Sow the large seeds under cover in April and May in pots or trays. A heated propagator will get them off to a swift start. Plant outside, 1m apart, when the risk of frosts has passed. Water well throughout the growing season and feed fortnightly as the fruits grow. As the fruits form, it's a good idea to restrict the number per plant, say four pumpkins or six butternut squash for example, and cut off any further shoots so that the plant puts all its energy into growing those fruits.

Powdery mildew, where the leaves become covered with a grey/white deposit, is common with pumpkins and other squash plants. It is usually a sign of conditions being too dry and/or hot. In light cases this shouldn't affect fruit production but if the leaves start to curl and dry up this will certainly weaken the plants. Water the plants often and, if it becomes a regular problem, try growing the plants in cooler parts of your plot.

Marrows can be made into wine and jam and are a great addition to chutneys. Pumpkins make great soup and pie. Butternut and other winter squashes also make good soup and are delicious when roasted. See our Macaroni 'Cheese' with butternut squash recipe in the chapter Cooking throughout the Year.

Storage

Marrows, pumpkins and winter squashes should be left on the plants until the first frost is expected. Then cut (with a few centimetres of stalk attached) and store in a cool dry building – either hung in nets or placed on shelves. They will stay in good condition until mid-winter.

> ### RECOMMENDED VARIETIES
>
> **ROUGE VIF D'ETAMPES:** A pumpkin with lobed fruits which have a good colour and mature quickly
>
> **JACK O'LANTERN:** The perfect pumpkin for Halloween! Stores well
>
> **HONEYNUT:** A butternut type, excellent for roasting
>
> **BUTTERSCOTCH:** A butternut type with small sweet fruits
>
> **TURKS TURBAN:** Often grown ornamentally but the pale yellow flesh is very tasty
>
> **VEGETABLE SPAGHETTI:** Produces strands of flesh that look like spaghetti, can be baked or boiled, a vigorous trailing plant

Radish

We all know the small red radishes grown for salad use, but don't overlook winter radishes which can be cooked or pickled.

Radishes are easy to grow. First sowings can be made under cover as early as February, then from April onwards sowing a short row every few weeks will ensure a constant supply of salad radishes. Pick them small and young before they get tough and before the slugs get to them.

Winter radishes need a longer growing period but will produce larger roots. Sow them June onwards for harvesting from October.

Flea beetles can be a problem, rapidly covering the leaves with tiny holes. Protect crops with horticultural fleece.

> ### RECOMMENDED VARIETIES
>
> *Spring and summer use:*
>
> **CHERRY BELLE:** Round red roots that grow fast and crop early, tasty white flesh
>
> **FRENCH BREAKFAST:** A favourite variety, elongated red roots with a white tip
>
> *Autumn and winter use:*
>
> **CHINA ROSE:** Tapered crimson roots with white flesh
>
> **MINOWASE (MOULI):** Long white roots – leave in the ground until required

The small, fast-growing radishes used fresh in salads should be harvested just a few weeks after sowing and used straight away, but the larger winter types can be stored in a number of ways, similar to other root vegetables.

Storage

Trim off the foliage and pack in damp sand in boxes – in a cool, frost-free building they should keep for several months. Winter radishes (below) can also be pickled: scrub the skins clean and slice before layering with salt (or putting in brine) and leaving for 24 hours. Rinse the salt off, pack into sterilised jars, and cover with pickling vinegar.

Raspberries

There are two main types of raspberries: those that fruit in the summer over a short season with heavy crops and those that fruit over the autumn with a protracted cropping period. Also worth trying are loganberries, tayberries and boysenberries that are all hybrid berries as a result of various crosses.

Raspberries can be obtained as bare-rooted canes or pot-grown plants and should be planted in the dormant season. They can be grown up canes, along a post and wire system or even in pots. Water well during dry periods.

Summer varieties should be pruned after all the fruits have been gathered. Cut down canes that fruited to ground level; leave about six young canes per plant to grow on and fruit next year. Autumn varieties should be cut down completely to ground level in February.

Pick the fruits when large and well-coloured, before they go soft. If your plants are attacked by raspberry beetle (you will find small white maggots inside the fruits) you may have to concentrate on growing autumn varieties which are less susceptible.

Storage

Raspberries are excellent for jam-making, bottling and freezing. To freeze them, remove the stalks then open-freeze on a tray in the freezer before bagging up. They can also be frozen as a purée after stewing and sieving.

> RECOMMENDED VARIETIES
>
> **GLEN AMPLE**: Good yields of large fruits ready in the summer
>
> **AUTUMN BLISS**: An autumn variety that will produce fruits from August until the first frosts

Rhubarb

Rhubarb can be sown as seeds but you'll get off to a faster start by buying a one-year-old crown, or a section of root from a neighbour.

Seeds can be sown in pots in April and then planted out in the autumn. Crowns (or split roots from a neighbour's plant) should be planted in the dormant season. Potted plants can be planted at any time and can be grown in large containers. They like a rich growing medium, plenty of compost, good drainage but watering well during dry spells. Don't harvest anything the first year after planting, but otherwise harvest a few stalks per plant up until June, then leave remaining stalks to grow on and strengthen the plant.

The practice of 'forcing' rhubarb (growing them in the dark) is often used for an early crop of tender, pale stems. The easiest way of doing this is to cover one or two crowns in January with a large pot, upturned dustbin or a special forcing pot. Check regularly for signs of shoots and cut as required.

When the leaves have died down in the winter remove them and leave the crowns exposed to frost to break dormancy. Established plants will crop for many years.

> ### RECOMMENDED VARIETIES
> **CHAMPAGNE**: An early variety often available as crowns
> **VICTORIA**: Reliable cropper that forces well
> **GLASKIN'S PERPETUAL**: A quick-growing variety that can be grown from seed

Storage

Rhubarb makes good jam, wine and chutneys. Use the young spring shoots for freezing and bottling. To freeze rhubarb, simply cut into chunks and open-freeze on a tray in the freezer before bagging up. Blanching for 1 minute will retain the colour, but it is not essential.

Spinach

With a selection of varieties you can have spinach ready for picking in the garden all year round. Perpetual spinach, which is a leaf beet rather than a true spinach, can withstand drier conditions than true spinach varieties without bolting.

Seeds can be sown from April through to August then thinned or planted out 15cm apart. Use the thinnings in salads. You may need to protect the young plants from pigeons with netting.

Pick a few leaves from each plant, and use or freeze as soon as possible after harvesting. Wash the leaves very well in several changes of water to get rid of any soil.

Storage

To freeze spinach, wash the leaves well then blanch for 2 minutes. Cool and squeeze out excess water before freezing in plastic bags. It will freeze as a solid lump so fill each bag with only as much spinach as you will need for one meal. To cook from frozen, boil for about 5 minutes.

> ### RECOMMENDED VARIETIES
> **CHAMPAGNE**: An early variety often available as crowns
> **VICTORIA**: Reliable cropper that forces well
> **GLASKIN'S PERPETUAL**: A quick-growing variety that can be grown from seed

Strawberries

A warm strawberry eaten straight from the plant is one of the joys of summer. They are easy to grow, whether in a bed or container.

Strawberries are generally obtained as potted plants or bare-rooted runners and planted in spring or autumn. Water well and feed every couple of weeks.

As the fruits start to form, lift them off the soil to avoid rot (straw is traditionally used for this). You may also need to protect the fruit from birds with netting.

At the end of the season remove old leaves (and straw if it was used). Plants should fruit well for about three years and can then be replaced. As the plants produce runners these can be cut off and potted up once they have started to take root.

If strawberries are planted too densely they can be susceptible to problems such as grey mould. If you see

RECOMMENDED VARIETIES

CHRISTINE: An early variety with good flavoured large fruits

CAMBRIDGE FAVOURITE: Mid-season, easy to grow and disease resistant

SYMPHONY: Late season with high yields of excellent flavoured fruits resistant to red core

Strawberry Jam

2kg strawberries
1 lemon
1.75kg sugar

Heat the strawberries with the juice of the lemon, stir and gently simmer until tender. Then add the sugar, stir, boil, and keep boiling hard until setting point. Ladle into sterilised jars and seal. If you have trouble getting your strawberry jam to set, try adding commercially available pectin.

fuzzy grey patches on leaves, remove all infected material and thin out the plants.

Storage

Smaller strawberries can be frozen by open-freezing on trays before packing into plastic bags or containers. They can also be frozen as a purée after processing. To dry strawberries, cut the fruit in slices before drying them in a food dehydrator. Once the fruit feels dry and squeezing produces no juice, the berries can be jarred up and sealed. The product can be eaten dry as a snack or soaked for a day in water before adding to recipes.

Swede

Swede is also known as rutabaga, Swedish turnip or yellow turnip. They were originally produced by crossing cabbages with white turnips and are hardy plants that taste sweeter after a frost.

Sow the seeds in April and thin or plant out 20cm apart a couple of months later.

If plants grow poorly, and/or wilt and die, they may have been attacked by cabbage root fly. The white larvae of the fly burrow down to eat the roots of the young plants – they can ruin entire swede roots. Practising crop rotation will help reduce the incidence of this; crops can also be protected with horticultural fleece. Otherwise, you can make collars for individual plants using a circle of cardboard, about 12cm across, placed at soil level around the stem of each plant. This prevents the fly laying eggs near enough to the swede.

Swede roots can be dug up as soon as they are large enough to use. They are very hardy and can be left in the soil until required. Expect to be harvesting from

RECOMMENDED VARIETIES

SWEDE YELLOW FRIESIAN: A traditional swede with delicious yellow flesh

SWEDE LOMOND: Easy to grow with good disease resistance

September to March. Try eating the yellow flesh from the roots mashed with carrots. Cut into chunks and boil until soft, drain, add seasoning but no liquid, mash or blend. Swede also goes well in winter stews in small cubes.

Storage

If hard frosts are expected pull up and gently remove the soil from undamaged roots. Twist off the foliage and pack the roots in damp sand in boxes – store in a cool, frost-free building. To freeze swede, wash, trim and cut into chunks before blanching for 3 minutes. Cool and freeze in plastic bags. To cook from frozen, boil for about 8 minutes.

Sweet Corn

Also known as maize or corn-on-the-cob, the kernels are so sweet when first picked they can be eaten raw in the garden straight from the cob! Otherwise they have a multitude of uses in the kitchen and are a good source of protein. They can be eaten together with beans, as each has an essential amino acid that the other lacks, so together they make a complete protein meal. This is the traditional way of eating them in Latin America.

Sow seeds in modules in April under cover then plant out when large enough in May or June, spacing the plants 45cm apart. As they are wind-pollinated they should be planted in blocks rather than rows. They are usually grown for the large cobs, but you can also try a baby corn variety – harvested up to 10cm long, they can be eaten raw or lightly boiled and they also freeze well.

In open, windy areas you may need to support the plants with canes. Mulch around the plants well. They can be intercropped with pumpkins which provide a kind of living mulch and will continue growing after the corn cobs have been harvested. Beans can also be planted amongst them to grow up the corn plants – this trilogy of growing sweet corn, pumpkins and beans together is known as the three sisters, and has been practised in the Americas for centuries.

Like peas, sweet corn loses its sweetness rapidly from the moment the cobs are picked as the sugar is converted to starch within minutes of harvesting. So pick the cobs only when you are going to eat or freeze them straight away. To harvest, wait until the silk tassels have turned brown then test for ripeness by exposing some kernels and pushing your thumbnail into one – if it's hard or squirts out a watery liquid it's not ripe, but if a milky fluid comes out it's ready.

Storage

Sweet corn can be frozen, dried for storage and later rehydrated (or for making into popcorn) or can be bottled or made into a tasty relish.

To freeze sweet corn, pull off the outer leaves and silks, trim the stalk, and blanch for 5 minutes. After cooling, wrap each cob in foil or cling film before placing in the freezer. Thaw before cooking in boiling water for 5 minutes, or 10 minutes from frozen. Alternatively, the kernels can be stripped from the cob using a knife, and then blanched for 1 minute before bagging up and freezing. Baby corn will also only need blanching for 1 minute before bagging up and freezing.

To dry sweet corn, leave the cobs on the plant longer than usual (until the kernels start to dry). Then hang them up indoors for a few weeks until fully dry. The kernels can then be stripped from the cobs and stored in airtight jars, until needed for popping or soaking before adding to soups and stews. Note that for successful popcorn the kernels must be completely dry and hard.

RECOMMENDED VARIETIES

MEDZI: Extra sweet flavour

DOUBLE STANDARD: Produces white and yellow kernels on the same cobs

MINIPOP: Harvest small for perfect baby corns

Tomatoes

Grown more than other fruit or vegetables due to their versatility – not only are they an essential constituent of most salads, but as a sauce they are the basis of many meals: pizza, chilli, curry, soup, pasta sauce and so on. Tomatoes are available in a wide range of colours, shapes, flavours and sizes, with fruits from 1cm diameter to weighing over 1kg each!

They will do best in a greenhouse or under cover but some varieties will crop well outdoors in a warm summer.

Sow the seeds under cover in March and pot on as required. Bush varieties are easy to grow with no support or pruning needed, but most others will need to grow up canes or other support and to have side shoots regularly pinched out. Once each plant has produced about six trusses of fruits, also pinch out the growing tip.

Feed the plants every fortnight with a liquid feed (ideally homemade from your nettles and comfrey) and/or a seaweed-based foliar feed. Water frequently as required.

They can be susceptible to blight (they are related to potatoes) so if this is a problem in your area choose varieties that have some blight resistance and grow them in a greenhouse or polytunnel. Dark patches at the bottom of tomato fruits are a sign of blossom end rot. This is actually caused by calcium deficiency as a result of inadequate watering. Remove rotted fruits and maintain a regular watering regime. If yellow blotches and grey mould appears on the leaves of the plants, this is a sign of poor ventilation. Open greenhouse doors and vents on warm days to create a through draught, and consider

RECOMMENDED VARIETIES

GARDENER'S DELIGHT: A favourite sweet cherry tomato with long trusses of fruits

ALICANTE: A medium-sized tomato with good resistance to mildew and greenback. An early cropper with good flavour.

TIGERELLA: Fruits are red with yellow stripes and of good flavour

ROMA: Plum variety, perfect for juices, soups and sauces

COUNTRY TASTE: Huge 'beefsteak' style tomato, great for slicing

TUMBLING TOM: Bush variety – low-growing plants, suitable for pots and hanging baskets and doing very well outdoors, producing very small but sweet tomatoes

Green Tomato Chutney

For 4 or 5 jars you'll need:

- 1kg green tomatoes
- 250g apples
- 250g onions
- 120g raisins
- 15g salt
- 250g sugar
- 300ml pickling vinegar
- Spices of your choice
  (e.g. ginger, pepper, chillies)

Finely chop the tomatoes, apples and onions and place all the ingredients in a large pan. Heat gently, stir, and simmer until a pulpy consistency is achieved. Jar up in sterilised jars and seal.

installing auto-vents that automatically open roof vents when a certain temperature is reached.

Harvested tomatoes will stay in good condition for a week or more. Pick when ripe with a deep colour. Green tomatoes make a great chutney (see recipe below) or can be encouraged to ripen by placing them in a plastic bag in a warm room with a couple of ripe tomatoes, apples or a banana.

Storage

Tomatoes can be stored in several different ways: frozen, bottled, dried, or juiced (and then frozen or bottled) or made into chutneys and ketchups etc.

The easiest way to freeze them is just to put them whole into the freezer. They can easily be skinned after freezing by immersing the frozen tomatoes in hot water for a minute or two, after which the skins will slide off when the fruit is squeezed. You can then add them to the dish. They can also be frozen after stewing to a purée for use as a base for pasta sauces etc. Simmer for 5 minutes then sieve before freezing in a plastic container. Tomatoes can be fully dried and stored in jars, or partly dried and stored in oil. Cut the tomatoes in half, lay on a rack in a low oven or in a food dehydrator, and sprinkle a little salt on the upturned face of each half. The drying process can take up to a day depending on the size of the tomatoes – remove them when they feel firm and dry. For oil storage, remove them while still a little squishy and pack into sterilised jars, covering with olive oil and sealing. Either way they will store for up to 6 months.

Turnips

Turnips grow quickly and can be used to fill gaps between other slower-growing vegetables on the plot.

Sow the seeds from April through to July and thin or plant out 20cm apart a couple of months later.

Plants that grow poorly, and/or wilt and die, may have been attacked by cabbage root fly. The white larvae of the fly burrow down to eat the roots of the young plants. Crop rotation will help reduce the incidence of this; plants can also be protected with horticultural fleece. Otherwise, you can make collars for individual plants using a circle of cardboard, about 12cm across, placed at soil level around the stem of each turnip. This prevents the fly laying eggs near enough to the plant.

Turnips are not fully frost-hardy, so later sowings should be lifted and stored before winter. To avoid wood-iness, the roots should be pulled when they reach no more than about 5cm in diameter.

Turnips can be steamed, stir-fried, mashed or roasted. The young leaves can also be harvested and eaten like spring greens.

Storage

Harvested turnips will keep fresh in the fridge for several weeks. For longer storage gently remove the soil from undamaged roots, twist off the foliage and pack the roots in damp sand in boxes. Store in a cool, frost-free building. They can also be frozen: wash, trim and cut into chunks before blanching for 3 minutes. Cool and freeze in plastic bags. To cook from frozen, boil for about 8 minutes.

RECOMMENDED VARIETIES

PURPLE TOP MILAN: Quick to mature. Sow in March for an early crop

WHITE GLOBE: Smooth roots with white tender flesh

GOLDEN BALL: Round golden roots with yellow flesh, stores well

12. CHALLENGING CROPS

In this section we discuss a few crops that aren't included in the Fruits and Vegetables chapter, page 63. By 'challenging', we simply mean plants that in one way or another require a little more care than many staple crops. It might be that they require higher temperatures, so will only thrive in a greenhouse for example, or they may need a different type of soil.

It's always interesting and fun to grow something brand new. You may discover a plant that loves your growing conditions and that you love to eat, which then becomes a regular crop for you for years afterwards. Seed catalogues and gardening magazines can be a source of inspiration for new and interesting varieties, but it's also important to look at heirloom plants. These are old cultivars, often handed down through generations. They are open-pollinated (rather than hybrids from crosses) and can deliver greater taste and nutritional value. In addition, as they produce less uniform plants, they will ripen over a longer period. You can also save your own seeds, knowing that they will produce plants that are true to type (which won't be the case if you save seeds from hybrid plants). You can order various heirloom varieties as seeds online. The organisation, Garden Organic, also run a Heritage Seed Library (see Resources, page 233), which you can join and then receive your choice of seeds as part of your membership. If you do so, you will be supporting the conservation of unusual varieties for future generations, as well as increasing biodiversity in your own garden.

The following are a few less commonly grown crops that we have recently tried.

Blueberries

These berries are actually relatively easy to grow, but they do require an acid soil, so are often best grown in pots. The berries will also need protection from birds. Blueberries are very healthy: high in antioxidants and vitamin C.

Although some varieties, like those recommended above, are self-fertile, they will usually crop more heavily if two or more different cultivars are grown near together. They require a soil pH of 5.5 or lower, so unless you have unusually acidic garden soil, you will need to purchase ericaceous compost to pot them on into larger pots. Containers of around 30-50cm diameter will be perfect. Only water with rainwater to maintain the acidity.

Once they start to fruit, either move the pots under cover or protect with netting. Harvest the fruits gradually once they turn dusty blue, between July and September.

Storage

Blueberries can be frozen easily as they are in bags or plastic containers. Alternatively, they can be made into preserves or dried in a dehydrator.

> RECOMMENDED VARIETIES
>
> **NELSON**: Hardy and self-fertile, large fruits produced late season
>
> **TOP HAT**: Self-fertile, a heavy cropper with very flavoursome fruits

Chickpea pods

Harvested chickpeas

Lemon plant

Chickpeas

These legumes are usually grown in the warm climes of the Mediterranean or Asia, but will produce pods of delicious peas in temperate climates too. In hot summers they will mature into the dried, sandy-coloured chickpeas we know so well, but can also be harvested while young, green and delicious, and eaten like ordinary green peas. The plants are attractive, nitrogen fixing and will grow to about 60cm tall.

Sow them in modules under cover, then plant out 20cm apart. Seeds sown in April will be ready for harvesting in September.

Storage

To freeze chickpeas, pick while tender, shell them, and then blanch for 1 minute before bagging up and freezing. To cook from frozen, boil for about 5 minutes.

If you have a long hot summer then you can dry them: Leave the pods on the plants until they turn yellow, before cutting the plant at ground level and hanging indoors to dry completely. When the pods have become brittle, shell the chickpeas and leave on trays for a few days, then store in a cool, dry place in airtight containers. Soak dried chickpeas overnight before cooking.

RECOMMENDED VARIETY

PRINCIPE: Grows well even in cool summers, producing small peas

Citrus

Citrus plants are not hardy and are generally grown in pots on a patio through the summer then brought into the shelter of a conservatory or frost-free greenhouse for the winter months. Lemons and kumquats are the most easily grown in cooler climates, but various others can thrive as described in the recommended varieties below. All are self-fertile and usually purchased as potted plants grown on dwarfing rootstocks. Fruits can take up to 12 months to ripen.

Placed in a sunny position, most citrus bushes will reach 1-2 metres tall. Feed the plants regularly from April to October using a nettle or compost tea or seaweed extract. Water regularly with rainwater during the summer but do not waterlog. When indoors, mist the plants daily – this helps with both humidity and pollination of the flowers.

RECOMMENDED VARIETIES

LEMON – EUREKA: A vigorous plant with excellent crops of thick-skinned fruits

LIME – TAHITI: A beautiful plant producing bright green seedless fruits

KUMQUAT – NAGAMI: Small oval fruits with a sweet skin and bitter pulp

ORANGE – BIGARADIER: Produces bright orange fruits suitable for making marmalade

MANDARIN – NOVA, also known as **CLEMENVILLA:** Produces medium-sized, sweet flavoured fruits

GRAPEFRUIT – WHITE MARSH: Vigorous and heavy cropping, producing fruits that are sweet when mature. Less hardy than other citrus and can reach a fair size, suitable for a large greenhouse

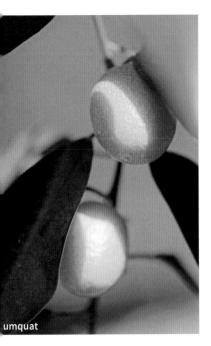
umquat

Ginger sprout

Mushrooms

In March each year, prune out overcrowded and over-long branches to reshape the plant, then either repot or replace the top 5cm of compost with fresh.

Storage

Fruits can generally be left on the plant until required. Harvested, they will keep in good condition in the fridge for several weeks. You may also want to extract the juice and freeze that in small cartons or ice cube trays for longer-term storage.

Ginger

The ginger rhizomes we see in supermarkets and green-grocers are from a tropical plant that is not frost-hardy, but can be grown under cover in temperate countries. In the early spring, choose a piece of rhizome that has a number of growth buds and break or cut it up into sections, each one with at least one bud. Plant these just under the surface of moist compost in pots or trays, with the buds facing up, and leave in a warm place such as a windowsill indoors or in a heated propagator. They will start to produce shoots and, once about 10cm high, can be transplanted into larger pots in the greenhouse. Eventually they will grow to about 1.5 metres tall with attractive grass-like foliage. The pots can be moved to a sunny location outside during the warm summer months.

The plants will mature in about nine months and then the foliage may start to die back. Before the first frosts in the autumn/winter you can dig up the rhizomes, which will have grown larger, and use some for cooking and some for growing more plants next year.

Storage

Ginger rhizomes will keep in the fridge in good condition for a month or two. The section that you want to use to grow new plants from next year can be kept in a pot of compost in a cool, frost-free room until February/March, when it should be moved to a warmer windowsill or heated propagator to start growing again.

Mushrooms

A source of protein as well as being packed with vitamins and minerals and with virtually no fat or calories, mushrooms are excellent for any diet. There are various methods for growing them, both indoors and out in the garden, depending on the varieties chosen.

White and brown cap mushrooms are traditionally grown on horse manure, but can equally be grown on coir compost (made from coconut husk fibre) or used coffee grounds, either of which can also be mixed with straw or waste cardboard. Coffee grounds can often be obtained free from cafés or from supermarkets with

RECOMMENDED VARIETIES

WHITE CAP: The common white mushroom often harvested young as buttons

BROWN CAP: Also known as chestnut mushrooms, a nuttier taste than white caps

OYSTER: A soft chewy texture, often used in stir-fries

SHITAKE: Full of flavour, often used in Oriental cooking and for making sauces

CHICKEN OF THE WOODS: A delicious yellow mushroom with a meaty texture

coffee machines. The fungi are obtained as spores, which are mixed in with the growing medium and left in a cool damp place to grow.

Oyster mushrooms can be grown on coffee grounds as well, but are also available as wooden dowels impregnated with their spawn. Shitake and chicken of the woods can also be obtained in this form. You drill holes in logs (usually freshly cut, hardwood logs like oak, beech or birch, though some types of oyster mushrooms prefer pine), insert the dowels and seal with wax. The logs can then be left in a shady position, for example under an evergreen shrub. It may be several months before the mushrooms appear, but they should continue fruiting for four or five years.

Storage

If you are drying or freezing mushrooms, this must be done as soon as possible after picking. To dry mushrooms, slice them then put in an electric dehydrator or warm oven (45-55°C) on a rack for a few hours. Alternatively, thread a string of small mushrooms on strong cotton and hang in a dry, airy place for several days. Store the dried mushrooms in airtight jars in a cool, dark place – this makes them a great addition to soups and stews, as the drying process gives the mushrooms new flavours and textures which are considered a delicacy.

You can also freeze them: button mushrooms can be frozen whole, while large ones can be sliced first. If frozen raw they will keep well only for about a month; if first cooked by frying for a few minutes they will keep up to three months. Add frozen mushrooms to soups, stews, casseroles and so on. Mushrooms can be pickled to be preserved and create a new taste experience: put clean mushrooms in a pan and cover with vinegar. Season with salt, pepper and spices if desired. Heat gently until the mushrooms have visibly shrunk, then jar up, covering with the hot vinegar. Seal and store in a dark cupboard.

Nuts

A valuable source of protein as well as vitamins and minerals, we really should grow and eat more nuts! As the plants they come from are often sizeable bushes or trees, they are not suitable for tiny gardens. For those who do have the space, however, the harvest (in terms of nutrients) compared to the space they take up is high. They are the perfect choice for a forest garden to provide the canopy and small tree layers. Many nuts are from trees that thrive only in tropical regions, but there are a number than can be grown in temperate areas.

Most nut plants are obtained as young potted specimens, sometimes grafted on to a rootstock.

Almonds should be grown against a south-facing wall or in a warm, protected spot. If frost threatens after the flowers have formed, you may want to protect them with horticultural fleece.

Hazels tolerate shade but prefer a sunny position. They will fruit after about three years, but are likely to need protection from squirrels, which can rapidly eat a whole harvest before you get to it. They could be grown as shrubs in a large fruit cage, for example.

Sweet chestnuts form large trees that will start to fruit after about six years. They can be kept to a more manageable size, however, by cutting to ground level every 12 years or so (coppicing).

Walnuts also mature into large trees but, like sweet chestnuts, can be pruned annually to keep them smaller.

Sweet chestnut leaves

Walnuts

Hazel catkins

RECOMMENDED VARIETIES

ALMOND – ROBIJN: Heavy crops, self-fertile, resistant to peach leaf curl

HAZEL – FILBERT KENTISH COB: Heavy crops of large well-flavoured nuts

SWEET CHESTNUT – MARIGOULE: Produces an early crop of deep brown nuts

WALNUT – BUCCANEER: Self-fertile, fast growing and disease resistant

WALNUT – RITA: For the smaller garden as it reaches only six metres tall, self-fertile

They will start to fruit after about five years. The crop may need protection from squirrels by wrapping smooth plastic around the trunk that the squirrels can't climb up. Ideally obtain a cultivar that has been grafted on to *Juglans regia* (English walnut) rather than *Juglans nigra* (black walnut), as the latter secretes chemicals that can inhibit other plants (known as allelopathy).

Storage

Mature nuts will store in their shells for a few months if well dried. Sweet chestnuts can be stored in boxes in a dry place. Almonds can be shelled and then kept in an airtight container in the fridge. Most nuts respond well to salting and this can be used for raw nuts, or after cooking in oil.

Hazelnuts do not store well as they tend to shrivel in their shells, but they can be salted to store for longer periods. Shell the nuts, rub the skins off and spread on a tray to dry in an oven at 40°C for an hour or two. Pack tightly in a jar with salt, finishing with a 1cm layer of salt over the top, then seal and store. Alternatively, the nuts can be cooked gently until golden brown in olive oil and then stored in airtight containers with a smaller quantity of salt (2 tbsp of salt and 5 tbsp of oil for 500g of hazelnuts).

To store walnuts, collect when the casing splits in the autumn. Remove the outer fibre from the nuts with a wire brush, then place in an oven at 40°C for a few hours until fully dry. Store in a cool, dry place. They can also be pickled: pick the walnuts while still green in early summer, before the shells have formed. Prick each walnut several times with a pin or fork and soak in brine for several days, then change the brine and soak several days further. Spread the nuts out on a tray and leave for a day or two until they have turned black. Pack into jars and cover with vinegar and leave for several months before eating. For sweet pickled walnuts, simply add 2 tsp of sugar to each jar and a combination of spices such as ginger, cinnamon, cloves, peppercorns and allspice.

Quinoa

Although originally grown high up in South American countries like Peru, quinoa can be grown at lower altitudes in temperate countries as well. The processing of the seeds is rather fiddly on a small scale, but it can be done quite effectively as described below.

Sow the seeds shallowly in fine compost in pots or trays under cover in the spring. Plant out 30cm apart when the plants are about 10cm tall and when the risk of frosts has passed. By August the plants will have reached up to 2 metres tall and will flower. The seeds will be ready to harvest in late September and October. Twenty plants should produce about 1kg of seeds.

Once the flower heads start to change colour, rub one between your hands – if some seeds are released they are ready. Cut the plants at ground level and hang in a dry building. After a few days, rub the flower heads over a large bowl (wearing rubber gloves may help with this task) to release the seeds and their flower bracts. Pick out any leaves or larger pieces of chaff (or pass through a suitable sieve). Spread the seeds/bracts out thinly on trays and dry for a few more days. Then rub further to extract the seeds from any remaining bracts. Finally, separate the seeds from any dust and small pieces of vegetation by tipping from one bowl or bucket to another several times. If you do this outside in a light breeze, the lighter chaff will blow away – this is an ancient technique known as winnowing.

Quinoa seed is covered with a bitter, soapy substance called saponin, which has to be removed by soaking and rinsing before they can be eaten. To do this, measure the amount of quinoa you want to cook with (50g per person, for example) and place it in a bowl with warm water, swirl it around for a minute or two then drain through a sieve. Repeat this procedure several times until the water is clear and not at all frothy or soapy. The seeds can then be simmered in water for 20 minutes. If they still taste a little bitter, try changing the cooking water halfway through.

RECOMMENDED VARIETIES

TEMUCO: A heavy cropper especially in cool summers

RAINBOW: Produces attractive flower heads in a range of colours

Storage

Fully dried quinoa seeds can be stored in airtight jars in a dark cupboard or pantry.

Quinoa head

Sweet Potatoes

Although we often cook them in the same way, sweet potatoes are only distantly related to regular potatoes – they are in the morning glory family and will need warmth and sunlight to thrive. They grow as a vine, with heart-shaped leaves (that can be eaten as greens) originating in the tropical Americas. The edible tubers they produce are vitamin-rich and high in the important minerals thiamin, manganese and potassium. Sweet potatoes usually have coloured flesh (commonly orange or red, though there are varieties with white or purple flesh) that is sweet tasting and very soft once cooked. They are usually obtained as cuttings known as 'slips'.

Plant the slips in pots of moist compost in the greenhouse or heated propagator in April, and repot into larger containers as the plant roots and grows. The foliage can be trained up canes. After about five months, around September time, the leaves will die back – this is the time to lift the tubers.

Once you have your own tubers, you can grow slips the following year. These will be better suited for growing in your climate than imported tubers bought from a supermarket. In early March, place a tuber in moist sand in a heated propagator (or airing cupboard). Once shoots have formed and are about 5-10cm long, gently pull them off and plant in pots as explained above.

Storage

Sweet potatoes can be stored in the same way as other potatoes in boxes or paper sacks in the dark in a frost-free but cool, dry building. They won't keep in good condition for so long, however, so use them as soon as possible or cook and freeze them as mash. Wrapping them individually in paper will help, and adding an apple to the box will prevent the tubers from budding. Don't forget to keep one or two for growing your own slips the following year!

RECOMMENDED VARIETIES

BEAUREGARD: Long roots with a red skin and sweet orange flesh

CAROLINA RUBY: High yielding with a deep red skin

Soya Beans

Originating in Asia, soya beans need a long hot summer to produce large mature beans, but in any case will produce young green seeds that can be eaten as edamame beans.

RECOMMENDED VARIETIES

BLACK JET: A good cropper even in poor summers

USTIE: Fast growing, suitable for temperate climates

Sow the beans in May under cover in pots or trays and plant out after about a month, 15cm apart. The plants will grow about 1 metre tall, but shouldn't need supporting unless they are in a windy spot. Keep well watered and hairy pods will start to form in August. By the end of September/early October, the leaves will start to fall off the plants and you can start to harvest the beans. Like most beans they contain toxins so should be boiled for 10 minutes before eating. Alternatively, you can pick the younger pods earlier in the season and cook them whole for 5 minutes. Serve salted as edamame beans – some people like to eat the pods too, but if they are tough they can be shelled as you eat them.

Storage

To freeze, shell and wash the beans, blanch for 2 minutes, freeze them spread out on a tray, then bag up. To cook from frozen, boil for about 10 minutes. Soya beans can also be dried: Leave the pods on the plants until they have turned yellow, then cut the plant at ground level and hang indoors to dry completely. When the pods have become brittle, shell the beans and leave on trays for a few days, then store in a cool, dry place in airtight containers. Soak the beans overnight before cooking.

13. COOKING THROUGHOUT THE YEAR

The following recipes all feature at least one main ingredient (often several) that are seasonal and will be available fresh from your plot if you have grown them. Even if you haven't, it's always best to cook with seasonal, local produce. Many of the other ingredients you may well have stored from previous harvests. We have allocated the recipes to months of the year, but of course many of them can be cooked at other times according to ingredient availability, so feel free to treat these as suggestions only.

Each month starts with a recap of which fruits and vegetables may be available fresh from your plot. Those you may have in storage are not listed as the variety could be huge, but, as discussed in earlier chapters, there are many that you could be self-sufficient in all year round, such as potatoes, onions and garlic. You may well dry your own beans and herbs for a constant supply, and of course, freezing can keep you stocked up with many fruits and vegetables. Some of the recipes include a few ingredients you will have to buy in, such as flour, salt and vegan margarine (spread).

As discussed in the Ingredients chapter, page 29, many of these recipes can be adapted and improvised around according to your taste, preferences and ingredients available; just because a recipe might suggest a certain herb or spice, for example, doesn't mean you can't make it. Simply substitute with something similar that you do have.

Weights, measures and temperatures

We use grams and millilitres in the recipes, but if you are using ounces or cups, here's a rough conversion guide:

20g = 0.7oz
50g = 1.75oz
100g = 3.5oz
200g = 7oz
500g = 18oz
240ml = 1 cup
120ml = ½ cup
60ml = ¼ cup

We do however also use tablespoons and teaspoons for ease of measuring smaller quantities:

1 tbsp (tablespoon) = 15ml
1 tsp (teaspoon) = 5ml

The temperatures we give are in degrees centigrade (°C or Celcius) for fan ovens as these are the most popular these days. If you are using a conventional non-fan oven, as a general rule you can increase the temperature by 15°C. If you use degrees Fahrenheit (°F), or gas marks, then here's a rough conversion guide:

150°C = 300°F = Gas mark 2
160°C = 325°F = Gas mark 3
180°C = 350°F = Gas mark 4
190°C = 375°F = Gas mark 5
200°C = 400°F = Gas mark 6
220°C = 425°F = Gas mark 7
230°C = 450°F = Gas mark 8
245°C = 475°F = Gas mark 9

JANUARY

Fresh from the plot

Artichoke, Jerusalem
Broccoli – early sprouting
Brussels sprouts
Cabbage
Carrots
Cauliflower
Celeriac
Kale
Leeks
Parsnips
Spinach, chard

Leek, Mushroom and Potato Pie

SERVES 4

A hearty and comforting dish that's good for the soul. The filling is hugely adaptable – try adding vegan mince or sun-dried tomatoes and cashew cheese for a Mediterranean twist! The pie can be served with a salad or vegetables.

FOR THE SHORTCRUST PASTRY

225g plain flour
Pinch of salt
100g vegan margarine (in chunks)
2½ tbsp cold water

FOR THE FILLING

1 large potato or several small ones
1 tbsp light olive or sunflower oil
2 leeks
200g mushrooms
Homemade or jarred vegan pesto
(see our recipe, page 166)
Salt and pepper

TO MAKE THE SHORTCRUST PASTRY

1. Add the flour, salt and margarine to a food processor and blend.

2. Gradually add the water until a ball of dough has formed.

3. Cover with cling film and put in the fridge until required.

TO MAKE THE FILLING AND ASSEMBLE THE PIE

1. Preheat the oven to 200°C.

2. Cut the potato into small chunks and steam for 10 minutes.

3. Roll out two-thirds of the pastry using a rolling pin until flat and even.

4. Carefully form the pie case by pressing the pastry around the edges and base of a pie tin. Place in the oven for 10 minutes.

5. Chop the leeks and mushrooms and fry in a pan over a medium heat with the oil for 5 minutes. Season with salt and pepper.

6. Add the cooked potatoes to the pan and combine.

7. Spread a generous amount of pesto over the pastry base before pouring in the filling. Dot more pesto on top of the mixture. Roll the remaining pastry into a circle shape to form the lid, and place carefully over the top, pressing the edges down. Make a slit in the lid to let steam escape and decorate with shapes of leftover pastry if you wish.

8. Place the pie back in the oven for a further 30 minutes.

Lentil, Split Pea and Sun-dried Tomato Bolognese

SERVES 2

Flavoursome, hearty and healthy, this sauce is especially good with spelt spaghetti.

40g lentils and / or split peas
1 onion
2 cloves garlic
40g sun-dried tomatoes
2 carrots
2 tbsp tomato purée
1 tbsp oregano
Pepper
150g dried pasta of your choice

1. Add the lentils/split peas to a saucepan of water and bring to the boil. Simmer for the required amount of time (usually about 30 minutes).

2. Meanwhile, chop the onion, garlic, sun-dried tomatoes and oregano and grate the carrots ready for the sauce.

3. Once the lentils are close to being ready, put the pasta on to boil.

4. Fry the onion in a large saucepan over a medium heat, adding the garlic once softened. Cook for 2 minutes.

5. Drain the lentils/split peas, leaving a little of the water, and pour into the frying pan, followed by the chopped sun-dried tomatoes, grated carrot and tomato purée. Cook for a further 5 minutes.

6. Chop the oregano and add to the sauce at the last minute.

7. Drain the pasta and add to the frying pan, stirring to combine. Serve.

Celeriac Mash

SERVES 4

This is our favourite winter mash, the celeriac adding a sweet, subtle taste. Note that vegan milk is not needed as the celeriac makes the mixture wetter than if it were potatoes alone. You can try other combinations of roots as a mash: Potatoes, parsnips, carrots, sweet potatoes, swede and turnips. It also works with the addition of winter squashes like pumpkins or butternut. Combining two or three vegetables seems to work best as the flavour can get confused if there are too many. The mash works well as an accompaniment to many dishes, including the classic sausages (vegan) and gravy.

500g celeriac (about 1 root)
500g potatoes (about 2 large)
250g carrots (about 2 large)
2 tbsp vegan spread
Salt and pepper
1 tbsp wholegrain mustard (optional)

1. Peel and cut up the roots into chunks.

2. Boil in salted water for 20 minutes.

3. Drain, then mash or blend with the vegan spread, salt and pepper. (Hand-mashing will produce a rougher texture – if you prefer it super-smooth use an electric processor/blender.)

4. Stir in the mustard.

Carrot Cake with Macadamia and Cashew Icing

An absolute favourite and classic – the perfect afternoon treat to nourish your soul. This version uses a healthy nut-based icing; alternatively you could make a classic 'butter' icing by combining 200g icing sugar with 50g vegan margarine and a little lemon juice.

FOR THE CAKE

140g self-raising white flour
140g self-raising wholemeal flour
1 tsp baking powder
170g coconut sugar or sweetener of your choice
1 tsp cinnamon
1 tsp ginger
1 tsp nutmeg
Pinch of salt
225g carrots
170g sultanas
200ml flavourless oil
200ml water
½ tsp cider vinegar
½ tsp vanilla essence

FOR THE ICING

60g raw macadamia nuts
60g raw cashews
60ml non-dairy milk
60ml agave nectar or sweetener of your choice
2 tbsp coconut oil (optional)
1 tsp vanilla extract
2 tsp lemon juice
½ tsp salt
Handful of sunflower seeds, to decorate

TO MAKE THE CAKE

1. Peel and grate the carrots and set aside. Grease a cake tin (approx. 24cm square).

2. In a large bowl, stir together the flours, baking powder, sugar, spices and salt.

3. Make a well in the centre of the mixture and add the remaining ingredients, combining well.

4. Spoon the cake batter into the cake tin and bake in the oven at 180°C for 40 minutes. Reduce the temperature to 150°C and cook for a further 30 minutes. Check to see if it's cooked in the middle by inserting a skewer or knife – if it comes out clean it's ready.

5. Remove from the oven and cool in the tin.

TO MAKE THE ICING

1. Soak the cashews and macadamia nuts in water for a few hours.

2. Drain the nuts then combine all the icing ingredients in a food processor and blend on high speed until completely smooth (around 2-3 minutes – you may have to scrape down the sides occasionally).

3. Chill in the fridge for 30 minutes before spreading over the cake, then sprinkle over the sunflower seeds to decorate.

FEBRUARY

Fresh from the plot

Broccoli – early sprouting
Brussels sprouts
Carrots
Cauliflower
Celeriac
Kale
Leeks
Parsnips
Spinach

Sprouting Broccoli Gratin with Homemade Vegan Parmesan

SERVES 2

A super healthy version of vegetable gratin, and just as scrumptious! Serve as a light lunch on its own, or alongside something protein-rich like a chickpea salad. The homemade 'parmesan' is also perfect to sprinkle over pasta dishes.

1½ tbsp light olive oil
1 onion
Salt and pepper
Small bunch of sprouting broccoli or a handful of florets
1 medium courgette
200ml vegan parmesan

FOR THE VEGAN PARMESAN

120g raw cashews
3 tbsp nutritional yeast
½ tsp salt
½ tsp garlic granules

TO MAKE THE GRATIN

1. Preheat the oven to 190°C.

2. Fry the onions over a medium heat in a dash of olive oil and the salt and pepper until lightly browned. Set aside.

3. Chop the broccoli and courgette and arrange on a large baking tray in a nice pattern.

4. Drizzle on the remaining olive oil and sprinkle the vegan parmesan over the top.

5. Bake in the oven for 25 minutes, allowing it to rest for a moment once out of the oven before dishing up.

TO MAKE THE VEGAN PARMESAN

Place all of the ingredients into a food processor and blend to a grain-like consistency.

Creamy Leek and Mushroom Pasta Sauce

SERVES 2

A filling lunch or supper; serve with a mixed salad. The vegan cream can be used for numerous other dishes, and adding a little sweetener, like agave nectar or date syrup, turns it into the perfect pouring cream for various desserts.

1 medium-sized leek

2 cloves garlic

Large handful of mushrooms

100g pasta (we use linguine, but feel free to substitute with your favourite)

1 tbsp pesto
(see our own delicious recipe in June, page 166)

1 tbsp light olive oil

FOR THE VEGAN CREAM

150g soaked cashew nuts

125ml filtered water

Juice of half a lemon

Salt and pepper

TO MAKE THE PASTA DISH

1. Place a pan of water on the hob, adding the pasta once the water is boiling.

2. Slice the leek and mushrooms, and mince or crush the garlic.

3. Heat a drizzle of olive oil in a large saucepan over a medium/high heat and add the vegetables, stirring for a few minutes.

4. Add the pesto and around half the cream (depending on how thick you want the sauce to be) to the vegetables.

5. Once the pasta is cooked, drain and add to the pan of sauce. Mix together and serve.

TO MAKE THE VEGAN CREAM

1. Cover the raw cashew nuts in water and leave to soak for at least 3 hours.

2. Drain the cashews, then place them into a food processor along with the water, lemon juice and a pinch of salt and pepper, blending for several minutes or until the consistency is smooth.

Note: You will only use around half of this quantity in the recipe, but having too few cashews makes the mixture harder to break down using a food processor. You can use the rest of the cream for whatever you like – it will keep in the fridge for a few days or can be frozen for longer periods.

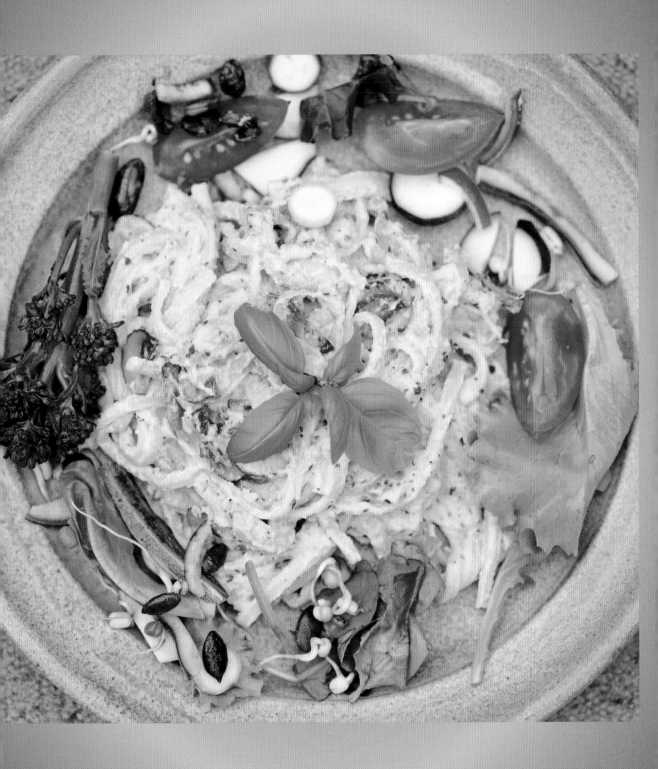

Parsnip Hash Browns

SERVES 4
Enough for about 12 hash browns

2 parsnips

1 leek

120g gram flour (also known as chickpea flour –
if you don't have any, ordinary plain flour will do)

1 tbsp sesame seeds
(or other seeds of your choice, such as flax)

½ tsp paprika
(or other spices/herbs of your choice –
chilli flakes for example)

Cold water

Salt and pepper

1 tbsp sunflower or avocado oil

1. Peel the parsnips and grate coarsely into a bowl.

2. Slice the leek thinly and add to the grated parsnips with the flour, seeds (optional), paprika and a little salt and pepper.

3. Mix together with a spoon and add small amounts of cold water until the mixture sticks together without being too wet.

4. Divide into about 12 small hash browns.

5. Heat the oil over a medium heat and fry the hash browns in a couple of batches until golden brown on both sides. When you first put them in the frying pan, press them down with a spatula so they aren't too thick and the insides cook properly.

6. The hash browns can be served on their own with ketchup for breakfast or as part of a vegan fry-up!

Beetroot Brownies

MAKES 12 BROWNIES

These rich and moist chocolate brownies are the epitome of melt-in-the-mouth decadence. An adaptable recipe, you can add chopped nuts or sultanas to the mixture instead of the chocolate chips if you fancy (or as well as!).

2 medium beetroot (raw or ready-cooked)
1 tbsp flavourless oil
225ml almond milk
1 tsp apple cider vinegar
170g coconut or granulated sugar or sweetener of your choice
55ml coconut oil (melted)
1 tbsp vanilla extract
135g plain flour
70g cocoa powder (plus more for topping)
1 tsp bicarbonate of soda
½ tsp baking powder
Pinch of salt
50g chocolate chips or chopped dark chocolate

1. To cook raw beetroot: remove the stem and most of the root from the beetroot and wash. Place the beetroot on a sheet of foil on top of a baking tray and drizzle with the flavourless oil. Wrap tightly in the foil and roast at 175°C for one hour. Once tender, place in a bowl in the fridge and leave to cool. Alternatively use ready-cooked beetroot.

2. When the beetroot is roughly at room temperature, blend in a food processor with 1 tbsp water.

3. In a large bowl, whisk together the almond milk and vinegar and set aside for a moment, allowing to curdle. Add the sugar, coconut oil, vanilla extract and puréed beetroot, and whisk until foamy.

4. Sift in the flour, cocoa powder, bicarbonate of soda, baking powder and salt, folding the mixture together before vigorously whisking (ideally use an electric whisk – you may also combine using a food processor). Gently stir through the chocolate chips or chopped dark chocolate.

5. Grease a suitable baking tray and pour the batter in, distributing evenly. Bake for 25 minutes at 175°C. Remove from the oven and allow to cool in the tray. Then, dust with cocoa powder, slice the brownies and serve with a scoop of vegan ice cream, page 220.

MARCH

Fresh from the plot

Broccoli – early sprouting
Brussels sprouts
Carrots
Cauliflower
Celeriac
Kale
Leeks
Lettuce
Parsnips
Rhubarb
Spinach, chard
Turnips

Purple Sprouting Broccoli Spring Salad

SERVES 2

As you can see from the ingredients, this is very much an improviser's dish – start with whatever you have ready that's suitable from your garden. The tamari nuts also make an irresistible snack on their own.

A few stems of purple sprouting broccoli
A large handful of baby broad beans
Lettuce or other salad leaves of your choice
A few spring onions or half a red onion
A few baby courgettes or one medium-sized one
A small handful of cherry or plum tomatoes
A large handful of bean sprouts
(we used a mixture of mung beans,
chickpeas and green peas)
A handful of homemade tamari nuts

FOR THE TAMARI NUTS

Any amount of mixed nuts and seeds of your choice (our favourite mixture includes walnuts, Brazil nuts, hazelnuts, cashews, pumpkin and sunflower seeds)
Tamari soy sauce

TO MAKE THE SALAD

1. Steam the broccoli and broad beans for 3 minutes.

2. Chop the vegetables and arrange in a bowl or on a large plate.

3. Sprinkle the tamari nuts over the salad just before serving.

TO MAKE THE TAMARI NUTS

1. Preheat the oven to 160°C.

2. Spread the mixed nuts evenly on a baking tray and bake for 5 minutes.

3. Pour the tamari soy sauce over the nuts, shaking the tray so that each nut gets covered evenly.

4. Place the nuts in the oven for a further 10 minutes in total, taking them out after 5 minutes to stir, before returning for the remaining 5.

5. Allow the nuts to cool.

Crunchy Baked Kale

SERVES 2

Crisp and tasty, our crunchy baked kale is a moreish delight!

2 large handfuls of curly kale

2 tbsp avocado or sunflower oil

Paprika

Salt and pepper

1. Tear the kale into bite-sized pieces and arrange on a baking tray with the oil.

2. Sprinkle on paprika, salt and pepper.

3. Bake in the oven at 200°C for 5-10 minutes, ensuring it doesn't burn. Once the kale becomes light and papery but not too brown, remove from the oven.

Cauliflower Steak with Tomato Sauce and Caper Relish

SERVES 2

This nutritious dish can form part of a roast, or is a fantastic centrepiece served with caper relish (page 136) and our Arrabbiata Tomato Sauce (see July for recipe, page 176)

Half a large head of cauliflower
1 tbsp capers
3 sun-dried tomatoes
1 tbsp sunflower or avocado oil
1 tbsp chopped parsley
1 tsp lemon juice
Salt and pepper

1. Cut the cauliflower head from the top into 2 slices about 1.5cm thick. Trim the stalk.

2. Heat a little oil in a large frying pan over a medium/high heat and fry the cauliflower steaks for 3 minutes on each side.

3. Transfer the steaks to a baking tray and cook in the oven at 200°C for 20 minutes, turning over halfway through.

4. While the cauliflower is baking, prepare the relish: chop the capers, sun-dried tomatoes and parsley and finely slice a few small florets from the rest of the cauliflower. Add the ingredients to a bowl along with the olive oil, lemon juice and salt and pepper. Mix well.

5. Serve the cauliflower steaks with our arrabbiata sauce and a spoonful of the caper relish.

Apple and Blackberry Crumble

SERVES 4

A homely classic, this crunchy crumble has hidden beneath the surface the perfect combination of sweet and tart. Ideally you will be using apples from your store and blackberries that you foraged and put in the freezer last autumn. If you don't have any, just leave out the blackberries or try with an alternative fruit. Serve with vegan ice cream (such as our Easy-Peasy Grape Ice Cream recipe in November, page 220) or custard.

FOR THE FILLING

3 apples (ideally a mixture of 2 cooking and 1 dessert)
Juice of 1 lemon
150g blackberries
80g demerara sugar
2 tsp mixed spice

FOR THE TOPPING

120g plain flour
1 tsp mixed spice
100g brown sugar
30g rolled oats
120g vegan margarine

1. Preheat the oven to 170°C.

2. Peel and core the apples and cut into slices. Place them in a crumble dish and squeeze over the lemon juice. Add the blackberries, sugar and spice and stir gently to mix.

3. To make the topping, place the flour, mixed spice, sugar and oats in a bowl and combine. Add the margarine to the mixture and rub it in with your fingertips until the consistency is like breadcrumbs.

4. Evenly distribute the crumble mixture on top of the fruit, and bake in the oven for 40 minutes or until the top is golden brown.

APRIL

Fresh from the plot

Broccoli – early sprouting
Cauliflower
Leeks
Lettuce
Rhubarb
Spinach, chard
Turnips

Artichoke and Broccoli Pizza

SERVES 4

This is one variant of our mouth-watering homemade pizza with a crispy polenta crust. You can alter the toppings depending on the season and what you fancy!

FOR THE TOMATO SAUCE

1 tbsp light olive oil
2 garlic cloves
Basil
Oregano
Paprika
300g passata

FOR THE CASHEW CHEESE

150g cashews
2½ tbsp lemon juice
2½ tbsp nutritional yeast
2 cloves garlic
Fresh parsley (optional)
60ml water
Salt and pepper

FOR THE PIZZA BASE

170g white bread flour
5g quick action yeast
½ tsp salt
1 tbsp olive oil
120ml water
2 tbsp coarse polenta

FOR THE PIZZA TOPPINGS

1 red onion
Sweet peppers
Handful of tenderstem broccoli
1 beef tomato or several cherry tomatoes
1 globe artichoke head
(from the garden or jarred, depending on the season)
Small handful of spinach
Cashew cheese

TO MAKE THE TOMATO SAUCE

1. Heat the olive oil in a pan over a low/medium heat, crush the garlic and lightly fry.

2. Finely chop the herbs and toss them in, along with the paprika.

3. Add the passata, stir together and simmer gently for a couple of minutes.

TO MAKE THE CASHEW CHEESE

1. Soak the cashews for at least 4 hours before adding them to a food processor, along with the lemon juice, nutritional yeast, garlic and a small handful of parsley (optional).

2. Blend the mixture to a coarse meal, before slowly adding the water bit by bit.

3. Once the consistency is similar to houmous, season with salt and pepper to taste.

TO MAKE THE PIZZA BASE AND ASSEMBLE THE PIZZA

1. Add the flour, yeast and salt to a large bowl and mix together.

2. Slowly pour in the water and add the olive oil.

3. Combine with a spoon, before removing the dough from the bowl and kneading for 5-10 minutes.

4. Place the dough back in the bowl, cover with cling film or a damp tea towel and leave to rise in a warm place for 10 minutes.

5. Preheat the oven to 190°C and oil a large baking tray.

6. Whilst the dough is rising, chop the vegetables ready to go on top.

7. Dust a clean worktop with a small handful of polenta and roll the dough over it until it is coated.

8. Spread the dough out evenly on the baking tray, ensuring it reaches each edge and corner.

9. Place the pizza base in the oven and cook for 10 minutes.

10. Pour the tomato sauce over the base and spread, leaving a thin crust around the edges.

11. Arrange the vegetables and spoon a few dollops of the cashew cheese on top. Put back in the oven and bake for a further 15 minutes.

Vegan Arancini

MAKES 12 BALLS

Serves 4 as a starter, side dish or light lunch. Arancini – a traditional Italian dish – are rice balls coated in breadcrumbs and then fried or baked. You can make the filling specially, like the scrumptious mushroom and olive risotto described below, or can even just use leftover risotto from a previous meal! Serve with our Arrabbiata Tomato Sauce (see July for recipe, page 176).

FOR THE RISOTTO

1 tbsp light olive or sunflower oil
2 shallots
1 garlic clove
120g mushrooms
10 queen olives or 20 smaller ones
120g arborio rice
1 glass white wine
½ tbsp soy sauce
300ml vegetable stock or bouillon
Handful fresh basil leaves
Salt and pepper

FOR THE COATING

2 or 3 tbsp gram (chickpea) flour
2 or 3 tbsp plant milk (such as almond)
2 or 3 tbsp dried breadcrumbs

1. Heat the oil in a large frying pan over a medium heat. Finely chop the shallots and fry gently for a few minutes until soft.

2. Crush the garlic clove and add to the pan.

3. Slice the mushrooms and the olives, add to the pan, and cook, stirring occasionally for a further 5 minutes.

4. Stir in the rice and cook for a further 2 minutes.

5. Add the wine and soy sauce and stir until absorbed.

6. Simmer gently, pouring in the stock a little at a time, adding more as it becomes absorbed, for around 20 minutes.

7. Stir in the chopped basil leaves. Season with salt and pepper.

8. Allow the risotto to cool completely, before forming the mixture into about 12 balls using your hands or an ice cream scoop.

9. Prepare a small plate with gram flour (plain flour will do), another with breadcrumbs, and a small bowl of milk.

10. Take each ball, cover in the flour, dip in the milk, then coat with the breadcrumbs.

11. Place the balls on an oiled baking sheet and bake in the oven at 200°C for 20 minutes, turning once halfway through. Alternatively they can be deep-fried, or shallow-fried in a frying pan until golden brown.

Aloo Gobi

SERVES 4 AS A SIDE
This flavoursome and comforting Indian favourite is the perfect accompaniment to other curries, as well as rice, naan bread and chutneys.

1 tbsp coconut oil
1 onion
2 garlic cloves
3cm piece of fresh ginger root
1 red chilli
1 tsp cumin seeds
1 tsp mustard seeds
1 tsp turmeric
250g potatoes
250g cauliflower
4 fresh tomatoes
200ml plant milk
(coconut or almond for example)
1 tsp garam masala
1 tsp lemon juice
1 tsp date or agave nectar
Salt and pepper
Handful of coriander leaves

1. Heat the oil in a large saucepan over a medium heat and add the sliced onion. Fry gently for 5 minutes.

2. Crush the garlic, grate the ginger, deseed and finely chop the chilli and add these to the pan along with the cumin and mustard seeds. Fry for a further 3 minutes.

3. Stir in the turmeric.

4. Cut the potatoes and cauliflower into bite-sized pieces and add to the pan with the milk and the quartered tomatoes (skinned if you wish).

5. Bring to the boil then reduce the heat. Cover and simmer for 20 minutes, adding more milk gradually if the mixture becomes too dry.

6. Add the garam masala, lemon juice, date nectar and salt and pepper along with half of the coriander, finely chopped. Cook for a further 5 minutes.

7. Serve with the remainder of the chopped coriander as a garnish.

Rhubarb and Orange Sorbet

SERVES 4

An easy sorbet to make (even without an ice cream maker), and it tastes unbelievably delicious.

250g rhubarb
100g coconut palm sugar or sweetener of your choice
50ml water
50ml orange juice
Juice of half a lemon
Half a fresh orange

1. Wash, trim and cut the rhubarb into 2cm pieces.

2. Place the rhubarb, water, sugar, lemon and orange juice in a pan over a low/medium heat and simmer gently for 20 minutes.

3. Let the mixture cool, then blend until smooth.

4. Pour into a plastic container with a lid and place in the freezer, stirring every 30 minutes to stop ice crystals forming (if you have an ice cream maker you can use this instead).

5. After about 4 hours the sorbet should be the right consistency. Ideally serve immediately before it becomes too solid.

6. Decorate with slices of fresh orange.

MAY

Fresh from the plot

Asparagus
Broad beans
Cabbage
Cauliflower
Chinese cabbage
Lettuce
Onions
Pak choi
Peas
Potatoes
Radish
Rhubarb
Spinach, chard
Turnips

Asparagus with Vegan Hollandaise Sauce

SERVES 2

This recipe makes a superb lunch but can be eaten at any time of the day. The hollandaise sauce works as a great accompaniment to numerous other dishes, or even as a substitute for mayonnaise.

120ml silken tofu
2 tbsp lemon juice
1 tbsp nutritional yeast
½ tsp salt
¼ tsp turmeric
⅛ tsp cayenne pepper
2 tbsp sunflower oil
8-12 asparagus spears
(depending on thickness)

1. Heat the silken tofu gently until lukewarm, then transfer to a food processor and blend until smooth.

2. Add the lemon juice, nutritional yeast, salt, turmeric and cayenne pepper, and continue to blend until well combined.

3. Then, with the food processor running, add the oil in a slow stream.

4. Transfer the sauce to a small pan over a low heat and warm through.

5. Trim the asparagus spears and steam for 3-4 minutes depending on thickness.

Note: Our favourite way of serving this is to lay the asparagus spears on a slice of toasted sourdough bread and then pour the sauce over the top.

New Potato and Chickpea Stew

SERVES 4

We're so used to using new potatoes for salads or roasts it's easy to forget all the other ways of cooking them. Here's a very tasty aromatic stew that makes a hearty supper – serve with garlic bread.

1 tbsp oil (coconut or sunflower)

1 medium onion

2 garlic cloves

1 small piece of fresh ginger root

1 chilli pepper
(or half, depending on how hot it is
and how hot you like it)

1 x 400g tin of peeled plum tomatoes

1 x 400g tin of chickpeas

400g new potatoes

8 pieces of sun-dried tomatoes

1 tbsp oregano

1 tsp Jamaican jerk seasoning
(if you don't have any you can
use allspice or mixed spice)

1 tbsp tomato purée

Salt and pepper

1. Peel and slice the onion and fry in the oil in a large non-stick pan over a medium heat for 5 minutes.

2. Finely slice or mince the garlic and ginger, adding to the pan. Slice and add the chilli pepper (deseed if it's a hot one). Stir and cook for a further 5 minutes.

3. Add the chopped plum tomatoes and chickpeas (including the water from the tin or add half a tin of water).

4. Slice the potatoes (no more than 1cm thick) and add to the pan.

5. While the stew is coming to the boil, chop and add the sun-dried tomatoes, oregano, jerk seasoning (or spice mix) and the tomato purée. Simmer for 30-40 minutes until the potatoes are tender, then taste for seasoning –sun-dried tomatoes are often very salty so you may not need much more.

Lentil and Spinach Burger

MAKES 4 BURGERS

This is the kind of dish that makes you wonder why EVERYONE isn't vegan. Perfect with salad, roast vegetables or homemade chips.

50g dried lentils
1 medium onion
2 garlic cloves
Salt and pepper
1 tsp cumin
Large handful of spinach
A few sprigs of parsley
60g breadcrumbs
2 tbsp tomato purée
1 tbsp avocado or sunflower oil

1. Start by boiling the lentils in a pan for their required cooking time (often around 30 minutes).

2. While they simmer, dice the onion and fry in a large frying pan over a medium heat.

3. Once softened, crush the garlic and add cumin, salt and pepper.

4. Roughly chop the spinach and finely chop the parsley, adding to the mixture after a couple of minutes. Cook for a further minute or two until the spinach has wilted.

5. Drain the lentils once they are ready and gently add them to the frying pan, along with the breadcrumbs (it's useful to keep a pot of breadcrumbs in the freezer at all times) and tomato purée.

6. Make sure all the ingredients are thoroughly combined before removing from the hob and setting aside.

7. Once the burger mixture is cool enough to handle, form into even patties using your hands and fry in a little oil in a clean frying pan, turning over halfway through until nicely browned.

Red Currant Shortbread

MAKES 12-16 BISCUITS

The addition of fresh red currants give this classic biscuit an exciting twist. Crumbly and scrumptious, you could improvise by using different currants or berries.

250g plain flour
100g golden caster sugar
(plus an extra 2 tbsp for sprinkling on top)
200g cold vegan margarine
250g fresh red currants

1. Preheat the oven to 170°C.

2. Combine the flour and sugar in a large bowl.

3. Add the margarine, using your fingers to rub it into the dry ingredients until the mixture resembles breadcrumbs.

4. Line a medium baking tray with greaseproof paper, and distribute onto it about two-thirds of the shortbread mixture, pressing it down firmly.

5. Scatter the red currants over the first layer of shortbread before sprinkling the rest of the mixture over the top, followed by the extra 2 tbsp sugar.

6. Bake in the oven for 30 minutes, or until the shortbread is golden brown. Allow to cool completely before cutting into squares.

JUNE

Fresh from the plot

Artichoke, globe
Asparagus
Broad beans
Cabbage
Cauliflower
Chinese cabbage
Courgettes
Currants – red
Florence fennel
French beans
Gooseberries
Lettuce
Onions
Pak choi
Peas
Potatoes
Radish
Rhubarb
Spinach, chard
Strawberries
Turnips

Broad Bean Risotto

SERVES 2

Our absolute favourite way of eating broad beans. Use small young beans if possible. The nutritional yeast will give the risotto a creamy consistency and a cheese-like flavour.

½ tbsp light olive oil
1 onion
100g risotto rice
1 medium glass of white wine
400ml litre hot vegetable stock
200g of broad beans, shelled
(and skinned if the beans are large).
Alternatively this can be made with peas
or half and half broad beans and peas
1 tbsp fresh mint
Salt and pepper
1 tbsp nutritional yeast
Vegan parmesan
(optional – see February for our recipe, page 122)

1. Heat the oil in a large frying pan over a medium heat. Finely chop the onion and fry gently for a few minutes until soft.

2. Add the rice and cook for a further 3 minutes, stirring occasionally.

3. Pour in the wine and stir until absorbed.

4. Simmer gently, adding the stock little by little as it becomes absorbed.

5. After 10 minutes add the broad beans (and/or peas) and cook for a further 10 minutes, pouring in the rest of the stock gradually.

6. Finely chop the mint and add to the mixture, along with some salt and pepper and the nutritional yeast.

7. After a couple of minutes, serve the risotto on warm plates or bowls and sprinkle with vegan parmesan if desired.

Asparagus Spanakopita

MAKES 12 SPANAKOPITA

We've given this traditional Greek dish a sumptuous vegan twist, substituting feta for our amazing home-made cashew cheese, which can be used in any number of recipes! The addition of asparagus makes our spanakopita the perfect summer lunch.

2 tbsp light olive oil
2 large onions or several shallots
Salt and pepper
270g filo pastry (about 8 sheets, big enough for your baking tray – you can buy pre-made vegan filo pastry, but do watch out for palm oil)
300g asparagus
2 tbsp dill
Cashew cheese – see below

FOR THE CASHEW CHEESE

150g cashews
2½ tbsp lemon juice
2½ tbsp nutritional yeast
2 garlic cloves
Parsley (optional)
60ml water
Salt and pepper

TO MAKE THE CASHEW CHEESE

1. Soak the cashews for at least 4 hours.

2. Drain the cashews and tip them into a food processor along with the lemon juice, nutritional yeast, garlic and parsley.

3. Blend the mixture to a coarse meal, before slowly adding the water, bit by bit.

4. Once the consistency is similar to houmous, add salt and pepper to taste.

FOR THE SPANAKOPITA

1. Preheat the oven to 170°C and lightly oil a baking tray.

2. In a frying pan, sauté the onions with the salt and pepper until they start to brown.

3. Carefully lay half the sheets of pastry on top of each other on the baking tray (roughly 4 sheets), brushing a little oil between each sheet. It is important that you do not over-oil the pastry.

4. Spoon the cashew cheese onto the base and spread evenly, before arranging the sprigs of asparagus and adding the onions.

5. Tear or chop the dill and liberally sprinkle over the top (you can use dried dill if fresh is not available).

6. Place the remaining layers of pastry over the filling, once again oiling each sheet lightly. Bake for 40-45 minutes, and serve with a salad or as part of a mezze spread.

Walnut Pesto

SERVES 2-4
Delicious as a pasta sauce, or a spread or dip.

A large bunch of fresh basil leaves
90g walnuts
2 garlic cloves
2 tbsp nutritional yeast or vegan parmesan cheese (optional)
100ml extra-virgin olive oil
Salt and pepper

1. Add the basil, walnuts and garlic to a food processor and blend (nutritional yeast/vegan parmesan can be added here too if using)

2. Slowly drizzle in the olive oil and continue to blitz.

3. Season with salt and pepper to taste.

Raspberry Truffles

MAKES AROUND 30 TRUFFLES
These delicious little trinkets won't last long! Simple, sweet and utterly devourable!

180g dark chocolate
6 tbsp full-fat coconut milk
180g fresh raspberries
2 tbsp unsweetened cocoa powder

1. Line a baking tray with parchment paper and roughly chop the chocolate.

2. Simmer the coconut milk in a small saucepan over a medium heat. Once warmed, stir in the chocolate until completely combined.

3. Drop the raspberries into the chocolate ganache a few at a time. Stir the mixture to coat the berries, and then remove them one at a time, allowing any excess ganache to drip back into the pan, before placing the berries on the parchment paper.

4. Place the baking tray of raspberries into the refrigerator and leave to set for at least an hour.

5. Spoon the cocoa powder into a sealable plastic bag. Once the raspberries have set, add them to the bag and gently shake to coat them in the cocoa powder. Store the truffles in the fridge until ready to be gobbled.

JULY

Fresh from the plot

Apricots
Artichoke, globe
Asparagus
Aubergine
Broad beans
Cabbage
Carrots
Cauliflower
Cherries
Chinese cabbage
Courgettes
Currants
Florence fennel
French beans
Garlic
Gooseberries
Lettuce
Melon
Onions
Pak choi
Peaches
Peas
Pepper, chilli, capsicum
Potatoes
Radish
Raspberries
Rhubarb
Runner beans
Spinach, chard
Strawberries
Turnips

Asparagus Quiche

SERVES 4

Our lovely vegan quiche can be made with almost any combination of your favourite vegetables to suit the time of year. We make this version in the summer, with asparagus, sprouting broccoli and mushrooms.

1 tbsp light olive oil
1 onion
4-6 asparagus spears, sliced
Handful of sprouting broccoli
Handful mushrooms
400g firm tofu
½ tsp turmeric
½ tsp salt
Pepper
12 fresh basil leaves (or 1 tsp of dried mixed herbs)
120ml plant milk
320g shortcrust pastry sheet
(see below for recipe or purchase ready-made, but make sure it's vegan and palm oil free)

1. Preheat the fan oven to 200°C.

2. Heat the olive oil in a saucepan over a medium heat and fry the chopped onion until soft.

3. Add the sliced asparagus, mushrooms and broccoli to the pan, stirring occasionally for a further 5 minutes.

4. Drain the tofu and crumble into a food processor. Add the turmeric, basil leaves, salt and pepper and milk and blend until smooth.

5. Add the tofu mixture to the pan of vegetables. Remove from the heat and mix together.

6. Take the sheet of pastry and line a pie tin.

7. Cover the base of the pastry with greaseproof paper and a layer of ceramic baking beans and bake for 5 minutes. If you don't have anything suitable to weigh the bottom down it will puff up a little and shrink from the sides, but all is not lost – you can push the base down before filling with the mixture, though it may crack a little. Another option would be to use a ready-baked vegan pie-crust, then there is no need for this initial bake.

8. Pour the tofu and vegetable mixture into the quiche-base, spread evenly, and bake for 30 minutes. The quiche can be eaten hot or cold – we like to serve it hot with salad and new potatoes.

HOMEMADE VEGAN PASTRY

100g vegan margarine
200g plain flour
Salt
2 tbsp cold water

1. Cut the vegan margarine into small pieces and put in a food processor with the flour and salt.

2. Blend together then add the water and blend further until a ball of pastry is formed.

3. Wrap in cling film and keep in the fridge until required (it can also be frozen for longer storage).

Spinach and Pea Gnocchi

SERVES 2 FOR A MAIN MEAL OR 4 AS A STARTER

With good carbs in the potato, protein in the peas and all your essential minerals and iron in the green veg, you can't go wrong with this divinely simple and delicious dish.

FOR THE GNOCCHI

The flesh of 2 baked potatoes, mashed without milk/butter
8-12 tbsp plain white flour
Mixed herbs
Salt and pepper

FOR THE SAUCE

2 tbsp vegan margarine
2 garlic cloves
Half fresh hot chilli
2 large handfuls of spinach
50g peas
Fresh herbs
Salt and pepper

TO MAKE THE GNOCCHI

1. Spoon the flesh from the potatoes into a large bowl. Keep the skins for a different dish.

2. Sieve half the flour into the bowl and add the mixed herbs, salt and pepper.

3. Combine the mixture, adding more flour as required, until the consistency is similar to bread dough.

4. Cut the dough into quarters. Remove each quarter from the bowl and roll into tube shapes, repeatedly cutting a couple of centimetres of dough to form the gnocchi and setting aside on a floured plate.

5. Drop the gnocchi into a pan of boiling water for around 3 minutes, or until it rises to the top. Remove with a slotted spoon.

TO MAKE THE SAUCE AND ASSEMBLE THE DISH

1. Heat the vegan margarine in a large pan over a low/medium heat.

2. Finely chop the garlic, chilli and fresh herbs and roughly chop the spinach. Shell the peas.

3. Fry the garlic and chilli lightly, before adding the rest of the ingredients and cooking for a few minutes.

4. Add the cooked gnocchi to the frying pan and coat in the sauce. Serve.

Arrabbiata Tomato Sauce

SERVES 2

This versatile sauce can be used as an accompaniment to many dishes, including our Cauliflower Steak and Vegan Arancini (page 144), or as a traditional pasta sauce. Make it in any quantity and freeze in portions for future use.

2 tbsp light olive oil
2 garlic cloves
1 red chilli
Handful fresh basil leaves
400g fresh tomatoes, tomato passata or tinned plum tomatoes
Salt and pepper

1. Heat the oil in a saucepan over a low/medium heat. Crush the garlic and fry gently for 2 minutes.

2. Deseed the chilli, finely slice and add to the pan with the chopped basil leaves. Cook for a further 2 minutes.

3. If you are using fresh tomatoes, skin them (immerse in boiling water for 1 minute then slide the skins off) then blend or chop and push through a sieve. If using tinned plum tomatoes, blend or chop and push through a sieve. Use passata as it is. Add to the pan and simmer for 5 minutes.

4. Season with salt and pepper to taste.

Chocolate and Strawberry Cake

A devilishly delectable cake from the heavens above:
simple to make and simply unforgettable.

FOR THE CAKE

370g self-raising flour

30g cacao or cocoa powder

240g coconut sugar or sweetener of your choice

2 tsp baking powder

400ml vegan milk

160ml flavourless oil

2 tbsp vanilla extract

400g fresh strawberries

Icing

FOR THE ICING

250g icing sugar

30g cacao or cocoa powder

100g vegan spread

TO MAKE THE CAKE

1. Lightly grease two sandwich tins (about 20cm diameter) and set aside.

2. Sieve the flour into a large bowl and add the cacao/cocoa powder, sugar and baking powder. Mix.

3. Make a well in the middle of the dry ingredients and pour in the milk, oil and vanilla extract, folding together until combined.

4. Chop about a quarter of the strawberries into small chunks and gently stir through the cake batter before spooning equally into the two sandwich tins.

5. Set the oven to 165°C and slide the tins inside (you do not need to preheat if you have a fan oven).

6. Bake for 30-35 minutes. Check to see if they're ready by sliding a skewer or knife into one of the cakes – if it comes out clean then it's ready – if it has some uncooked cake mixture stuck to it, cook for a few minutes longer then check again. Once ready, remove the cakes and allow to cool inside the tins for 10 minutes, before transferring to a wire rack.

7. Once they are completely cool, place one on a plate, upside down. Spread half the icing over the first sponge, before carefully placing the other half on top, this time the same way up that it was in the oven. Distribute the rest of the icing on top and spread evenly. Decorate with the remaining strawberries.

TO MAKE THE ICING

1. Sieve the icing sugar into a bowl and add the cacao powder, stirring to combine.

2. Soften the vegan spread slightly under a gentle heat, then add to the bowl.

3. Whisk until smooth.

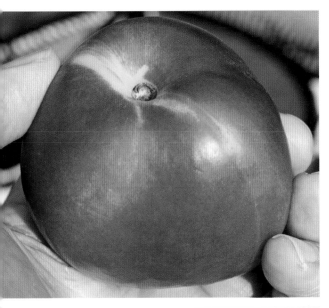

AUGUST

Fresh from the plot

Apples
Apricots
Artichoke, globe
Aubergine
Beetroot
Broccoli – calabrese
Carrots
Cauliflower
Celery
Cherries
Chinese cabbage
Courgettes
Cucumber
Currants – black
Figs
Florence fennel
French beans
Garlic
Grapes
Lettuce
Melon
Onions
Pak choi
Peaches, nectarines
Pears
Peas
Pepper, chilli, capsicum
Plums
Potatoes
Pumpkins/squashes
Radish
Raspberries
Runner beans
Spinach, chard
Strawberries
Tomatoes
Turnips

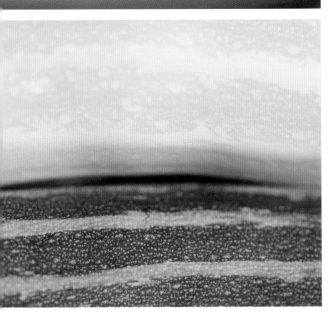

Stuffed Aubergine

SERVES 2

Baking aubergines is the best way to get a beautiful tender texture, and stuffing them makes them even more delicious! You can adapt the stuffing by swapping any of the vegetable ingredients for alternatives of your choice. You can substitute the breadcrumbs for some homemade vegan parmesan if you prefer (page 122), and it's extra good with a tahini sauce drizzled on top (page 164). Serve with a salad or tomato sauce and roasted vegetables.

1 large aubergine
2 tbsp light olive oil
100g dry quinoa
1 medium onion
4 chestnut mushrooms
1 spring onion
Half a bell pepper
Half a chilli
5 cherry tomatoes
2 garlic cloves
1 tbsp tomato purée
Fresh parsley
Fresh coriander
½ tsp cumin
½ tsp paprika
Salt and pepper
4 tbsp breadcrumbs

1. Preheat the oven to 180°C. Cut the aubergine in half and place cut side up on a piece of tin foil on a baking sheet. Drizzle with olive oil and wrap in the foil. Bake in the oven for an initial 40 minutes.

2. Meanwhile, simmer the quinoa in a pan of water for 20 minutes and chop the vegetables into small pieces.

3. Fry the onion for a few moments over a medium heat before adding the garlic and the rest of the vegetables, excluding the tomatoes.

4. Once the quinoa is cooked, add it to the pan of vegetables along with the tomatoes, tomato purée, chopped herbs, spices and a little salt and pepper. Stir. After cooking the stuffing for a few minutes, set aside.

5. When the aubergine has been in the oven for 40 minutes, remove it and unwrap. Using a spoon, push the flesh to either side of the skin, creating room for the stuffing, before spooning it in.

6. Sprinkle with breadcrumbs, drizzle with a little olive oil, and place back into the oven for 20 more minutes.

French Beans with Crispy Shallots and Toasted Almonds

SERVES 2

Crunchy, healthy and packed full of flavour, our French bean dish makes a glorious accompaniment to many meals, and is great for lunch, served with crusty bread.

1 tbsp coconut or avocado oil
6 shallots
20g flaked almonds
2 handfuls of French beans
4 tbsp homemade tahini sauce (see below)

1. Slice and fry the shallots in the coconut oil over a medium/high heat. You want them to be crispy but not burnt, so this may take a while.

2. While the onions are on the hob, dry-toast the almonds in a separate pan. Stir regularly until golden brown.

3. Top and tail the beans and steam for 5 minutes.

4. Toss the beans in the tahini sauce and sprinkle with the toasted almonds and crispy shallots.

Tahini Sauce

Well known as an ingredient in houmous (and also delicious simply spread on toast), tahini is made from roasted pulped sesame seeds. It can be made into a dressing/sauce simply by mixing with an equal quantity of water and some lemon juice, but a more luxurious version, ideal for our French bean recipe, can be made with the following ingredients:

3 tbsp tahini
3 tbsp water
Juice of half lemon
½ tsp agave or date nectar
2 tsp cider vinegar
1 tsp tamari
1 tsp garam masala (optional)
1 tbsp extra-virgin olive oil
2 tsp sesame seeds
A pinch of sea salt
1 garlic clove, crushed

1. In a glass jar, add the ingredients and shake thoroughly to combine.

2. If the sauce is too thick for your needs, simply add a little more water and shake.

3. Experiment with your favourite spices to make your own version!

Spitfire Sauce

MAKES 200ML

A sizzling hot sauce to spice up any meal. This is our version of a recipe that originates from the West Indies, but you can try making it with a variety of different chillies and spices according to your taste. Using habanero chilli peppers, for example, will give you an extremely hot version, but even the more common long, tapered peppers produce a wonderfully flavoured spicy sauce. Multiply the following quantities depending on how much sauce you are making.

10-30 chilli peppers depending on type and size (we use 20 of the long red ones, such as the variety Ring of Fire)
1 green capsicum pepper
1 onion
2 garlic cloves
1 tsp brown sugar
1 tsp salt
150ml cider vinegar or white wine vinegar

1. Roughly chop the chilli peppers (removing the seeds will produce a better flavour to heat ratio). Beware of the stinging juices, being especially careful not to touch your eyes. One method to help with this is to use a fork and a sharp knife to chop and deseed the chilli peppers so that you're not touching them with your bare hands.

2. Chop the onions and garlic and heat in a pan over a medium heat with the chilli peppers and the other ingredients. Cover the pan, bring to the boil then simmer for 30 minutes.

3. Blend in a food processor or with a stick blender before pouring into sterilised glass bottles and sealing. Once opened, keep in the refrigerator, and use within 3 months of opening.

Nectarine Delight

SERVES 4

A lovely light dessert, perfect for summer evenings.

400g silken tofu

3 ripe nectarines

1 tsp vanilla extract

1-2 tbsp maple syrup or sweetener of your choice

1. Chop the flesh from two of the nectarines and put in a blender with the tofu, vanilla extract and maple syrup. Blend well until smooth and creamy.

2. Taste and add more maple syrup if required.

3. Serve chilled in wine glasses. Thinly slice the other nectarine and place on top as decoration.

SEPTEMBER

Fresh from the plot

Apples
Aubergine
Beetroot
Broccoli – calabrese
Brussels sprouts
Carrots
Cauliflower
Celery
Chinese cabbage
Courgettes
Cucumber
Figs
French beans
Grapes
Leeks
Melon
Pak choi
Peaches
Pears
Pepper, chilli, capsicum
Plums
Pumpkins/squashes
Raspberries
Runner beans
Spinach, chard
Strawberries
Swede
Sweet corn
Tomatoes
Turnips

Vegan Paella with Artichoke Hearts

SERVES 2

This colourful feast is as delicious as it is adaptable in that you can include any vegetables you desire. We like to use brightly coloured peppers and artichoke hearts, but you could try it with various combinations of carrots, broccoli, cauliflower, leeks, asparagus, squash, mushrooms and any type of beans. The bright yellow colour can come from saffron, but we prefer to use turmeric, known as one of the most healing spices on the planet! One of the differences between paella and risotto is that paella is not stirred as the rice cooks, ensuring it doesn't become too creamy.

1 tbsp light olive or sunflower oil

1 red onion

Half a large red pepper

Half a large yellow pepper

2 garlic cloves

120g rice (ideally paella bomba rice but you can also use arborio or even get away with basmati)

1 tbsp turmeric

1 tsp paprika

400ml vegan stock or bouillon

2 fresh tomatoes

60g peas (fresh or frozen)

140g sliced artichoke hearts

Salt and pepper

2 tbsp parsley or coriander

Half a lemon cut into wedges

1. Slice the onion and fry gently in the oil for 3 minutes over a low/medium heat, using a paella pan or large flat-bottomed frying pan.

2. Slice the peppers and crush the garlic, adding to the pan and stirring for a further 3 minutes.

3. Add the rice, turmeric and paprika and stir occasionally for 1 minute.

4. Add the tomatoes (chopped into quarters) and half the stock. Stir initially then leave to simmer gently for 5 minutes.

5. Add the other half of the stock and continue to simmer for a further 5 minutes.

6. Add the peas and artichoke hearts to the surface of the mixture and season with salt and pepper.

7. Cover the pan with a lid or tin foil and cook gently for 15 minutes.

8. Turn off the heat, stir in half the parsley (or coriander), re-cover and allow to rest for 5-10 minutes.

9. Garnish with the rest of the parsley/coriander and serve with the lemon wedges to squeeze.

Ratatouille

SERVES 4

Ratatouille is a classic late summer dish, useful for using a glut of courgettes, aubergines, peppers and tomatoes. Make loads and store it by bottling or freezing. Serve with hunks of crusty bread or some vegan sausages.

1 large or 2 medium aubergines
3 courgettes
2 red peppers
2 tbsp light olive oil
8 tomatoes (or 400g tinned plum tomatoes)
2 red onions
3 garlic cloves
1 red chilli (optional) if you like it hot!
2 tbsp tomato purée
Handful fresh basil
1 tbsp mixed herbs
1 tbsp balsamic vinegar
1 tsp date nectar (or agave nectar or brown sugar)
Salt and pepper

1. Chop the aubergines, courgettes and peppers into bite-size pieces.

2. Skin the tomatoes (cover with boiling water for 1 minute then slide the skins off).

3. Heat 1 tbsp oil in a large frying pan over a medium/ high heat and fry the chopped aubergines, courgettes and peppers for 5 minutes, along with a good pinch of salt, stirring occasionally before spooning into a bowl and setting aside.

4. Heat the remaining oil in the same pan and fry the chopped onions for 3 minutes.

5. Crush the garlic and add to the pan, along with the finely sliced chilli if you fancy a fiery ratatouille! Fry for a further minute.

6. Add the chopped tomatoes, the purée, herbs, vinegar and date nectar. Stir and cook for a couple of minutes.

7. Add the aubergines, courgettes and peppers and cook for 10 minutes, pouring in a little water if the mixture seems too dry.

8. Season with salt and pepper.

Green Houmous

This is a mouth-watering take on traditional houmous. Flavoursome and healthy, it's the perfect addictive accompaniment to almost any dish. A vegan staple!

400g fresh chickpeas
(or 1 tin of cooked or 150g dried chickpeas)
3 tbsp tahini
1 large lemon
2 tbsp extra-virgin olive oil
2 small cloves garlic (or 1 large)
3 tbsp fresh parsley, chopped
3 tbsp fresh dill, chopped
3 tbsp chives, chopped
Salt
3 tbsp water
Paprika, olive oil and a few spare chickpeas, to decorate

1. If you're not using tinned chickpeas you'll have to cook them first. If fresh from the pod, you only need to simmer them in water for about 5 minutes. If dried, soak them overnight, then simmer for 60–90 minutes. Alternatively, you can let them sprout for a couple of days after soaking, and then blend them in this form to make the houmous – see the chapter Sprouting, page 51, for further information.

2. Blitz the tahini and juice from the lemon for a minute in a food processor or blender.

3. Add the cooked or tinned chickpeas (leaving a few aside), along with the olive oil, garlic, salt and the herbs. Pulse until it becomes a coarse paste, then slowly add the water, keeping an eye on it until you're satisfied with the consistency.

4. Spoon the houmous into a bowl to serve, decorating with a sprinkle of paprika, the chickpeas you saved and a drizzle of olive oil.

Blueberry Flan

SERVES 6–8

This raw flan with its delicate and authentic flavours is the perfect combination of sweet and tart.

Note: it takes a while to make due to the lengthy chilling process, but is well worth the wait.

FOR THE BASE

85g ground almonds
Pinch of sea salt
160g pitted dates (medjool are the best)

FOR THE FILLING

170g cashews
Pinch of sea salt
75ml coconut oil (melted)
1 tsp vanilla extract
30ml lemon juice
60ml agave nectar

FOR THE BERRY COMPOTE

200g blueberries
1 tsp lemon juice
1 tbsp agave nectar

TO MAKE THE BASE

1. Place the ground almonds and sea salt in a food processor with the pitted dates and pulse until the mixture forms a sticky dough.

2. Distribute the mixture and press evenly into the bottom of a small flan tin.

TO MAKE THE FILLING

1. Blend all filling ingredients together in a food processor on high speed until silky-smooth (you may need to stop every so often to scrape down the sides).

2. Pour the mixture over the base and spread evenly.

3. Place the flan in the freezer for at least 2 hours to set, then transfer it to the fridge for a further hour. (Or, you can take it out of the freezer after one hour and then leave it to set in the fridge overnight.)

TO MAKE THE BERRY COMPOTE

1. Once the flan has set, blend 150g of the blueberries, the lemon juice and the agave nectar in a food processor.

2. Transfer to a small bowl and stir in the remaining blueberries.

3. Pour the mixture over the flan (or over individual slices if you prefer).

OCTOBER

Fresh from the plot

Apples
Beetroot
Brussels sprouts
Carrots
Cauliflower
Celeriac
Celery
Chinese cabbage
Cucumber
Figs
Grapes
Leeks
Parsnips
Pears
Pepper, chilli
Plums
Pumpkins/squashes
Raspberries
Spinach, chard
Strawberries
Swede
Tomatoes
Turnips

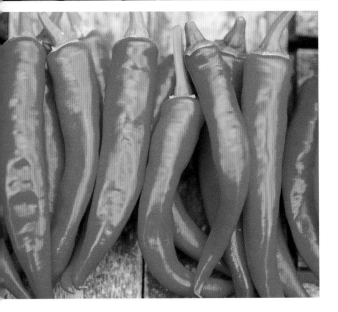

Sweet Potato Shepherd's Pie

SERVES 4

The ultimate in comfort food, this simple, flavoursome pie will fill you up and put a smile on your face. Serve with green vegetables and gravy (see gravy recipe on page 204).

FOR THE FILLING

1 tbsp light olive or sunflower oil
1 onion
2 garlic cloves
100g chestnut mushrooms
250g dried lentils
800ml vegetable stock or bouillon
1 bay leaf
2 carrots
1 celery stick
1 tbsp chopped thyme (or mixed herbs)
50ml red wine (optional)
2 tbsp tomato purée

FOR THE TOPPING

1kg sweet potatoes
30g vegan margarine
Salt and pepper

1. In a large saucepan, sauté the onion in the olive oil over a medium heat until golden. Add the crushed garlic, sliced mushrooms and a pinch of salt and pepper, frying for a couple of minutes, before stirring in the lentils, vegetable stock and bay leaf.

2. Chop the carrots and celery stick into small chunks.

3. Once the lentils are half-cooked (about 15 minutes), add the remaining ingredients, bring to the boil then turn down the heat, stirring occasionally and allowing to simmer for around 10 minutes.

4. Meanwhile, peel and chop the potatoes into large chunks, boiling for around 20 minutes. Once cooked, drain, and mash with the margarine, adding salt and pepper to taste.

5. Preheat the oven to 180°C.

6. Pour the lentil mixture into a large ceramic dish. Gently spoon the sweet potato mash evenly over the top of the filling.

7. Bake in the oven at 180°C for 20 minutes. Remove and allow to cool for a few minutes before serving.

Homemade Vegan Gravy

MAKES 600ML

This delicious gravy is easy to make, and many of the ingredients are optional, so don't worry if you don't have them all.

1 tbsp light olive or sunflower oil

1 onion

1 carrot

1 celery stick

1 tsp mixed herbs

1 tbsp plain flour

1 tbsp nutritional yeast

1 glass red wine

1 tsp Marmite

1 tbsp tomato purée

1 tbsp red wine vinegar

500ml vegan bouillon

Salt and pepper

1. Chop the onion, carrot and celery and fry in the oil over a medium heat for 10 minutes.

2. Stir in the herbs, flour and nutritional yeast and cook for another 2 minutes.

3. Add the red wine and simmer for 2 minutes.

4. Add the rest of the ingredients and simmer for 5 minutes while stirring.

5. Taste and season with salt (if required) and pepper.

6. Pass through a sieve before serving if you want it smooth – otherwise enjoy the chunky vegetables too!

Saint's Love Soup

SERVES 4

This comforting soup is adapted from a recipe of a friend of ours called Saint. Feed your soul and feel the love.

150g broccoli
150g cauliflower
2 garlic cloves
Half a fresh chilli
1 litre vegetable stock
125ml vegan cream (see our recipe in February for Creamy Leek and Mushroom Pasta Sauce, page 124, or use a ready-made vegan cream)
1 tbsp light olive oil
2 medium onions
250g mushrooms
Salt and pepper
Parsley/coriander (to garnish)

1. Chop the vegetables and place the broccoli, cauliflower, garlic and chilli into a saucepan, along with the vegetable stock. Bring to the boil and simmer until tender.

2. Add the vegan cream and stir.

3. Pour the mixture into a food processor (or use a hand blender), and blend until smooth.

4. Sauté the chopped mushrooms and onions in the olive oil over a medium heat until the mushrooms are soft and the onions are turning brown (at least 5 minutes).

5. Stir the mushrooms and onions into the soup until evenly distributed. Season with salt and pepper.

6. Serve hot and garnish with fresh parsley/coriander.

Caponata

SERVES 2-4

This sweet and sour stew delivers the taste of the Mediterranean. Delicious hot, served with crusty bread, or at room temperature as a tapas dish.

1 tbsp light olive oil
1 aubergine
1 tsp dried mixed herbs
Pinch of salt
1 red onion
1 celery stalk
1 garlic clove
8 tomatoes (or 400g tin of plum tomatoes)
30g olives
30g sultanas
1 tbsp capers
1 tbsp balsamic vinegar
1 tsp date nectar
Salt and pepper
Small handful of parsley

1. Cut the aubergine into chunks and fry in the oil over a medium heat with the mixed herbs and a pinch of salt for 5 minutes.

2. Add the sliced onion and celery and cook for a further 2 minutes.

3. Crush the garlic clove and stir in, frying for 1 minute more.

4. Skin, de-core and chop the tomatoes (or chop a tin of plum tomatoes) and add to the pan.

5. Remove the pits from the olives, halve them and add, along with sultanas, capers, vinegar and date nectar.

6. Stir well and allow to simmer for 10 minutes, adding a little more water if it gets too dry.

7. Taste and season with salt and pepper as required. Garnish with chopped parsley.

Fig and Dark Chocolate Tart

SERVES 6-8

Truly heaven-sent, this delectable and decadent tart is so good, you'll want it every day. It's gluten-free too, and can be refined-sugar-free depending on the chocolate you choose to cook with.

FOR THE BASE

125g ground almonds
⅛ tsp salt
⅛ tsp bicarbonate of soda
3 tbsp date nectar
2 tbsp coconut oil, melted

FOR THE TOPPING

8 fresh figs
1 tbsp date nectar
120ml coconut milk
120g dark chocolate

1. In a bowl, stir together the ground almonds, salt and bicarbonate of soda. After melting the coconut oil, form a well in the middle of the dry ingredients and pour in the coconut oil and the 3 tbsp of date nectar. Combine well using a fork.

2. Place the dough into a tart tin. Using a spoon and/or your fingers, create the tart case by pressing it evenly to the base and around the sides of the tin.

3. Let the dough firm and chill in the fridge for 30 minutes or more.

4. Preheat the oven to 160°C and bake the chilled tart case for 10 minutes.

5. Meanwhile, cut off the stems of four of your figs and slice them into circles about 0.5cm thick.

6. Lay the sliced figs on greaseproof paper on a baking tray and drizzle with the 1tbsp of date syrup. Place under the grill for around 5 minutes, until the syrup starts to bubble. Keep a close eye on them to ensure they don't burn.

7. To make the chocolate ganache, heat the coconut milk in a small saucepan. As soon as it starts to bubble, remove the pan from the heat and add the chopped chocolate. Stir the mixture until the chocolate has completely melted.

8. Once the tart case has cooled, arrange the chopped figs around the base and pour over the ganache. Chill in the fridge for a further 30 minutes or more. Remove the stalks from the remaining four figs and chop into quarters. Once the ganache has set, arrange them on the surface. Slice and serve with vegan cream, ice cream, on its own or with a cup of tea.

NOVEMBER

Fresh from the plot

Apples
Artichoke, Jerusalem
Beetroot
Brussels sprouts
Cabbage
Carrots
Cauliflower
Celeriac
Chinese cabbage
Grapes
Kale
Leeks
Parsnips
Spinach, chard
Swede
Turnips

Pumpkin Soup

SERVES 6–8
(DEPENDING ON THE SIZE OF THE PUMPKIN)
The classic Halloween soup. We've been using this recipe for many years after hollowing out pumpkins to make lanterns. Save some for bonfire night – or make more!

1 medium-sized pumpkin (around 2kg)
1 tbsp light olive oil
2 onions
1 litre vegetable stock or bouillon
2 tsp mixed herbs
1 tsp mixed spice (optional)
Salt and pepper

1. Scoop the flesh out of the pumpkin with strong metal spoons and roughly chop.

2. Take a large pan and fry the chopped onions in oil over a medium heat for 5 minutes.

3. When the onions are soft, add the pumpkin flesh and fry for a further 5 minutes.

4. Add a litre of stock and season with the herbs, spices, salt and pepper.

5. Bring to the boil and simmer for 15-20 minutes until the flesh is soft.

6. Blend the soup (a hand-held blender is ideal for this) until smooth. If the soup is too thick, add more water.

7. Taste the soup and add more seasoning if required.

Note: If you have several pumpkins to use for soup, why not experiment by including other vegetables like potatoes and celery, or mix in some chopped plum tomatoes? Add a chilli to give it a kick!

Homemade Baked Beans

SERVES 2 AS A MAIN MEAL OR 4 AS A SNACK

This comforting bean stew can be made with fresh beans straight from the pod, or with frozen or dried beans that you have in storage. It works well with any type of bean, but we often use French beans that have been left to develop in the pods. It's a very versatile dish – have it on toast for breakfast or lunch, or as part of a main meal with vegan sausages and/or rice, quinoa or couscous. Note that haricot beans are not an actual variety, but the name for the type used in tinned baked beans which are usually Boston navy beans or white beans.

150g dried beans
or 400g fresh or tinned haricot beans
1 tbsp light olive or sunflower oil
1 onion
1 garlic clove
1 small/medium red pepper
1 tbsp paprika
2 tbsp tomato purée
400g tinned or fresh tomatoes
120ml water
1 tsp mixed herbs
Salt and pepper

1. If you are using dried beans, soak them overnight in cold water, then drain and cook in boiling water for 45 minutes. Fresh beans do not need soaking but can take anything between 10 and 45 minutes to cook, depending on their size and freshness.

2. Meanwhile, slice the onion and fry gently in a pan with the oil over a medium heat for 5 minutes.

3. Add the crushed clove of garlic and fry for a further 2 minutes.

4. Chop the red pepper into small cubes and add to the pan with the paprika, stirring occasionally for 5 minutes more.

5. Add the tomato purée, chopped tomatoes, water and mixed herbs. If you are using fresh tomatoes we recommend you skin them first (cover with boiling water for 1 minute then pull the skin off). If you are using fresh or tinned beans (which are already cooked) add them at this stage.

6. Bring to the boil, cover, and simmer for 10 minutes, adding salt and pepper to taste.

Butternut Squash Pasta

SERVES 4

An alternative to macaroni cheese, this pasta dish goes above and beyond when it comes to both nutritional value and yumminess! Use any pasta you like. We used linguine – one of our favourites.

2 tbsp light olive oil or avocado oil
20 fresh sage leaves
1 medium onion
1 butternut squash (approx 700g)
3 garlic cloves
½ chilli
400ml vegetable stock
2 tbsp nutritional yeast
300g pasta
25g pine nuts
Salt and pepper

1. Heat the oil in a large frying pan over a medium/high heat and fry the sage leaves for a couple of minutes, taking care that they don't burn. Lift them out with a fork on to a plate and set aside – they will crisp up as they cool.

2. Roughly chop the onion and garlic, and peel and chop the butternut squash.

3. In the same frying pan, with the oil that will now be wonderfully flavoured with sage, add the onions, butternut squash, garlic and chilli and fry for 5 minutes over a medium heat.

4. Pour the stock over the vegetables, add the nutritional yeast, bring to the boil and simmer for 15 minutes.

5. In another large pan, begin to cook the pasta.

6. Dry-toast the pine nuts in a small frying pan for a few minutes, taking care they don't burn, and set aside.

7. Gently transfer the stock and vegetables to a food processor and blend until smooth, before pouring back into the pan. Season with salt and pepper.

8. Once the pasta is cooked, drain and add to the pan of butternut squash sauce. Tip in the toasted pine nuts, gently mixing everything together.

9. Serve topped with the crumbled crispy sage leaves.

Easy-Peasy Grape Ice Cream

SERVES 4

This recipe is unbelievably simple, but the results are sublime – you certainly won't feel treat-deprived.

3 ripe bananas

Around 30 red grapes

1. Peel the bananas and chop into large chunks. Place in the freezer overnight, or for a few hours, along with around 20 of the grapes.

2. Remove the frozen bananas and grapes and allow to soften for around 10 minutes. Tip them into a food processor and pulse until smooth. You may need to stop and give the mixture a stir by hand before pulsing again.

3. Serve immediately, decorated with the remaining grapes. If the mixture has become too runny, return it to the freezer for 20 minutes or so.

DECEMBER

Fresh from the plot

Artichoke, Jerusalem
Brussels sprouts
Cabbage
Carrots
Cauliflower
Celeriac
Kale
Leeks
Parsnips
Spinach, chard
Swede
Turnips

Swede, Sweet Potato and Bean Goulash

SERVES 6

This vegetable stew is the ultimate winter soul-food. It can be served with a variety of accompaniments including bread, wholegrain rice or quinoa. Serve with a side of winter greens.

1 tbsp light olive oil

2 onions

2 garlic cloves

2 carrots

400g swede

400g sweet potatoes

2 tbsp paprika

2 tbsp tomato purée

600ml vegetable stock

400g skinned tomatoes (or tinned plum tomatoes)

1 red capsicum

400g beans, frozen or dried and soaked overnight (we used borlotti beans that we had dried from earlier in the year but you could use all sorts of beans such as canellini, butter beans or a mixture of several different types)

2 tsp dried mixed herbs

Salt and pepper

1. Preheat the oven to 150°C. Peel (if necessary), and chop all the vegetables according to your preference on the texture of the stew, and set aside.

2. Heat the oil in a large frying pan over a medium heat. Sauté the onions until soft, then add the garlic, frying for a further 2 minutes.

3. Add the carrots, swede, sweet potatoes and paprika and fry for 5 more minutes. Stir in the tomato purée, vegetable stock, chopped tomatoes, red pepper, beans and herbs and bring to the boil (you may need to transfer to a large pan if your frying pan is not big enough).

4. Season with salt and pepper.

5. Pour the mixture into a large preheated casserole dish with a lid, and bake in the oven for 1.5-2 hours.

Cauliflower Couscous

SERVES 2–4

This ingenious method of blitzing cauliflower creates a low-carb alternative to couscous or rice. Once made, you can eat it raw or fry it up and add any vegetables, herbs and spices you fancy – the recipe below is just a suggestion. If you make more couscous than you need, you can freeze it raw.

Half a head cauliflower
2 handfuls of spinach
1 tbsp light olive or sunflower oil
2 spring onions
1 cooked beetroot
4 cherry tomatoes
2 tbsp sultanas
½ tsp garam masala
½ tsp paprika
1 tbsp chopped parsley
1 tbsp chopped oregano
1 tbsp capers
Salt and pepper

1. Prepare the cauliflower by slicing off the florets and putting into a food processor. Pulse until the consistency is similar to couscous, but be careful not to overdo it! Pour the blitzed cauliflower into a large bowl and remove any lumps that haven't been processed properly. Place them back in the food processor and pulse again.

2. Steam the spinach for a couple of minutes, and chop the rest of the vegetables.

3. Heat the oil in a large frying pan over a low/medium heat before adding the cauliflower couscous. Fry gently for 3 minutes, then add the spices and cook for a further 2 minutes.

4. Place the cooked couscous back in the bowl and add the spinach, raw vegetables, capers, herbs and sultanas along with a little salt and pepper. Mix together.

Parsnip, Orange and Chestnut Winter Salad, with Homemade Tahini Sauce

SERVES 2

An amazing and unusual festive salad!

2 parsnips

1 orange

Handful of chestnuts (pre-cooked)

2 tbsp avocado or sunflower oil

1 tbsp of black cracked peppercorns
or rainbow peppercorns

Homemade tahini sauce

FOR THE TAHINI SAUCE

3 tbsp tahini

3 tbsp water

1 garlic clove, crushed

1 tbsp lemon juice

Salt and pepper

TO MAKE THE SALAD

1. Preheat the oven to 180°C. Peel and core the parsnips, chopping into quarters or eighths.

2. Slice the orange into several fine segments and chop the chestnuts in half.

3. Arrange the parsnips on a large baking tray, drizzle with the oil, and add the slices of orange. Sprinkle the peppercorns over the top.

4. Place in the oven for 30 minutes, before adding the chestnuts and returning to the oven for a further 10.

5. Once cooked, serve warm and drizzled with the tahini sauce.

TO MAKE THE TAHINI SAUCE

1. In a small jar, add the tahini, water, garlic and lemon juice and shake thoroughly.

2. Taste before seasoning with salt and pepper, and shake again.

Apple and Oat Cookie-cakes

MAKES 18

Chewy and zesty, crunchy on top with a soft centre
– the perfect accompaniment to a cup of rooibos tea.

60g wholemeal flour
60g plain flour
100g rolled oats
130g brown sugar
½ tbsp cornflour
½ tsp baking powder
¼ tsp salt
¼ tsp cinnamon or mixed spice
4 tbsp flavourless oil
4 tbsp vegan milk
1 small or medium apple
50g sultanas (optional)

1. Preheat the oven to 170°C and line a baking tray with parchment paper.

2. Combine all of the dry ingredients in a large bowl. Make a well in the centre of the mixture and pour in the oil and milk. Stir together.

3. Peel and core the apple and chop into small pieces before folding it into the mixture with the sultanas (if desired).

4. Drop heaped tablespoon-sized blobs of the mixture onto the baking tray, allowing them to settle into round cookie-like shapes. Bake for 15-20 minutes, or until the edges are lightly browned. For a crunchier cookie you can bake for up to 30 minutes.

RESOURCES

What follows is a selection of resources and further reading that we've found useful and inspirational.

Organisations

Garden Organic

is a charity that brings together thousands of people who share a common belief – that organic growing is essential for a healthy and sustainable world. Through campaigning, advice, community work and research, their aim is to get everyone growing 'the organic way'.
www.gardenorganic.org.uk

GreenSpirit

is a network of people who celebrate the human spirit in the context of our place in the natural world and Earth's own evolutionary journey. Their radical vision brings together the rigour of science, the creativity of artistic expression, the passion of social action and the wisdom of spiritual traditions of all ages. Attracting those of many faith traditions, they are a body of people who believe that human life has both an ecological and a spiritual dimension.
www.greenspirit.org.uk

PETA

(People for the Ethical Treatment of Animals) produce a free 'Vegan Starter Kit' full of useful information and suggestions.
www.peta.org.uk

Permaculture Association

is a registered charity founded in 1983. They support members and the public with advice, support, information and training about the theory and practice of permaculture.
www.permaculture.org.uk

The Soil Association

As the UK's leading food and farming charity and organic certification body, The Soil Association works to save our soils and make good food the easy choice for everyone.
www.soilassociation.org

The Vegan Society

Their mission is to make veganism mainstream. They work to achieve this by providing information, supporting and advising individuals and health professionals, caterers and manufacturers, and influencing policy makers. They also fund vegan initiatives set up by members and supporters, and work with volunteers and partners towards making their vision a reality. They also work with the media to help reinforce a positive view of veganism and to help a larger audience see that veganism is a rewarding, enjoyable and viable lifestyle.
www.vegansociety.com

Vegan Organic Network

was founded in 1996. VON is an ambitious UK registered charity with an international network of active supporters. Their aims are to research and promote vegan organic (also known as stockfree organic) methods of agriculture and horticulture throughout the world, so that green, clean and cruelty-free food becomes widely available.
www.veganorganic.net

VIVA!

are very active in campaigning against animal cruelty, plus delivering excellent nutritional advice. They have produced The Incredible Vegan Health Report (what science and experience say about vegan diets and human health), packed full of the latest findings with many scientific references. It can be downloaded free from: www.vivahealth.org.uk/veganhealth/report
www.viva.org.uk

Blogs/Websites

There are many thousands of vegan blogs, websites and social media groups on various platforms, and the number grows daily! Here are just a few we have found useful:

Deliciously Ella

is a hugely popular blog by the author of the book of the same name, which was the fastest-selling debut cookbook of all time! The focus is on diet for health – and it's all vegan.
www.deliciouslyella.com

Essential Vegan

Vanessa Almeida is a Brazilian vegan chef based in London. Her desire is to educate and inspire others in the kitchen.
www.essentialvegan.uk

Nutritionfacts.org

The latest in nutrition-related research delivered in easy to understand video segments brought to you by Dr. Michael Greger MD.

Oh She Glows

is filled with creative vegan recipes, mouth-watering photos and a heart-on-her-sleeve writing style.
www.ohsheglows.com

The Vegan Apprentice

has a mission to spread veganism through education and community and to build a hub for all things vegan, including the lifestyle that comes with it.
http://theveganapprentice.blogspot.co.uk

Vegan Family House

from Scotland includes recipes, book reviews, photos and more.
www.veganfamily.co.uk

Vegan Sidekick

makes comics explaining why it is absurd to defend animal abuse.
http://vegansidekick.com and www.facebook.com/vegansidekick

YouTube Channels

Many vegan activists have harnessed the power of posting short films to YouTube, an effective way of reaching people and getting their message across. There are numerous channels, some of which have many thousands of subscribers. Here are a few of our favourites:

Anneka Svenska (GreenWorldTV)

works with animals in conservation, exploring wildlife crime and supporting vegan and animal charities.
www.youtube.com/channel/UCfsRp0AAJQII4EIfZeVoeRw

Ask Yourself

shares and creates videos on whatever is currently on his mind – strong vegan focus.
www.youtube.com/channel/UCQNmHyGAKqzOT_JsVEs4eag

Banana Warrior Princess

is a UK-based online activist, showing you how easy it is to go vegan overnight with minimal effort required.
www.youtube.com/channel/UCKZIqLWqUgW541ldU_MNmkA

Bite Size Vegan

Learn about veganism and the many interconnected issues within the vegan world. Vegan education in the form of 'vegan nugget' videos with loads of information distilled down to fast, powerful clips.
www.youtube.com/user/BiteSizeVegan

Earthling Ed

is passionate about saving the planet and non-human animals and creates content to be used as educational resources related to veganism.
www.youtube.com/channel/UCVRrGAcUc7cblUzOhI1KfFg

Erin Janus

is a passionate vegan, activist, writer, journalist, video producer and aspiring musician.
www.youtube.com/user/erinsotherstuff

Finding Gemma

shares her journey of health and spiritualism.
www.youtube.com/channel/UCDsNofehuLc_mnGMG5fU3rQ

Freelee the Banana Girl

runs a hugely popular channel critiquing various other diets, giving advice, and promoting veganism.
www.youtube.com/user/Freelea

Gary Yourofsky

The official YouTube channel of vegan animal liberation activist, Gary Yourofsky. Gary has given thousands of lectures and is often quoted as a major factor for people becoming vegan.
www.youtube.com/channel/UCLW0TEV3YEt-J56pYZm-TgA

Hench Herbivore

is a personal trainer and nutritional advisor specialising in veganism. He aims to show the world that animals need not suffer in order for us to reach ultimate health and fitness.
www.youtube.com/channel/UC2ZWX3GJfAIeRFWN91t09ww

Plant Based News!

contains news about animal rights, ethical consumerism, food trends and more.
www.youtube.com/channel/UCJRjK20fHyIJyf-HiBtqI2w

The Vegan Activist

creates excellent educational videos, inspiring short films and powerful documentaries about veganism and activism.
www.youtube.com/channel/UCE0yGL4Bgs2QNomOrslyLtw
He has also produced the excellent *Complete Guide to Vegan Food* which can be viewed at www.youtube.com/watch?v=htf5eCgyt5Q plus can be downloaded as a free eBook.

The Vegetable Police

is a health based comedy channel with a lot of practical tips to help you overcome your diseases, lose weight, get rid of acne and slow the aging process!
www.youtube.com/user/canadianwargod

Vegan Geezer

Thrown by the details? Confused by the science? Feel it's miles away from your thinking? Vegan Geezer likes to tell it how it is: no nonsense, no tricks, just truth – in a way we can all relate to.
www.youtube.com/user/VeganGeezer

Vegan Speak

Empowering others to speak up against institutionalised animal abuse.
www.youtube.com/channel/UCHzHZkCwYjRfDjts4O9OL1Q

Many of these channels have associated Facebook pages with frequent activity and numerous followers.

Magazines

Ethical Consumer
Each issue features detailed product guides, news of ethical products and campaigns, in-depth features, opinion, comment, boycott updates, readers' letters, and more. Discover the truth behind the products we buy and the companies we buy them from.
www.ethicalconsumer.org

Growing Green International
is the twice-yearly magazine published by the Vegan Organic Network, and is free to members. It reflects a broad range of information and opinions, covering the 'why' and the 'how' of vegan organic growing, featuring a mixture of articles that cover practical, technical and ethical issues, as well as hints and tips.
www.veganorganic.net/growing-green-international

Grow Your Own
provides a monthly guide to edible crops to grow in your garden or allotment and how to do it. Issues often include free packets of seeds.
www.growfruitandveg.co.uk

Permaculture magazine – earth care, people care, future care
Full of articles, reviews and lists of courses on all things permaculture, from all over the world.
www.permaculture.co.uk

Plant Based
is more than just a collection of recipes; it also includes lots of information about plant-based ingredients and techniques, produced by the team behind Vegan Life.
www.plantbasedmag.com

Vegan Food and Living
magazine is dedicated to celebrating the vegan lifestyle. Every issue is packed with 75 tasty recipes, plus informative features which resonate with all vegans.
www.veganfoodandliving.com

Vegan Life
aims to encompass social, economic, ecological and political considerations to assist in bringing about a change in attitudes by encouraging the adoption of a plant-based diet, bringing Vegan into Vogue.
www.veganlifemag.com

Books

101 Uses for Stinging Nettles (Wildeye, 2006) by Piers Warren explores the diverse uses of this fascinating plant – in the garden and the kitchen, for their medical and fibrous properties, and so on. It is packed with practical suggestions, as well as a guide to the botany of stinging nettles, and how to collect and store them.

Forest Gardening in Practice: An Illustrated Practical Guide for Homes, Communities and Enterprises (Permanent Publications, 2017) by Tomas Remiarz is an in-depth review of forest gardening with living, best practice examples. It highlights the four core skills of forest gardeners: ecology, horticulture, design and cooperation.

Growing Green (The Vegan Organic Network, 2010) by Jenny Hall and Iain Tolhurst is a reference guide for organic growers, gardeners, researchers and students. The book introduces the concept of stockfree organic and shows, through case studies, that when growers abandon slaughterhouse by products and manures, they can be rewarded with healthy crops. The reader is taken through each organic standard step by step and learns how to grow and sell 60 different vegetables with confidence.

How Not to Die (Macmillan, 2016) by Michael Greger MD gives effective, scientifically-proven nutritional advice to prevent our biggest killers – heart disease, breast cancer, prostate cancer, high blood pressure and diabetes – and reveals the astounding health benefits that simple dietary choices can provide.

How to Make a Forest Garden (Permanent Publications, 2012) by Patrick Whitefield is a step-by-step guide to creating a maximum output for minimum labour food producing garden, designed using the ecological principles of a natural woodland.

How to Store Your Garden Produce – The Key to Self-sufficiency (Green Books, 2008) by Piers Warren is packed with ideas for making your produce last for months and to help you embrace the wonderful world of self-sufficiency. Includes simple and enjoyable techniques for bottling, clamping, fermenting, drying, freezing and salting, as well as delicious recipes for jams, jellies, pickles and chutneys, relishes and ketchups and fruit butters and cheeses.

Sort Out Your Soil is a guide to using green manures produced by Garden Organic and Cotswold Seeds. It's available free as a PDF download or printed booklet via www.gardenorganic.org.uk/green-manures

The China Study (BenBella, 2006) by Dr T. Colin Campbell and Thomas M. Campbell II, details the connection between nutrition and heart disease, diabetes and cancer. The report also examines the source of nutritional confusion produced by powerful lobbies, government entities and opportunistic scientists.

The Forest Garden Greenhouse (Chelsea Green Publishing, 2015) by Jerome Osentowski shows how bringing the forest garden indoors is not only possible, but doable on unlikely terrain and in cold climates, using near net-zero technology. Different from other books on greenhouse design and management, this book advocates for an indoor agriculture, using permaculture design concepts, integration, multi-functions, perennials and polycultures, that take season extension into new and important territory.

The Sprouters Handbook (Argyll Publishing, 2011) by Edward Cairney is packed with sprouting methods, nutritional information, charts and recipes.

The Vegan Book of Permaculture (Permanent Publications, 2014) by Graham Burnett demonstrates how understanding universal patterns and principles – and applying these to our own gardens and lives – can make a very real difference to both ourselves and the health of our planet. Interspersed with an abundance of delicious, healthy and wholesome exploitation-free recipes, Graham provides solutions-based approaches to nurturing personal effectiveness and health, eco-friendly living, home and garden design, veganic food growing, reafforestation strategies, forest gardening, reconnection with wild nature, and community regeneration, with plenty of practical ways to be well fed with not an animal dead!

World Peace Diet (Lantern Books, 2016) by Dr Will Tuttle is a bestselling, in-depth study of our food and culture with a spiritual thread throughout.

Documentaries/Movies

Carnage from the BBC directed by Simon Amstell. It's 2067, the UK is vegan, but older generations are suffering the guilt of their carnivorous past. Simon Amstell asks us to forgive them for the horrors of what they swallowed. Excellent and hilarious mockumentary.
Available on BBC iPlayer.

Cowspiracy is a groundbreaking feature-length environmental documentary, following film-maker Kip Andersen as he uncovers the most destructive industry facing the planet today, and investigates why the world's leading environmental organisations are too afraid to talk about it. Although some of the statistics in the film are questionable, the message is sound.
www.cowspiracy.com

Earthlings is a hard-hitting documentary about humankind's total dependence on animals for economic purposes.
www.nationearth.com/earthlings

Forks Over Knives examines the profound claim that most, if not all of the degenerative diseases that afflict us, can be controlled or even reversed by rejecting animal based and processed foods.
www.forksoverknives.com/the-film

These last three films together make a great package as between them they cover environment, ethics and health.

Festivals

There are increasing numbers of vegan festivals and events throughout the world. Many of those in the UK are promoted and supported by

Vegfest

who also organise some of the biggest British vegan festivals. In particular there are major Vegfest festivals in Brighton, Bristol, London and Glasgow. Their website is a great resource of information about many different vegan events including festivals organised by other people which are springing up in cities all over the UK.
www.vegfest.co.uk

The annual Vegan Abundance Festival

is organised by Vegan Organic Network (www.veganorganic.net/upcoming-events), and includes workshops, talks, stalls and much more.

Courses

Vegan Permaculture Design Certificate is a course adapted from the 72-hour international Permaculture Design Course syllabus, and is accredited by the Permaculture Association (Britain). It covers universal permaculture ethics, principles and design methods. The focus, however, is on non-animal based and stockfree systems and alternatives to animal exploitation.

spiralseed.co.uk/vegan-permaculture
and www.emptycagesdesign.org/vegan-permaculture-design-course

Other courses and events are listed on the Vegan Organic Network page www.veganorganic.net/upcoming-events

Suppliers

The Organic Gardening Catalogue
suppliers of organic seeds and plants
www.organiccatalogue.com

Garden Organic
runs a Heritage Seed Library
www.gardenorganic.org.uk/hsl

Suma
is the UK's largest independent whole food wholesaler/distributor, specialising in vegetarian, fairly traded, organic, ethical and natural products. They are a workers' co-operative committed to ethical business.
www.suma.coop

INDEX

Recipes
Aloo Gobi 146
Apple and Blackberry Crumble 138
Apple and Oat Cookie-cakes 230
Arrabbiata Tomato Sauce 176
Artichoke and Broccoli Pizza 142
Asparagus Quiche 172
Asparagus Spanakopita 164
Asparagus with Vegan Hollandaise Sauce 152
Beetroot Brownies 128
Blueberry Flan 198
Broad Bean Risotto 162
Butternut Squash Pasta 218
Caponata 208
Carrot Cake with Macadamia and Cashew Icing 118
Cauliflower Couscous 226
Cauliflower Steak with Tomato Sauce and Caper Relish 136
Celeriac Mash 116
Chocolate and Strawberry Cake 178
Creamy Leek and Mushroom Pasta Sauce 124
Crunchy Baked Kale 134
Easy-Peasy Grape Ice Cream 220
Fig and Dark Chocolate Tart 210
French Beans with Crispy Shallots and Toasted Almonds 184
Green Houmous 196
Homemade Baked Beans 216
Homemade Vegan Gravy 204
Leek, Mushroom and Potato Pie 112
Lentil and Spinach Burger 156
Lentil, Split Pea and Sun-dried Tomato Bolognese 114
Nectarine Delight 188
New Potato and Chickpea Stew 154

Parsnip Hash Browns 126
Parsnip, Orange and Chestnut Winter Salad, with Homemade Tahini Sauce 228
Pumpkin Soup 214
Purple Sprouting Broccoli Spring Salad 132
Raspberry Truffles 168
Ratatouille 194
Red Currant Shortbread 158
Rhubarb and Orange Sorbet 148
Saint's Love Soup 206
Spinach and Pea Gnocchi 174
Spitfire Sauce 186
Sprouting Broccoli Gratin with Homemade Vegan Parmesan 122
Stuffed Aubergine 182
Swede, Sweet Potato and Bean Goulash 224
Sweet Potato Shepherd's Pie 202
Vegan Arancini 144
Vegan Paella with Artichoke Hearts 192
Walnut Pesto 166

aduki beans 52
agave nectar 32
agriculture 7, 17, 18
alfalfa 52
alliums 15
    see also chives, garlic, leeks, onions
allotments 21, 22
allspice 37
almonds 35, 104
    with French beans and shallots 184
    and oil 31
    and sprouting 52
aloo gobi 146
amaranth 33
animal products 7, 31

animal welfare 3, 5
anise 37
annual calendar 55-61
    and cooking 109
    see also individual months
annuals
    herbs 41
aphids 13, 15
apples 63
    and blackberry crumble 138
    and juice concentrate 32
    and oat cookie-cakes 230
    and seed saving 27
apricots 64
April 57
    recipes 141-9
area 21, 22
arrabbiata tomato sauce 166
artichokes 57, 61, 64-5
    and broccoli pizza 142
    hearts with paella 192
Asian leaves lettuce 48
asparagus 60, 66
    quiche 162
    spanakopita 164
    with vegan hollandaise sauce 152
aubergine 66-7
    stuffed 182
August 59
    recipes 181-9
avocado oil 30

bakes
    asparagus spanakopita 164
    crunchy kale 134
    sprouting broccoli gratin 122
baking 30
    see also biscuits, cakes
barley 33
barriers 14
base maps 19
basil 42
batavia lettuce 48
bats 13
bay 42

beans 68-70
  and dried 34
    homemade baked 216
    and seed saving 27
    and swede and sweet potato
      goulash 224
    see also broad beans, soya
      beans, sprouting
beauty products 5
bees 8, 31-2
beetles 13, 14
    and asparagus 66
    and flea 85, 93
beetroot 70
    brownies 128
biodiversity 7, 12
birds 13, 14
    see also pigeons
biscuits
    apple and oat 230
    red currant shortbread 158
black pepper 37
black plastic 10
blackberry and apple crumble
    138
blight 58, 91, 98-9
blogs 233-4
blueberries 101
    flan 198
bonechar 31
books 235-6
bottling 26
bouillon 39
brambles 12
brassicas 12
    and pests 14, 58
    see also broccoli, Brussels
      sprouts, cabbage,
      cauliflower, kale, pak choi
Brazil nuts 35
broad beans 57, 58, 67-8
    risotto 30, 162
broccoli 71
    and artichoke pizza 142
    gratin with vegan parmesan
      122
    and predators 14
    saint's love soup 206
    spring salad 132
    and sprouting 52
brown rice syrup 32

brown rot 87
brown sugar 32
brownies 128
Brussels sprouts 71
buckwheat 33
    and sprouting 52
bulgur wheat 33
burgers
    lentil and spinach 156
butterflies 14
butterhead lettuce 48
butternut squash pasta 218

cabbage 72, 76
    see also root fly
cakes
    apple and oat 230
    beetroot brownies 128
    carrot with macadamia and
      cashew icing 118
    chocolate and strawberry
      168
calabrese *see* broccoli
calcium 3, 4
canes 57, 58, 68
caper relish 136
caponata 208
capsicum peppers 88-9
caraway 37
carbohydrates 4
carbon footprint 5, 7
cardamom 38
cardboard 10
carrots 55, 73
    cake with macadamia and
      cashew icing 118
    see also root fly
cashews 35
    icing with carrot cake 118
    vegan cream 124
    vegan parmesan 122
catalogues 22
cauliflower 73-4
    aloo gobi 146
    couscous 226
    saint's love soup 206
    steak with tomato sauce and
      caper relish 136
celeriac 60, 74
    mash 116
celery 74-5

centipedes 13
chard 75
'cheese'
    cashew 142, 164
    vegan parmesan 122
cherries 75-6
chestnuts 35, 104
    parsnip and orange salad
      with tahini 228
chia 36
chickpeas 52, 102
    green houmous 196
    and potato stew 154
chicory 49
chilli peppers 38, 89-90
    spitfire sauce 186
Chinese cabbage 76
chives 42
chlorophyll 10
chocolate
    beetroot brownies 128
    and fig tart 210
    raspberry truffles 168
    and strawberry cake 168
chutney 26
    apple 63
    gooseberry 81
    green tomato 98
    plum 90
    see also relishes
cider 63
cinnamon 38
citrus plants 102-3
climate change 3, 5
    and ingredients 29
climbers 19
cloches 14, 23, 24
clothing 5
cloves 38
coconuts 35
    and oil 31
    and sugar 32
coffee grounds 103-4
cold frames 23, 24
comfrey 11, 57
companion planting 15
compost 8-9, 10
    and salad leaves 47
    and teas 11
conservatories 23
containers 18, 22

cooking
  and asparagus 66
  and aubergine 67
  and broad beans 67-8
  and French beans 69
  and squashes 93
  and turnips 99
  see also individual recipes
coriander 38, 41, 42
corn 30, 33
  see also sweet corn
cos lettuce 48
courgettes 76-7
courses 19, 236
couscous 33
creamy leek and mushroom
  pasta sauce 124
cress 49
crisphead lettuce 48
crop rotation 11-12
crunchy baked kale 134
cucumber 77
cumin 38, 42
currants 78
  red currant shortbread 158
curries
  aloo gobi 146
cuttings 41

dairy industry 3, 4-5
dandelions 12
date nectar 32
December 61
  recipes 223-31
deforestation 5, 29
dehydrators 24
design 19
desserts
  apple and blackberry crumble
  138
  blueberry flan 198
  fig and dark chocolate tart
  210
  nectarine delight 188
  see also ice cream, sorbet
diet 21
dill 42
documentaries 236
drying 24
  and apples 63
  and beans 69, 70

and broad beans 68
and cherries 76
and chickpeas 102
and chilli peppers 89-90
and figs 78
and herbs 41
and mushrooms 104
and peaches 87
and peas 88
and soya beans 107
and strawberries 96
and sweet corn 97
and tomatoes 99

earth care 17
easy-peasy grape ice cream 220
ecosystems 10, 13
egg industry 3
endive 49
engevita 39
equipment
  sprouting 51
ethics 17

farm shops 29
fats 4
February 56
  and recipes 121-9
feeds 11, 57, 58
fennel 38, 42
  see also Florence fennel
fenugreek 53
fertilisers 11
festivals 236
fibre 4
figs 78
  and dark chocolate tart 210
fishing industry 3
flaxseed 31, 36
fleece 14, 23
Florence fennel 79
flowering plants 15
food miles 29
forest gardening 19, 24
fossil fuels 7
freezing 24, 26
  and apples 63
  and beans 70
  and blueberries 101
  and broad beans 68
  and Brussels sprouts 71

and celery 75
and cherries 76
and chickpeas 102
and courgettes 77
and currants 78
and Florence fennel 79
and gooseberries 80
and herbs 41
and kale 83
and leeks 83
and mushrooms 104
and parsnips 86
and peas 88
and peppers 89
and raspberries 94
and rhubarb 95
and soya beans 107
and spinach 95
and strawberries 96
and swede 97
and sweet corn 97
and tomatoes 99
French beans 68-9
  with shallots and almonds
  184
French marigold 15
frogs 13
frost 23
fructose 31, 32
fruit 22
  and cages 14
  and jam 26-7
  and January 55
  and storage 24
  and trees 58, 59
  see also apples, apricots,
    blueberries, cherries,
    citrus plants, currants,
    figs, gooseberries, grapes,
    melon, nectarines,
    oranges, peaches, pears,
    plums, raspberries, rhubarb,
    strawberries

garam masala 38
Garden Organic 18, 101, 233
gardens 21-2
garlic 79-80
ginger 38, 103
globe artichokes 57, 61, 64-5
glucose 31, 32

glyphosate 8
gnocchi
   spinach and pea 164
goals 18
golden syrup 32
gooseberries 80-1
grains 33
grapes 61, 82
   ice cream 220
gravy 204
green houmous 196
green lentils 52
green manure 10, 12, 60
greenfly 58
greengrocers 29
greenhouses 23-4, 66-7
   May 57
   June-July 58
   October 60
   November 61
GreenSpirit 233
ground cover 19
groundnut oil 31
growing 7-8
   and choice 22
   and under cover 23-4, 47-8
   and through the year 55-61

harvesting
   January 55
   February 56
   March 56
   April 57
   May 57
   June 58
   July 58
   August 59
   September 60
   October 60
   November 61
   December 61
   and apples 63
   and apricots 64
   and artichokes 65
   ash browns 126
hazelnuts 35, 104
health benefits 3-4, 5, 7, 12
   and herbs 41
hedgehogs 13
heirloom varieties 18, 101
hemp 31, 36

herbicides 7-8
herbs 15, 30, 41-5
   and location 17
   and salads 47
heritage varieties see heirloom
   varieties
high fructose corn syrup (HFCS)
   32
hoeing 12
homemade baked beans 216
homemade vegan gravy 204
honey 31-2
houmous 34, 196
household products 5
hoverflies 13

ice cream
   grape 220
Incredible Vegan Health Report,
   The 4
ingredients 29-30, 109
intercropping 12
iron 4
Italian blend lettuce 48

jam 26-7
   apple 63
   apricot 64
   gooseberry 80
   plum 90
   strawberry 96
January
   and recipes 111-19
Jerusalem artichokes 61, 65
jobs
   January 55
   February 56
   March 56
   April 57
   May 57
   June 58
   July 58
   August 59
   September 60
   October 60
   November 61
   December 61
juices
   and apple concentrate 32
   and beetroot 70
   and black currant 78

   and grapes 82
   and wheatgrass 51, 53
July 58
   recipes 171-9
June 58
   recipes 161-9

kale 82-3
   crunchy baked 134

lacewings 13
ladybirds 13
lambs lettuce 49
lavender 43
leaf mould 9, 10, 60
leeks 83
   and mushroom and potato
   pie 112
   and mushroom pasta sauce
   124
legumes 12, 34
   see also beans, chickpeas,
   lentils, peas
lemon balm 43
lentils 34
   and spinach burger 156
   and split pea and sun-dried
   tomato bolognese 114
   and sprouting 52
lettuce 48
livestock industry 3, 4-5, 17
location 17-18
loose leaf lettuce 48

macadamia nuts 36
   icing with carrot cake 118
magazines 235
mail-order organic wholesalers 29
maintenance 19, 56
   see also jobs
maize *see* corn
maple syrup 32
March 56
   recipes 131-9
margarine 29, 30
marjoram 43-4
marrow 93
May 57
   recipes 151-9
melon 84
mesh 14, 23

milk 3-4
millet 33
minerals 4
mint 15, 44
miso 35
mixed lettuce 48
molasses 32
mulch 9-10, 17, 61
    and apples 63
multisalad lettuce 48
mung beans 53
muscovado sugar 32
mushrooms 103-4
    and leek and potato pie 112
    and leek pasta sauce 124
mustard 38, 49

nasturtiums 15
nectarines 86-7
    delight 188
neonicotinoids 8
netting 14, 57
nettles 11, 12, 57
new potato and chickpea stew
    154
newts 14
nitrogen 10
no-dig method 10
November 61
    recipes 213-21
nutmeg 38
nutrition 4
nuts 35-6, 104-5
    tamari 132

oats 33
    and apple cookie-cakes 230
October 60
    recipes 201-11
oils 30-1
olive oil 31
olives 30
omega 3 4
onion white rot 83, 85
onions 15, 22, 84-5
    and drying 59
    and storage 24
oranges
    parsnip and chestnut salad
    with tahini 228
    and rhubarb sorbet 148

oregano 43-4
organic growing 7-8
Oriental leaves 49
oxidisation 65

pak choi 85
palm oil 29, 31
paprika 38
parsley 44
parsnips 60, 86
    hash browns 126
    orange and chestnut salad
    with tahini 228
pasta
    butternut squash 218
    leek and mushroom sauce
    124
    lentil, split pea and tomato
    bolognese 114
pea shoots 49
peaches 86-7
peanuts 36
pears 87
peas 88
    and dried 34
    and seed saving 27
    and spinach gnocchi 164
    and sprouting 53
pecan nuts 36
people care 17
peppers 88-90
    and seed saving 27
    spitfire sauce 186
perennials 19
    and herbs 41
permaculture 7, 17-19
Permaculture Association
    233
pesticides 7-8, 13
pesto
    walnut 166
pests 12-15
    and aubergine 67
    and broad beans 67
    and cabbage 72, 76
    see also beetles, root fly,
    slugs, snails
PETA 233
piccalilli 74
pick-your-own (PYO) enterprises
    29

pickling 26
    and beetroot 70
    and courgettes 77
    and cucumbers 77
    and mushrooms 104
    and onions 85
    and peppers 89
    and radish 94
    and red cabbage 72
pies
    leek, mushroom and potato
    112
    sweet potato shepherd's 202
pigeons 12, 14, 69
pine nuts 36
pizza
    artichoke and broccoli 142
planning 17, 18-19
    and quantities 22
plant teas 11
planting
    January 55
    February 56
    March 56
    April 57
    September 60
    October 60
    December 61
planting out
    April 57
    May 57
    June 58
    July 58
    August 59
    September 60
plums 90
polyculture 12
polytunnels 23
pomegranate seeds 36
ponds 13, 14
poppy seeds 36
potatoes 12, 22-3, 91
    aloo gobi 146
    and blight 58, 91
    and chickpea stew 154
    and chitting 55
    gnocchi with spinach and
    peas 164
    and harvesting 57
    and leek and mushroom pie
    112

and saving 27
and storage 24
see also sweet potatoes
pots *see* containers
potting sheds 23
powdery mildew 76, 93
predators 13-14
preparation 56
protein 3, 4, 10
prunes 90
pruning 56, 58, 59, 61
and apples 63
and apricots 64
and cherries 75-6
and figs 78
and gooseberries 80
and grapes 82
and pears 87
and plums 90
and raspberries 94
pulses 34-5
pumpkins 10, 93
and seeds 27, 36
soup 214
and sprouting 53
purple sprouting broccoli
spring salad 132

quantities 22
quinoa 33, 105

rabbits 14
radish 53, 93-4
raisins 82
rapeseed oil 31
raspberries 94
truffles 168
ratatouille 194
raw food 5
recipes 30
see also individual months,
recipes
red clover 53
red currant shortbread 158
red pepper relish 89
red spider mite 67, 78, 88-9
relishes
caper 136
piccalilli 74
red pepper 89
relocation 14-15

resources 233-6
rhubarb 60, 95
and 'forced' 55
and orange sorbet 148
rice 33
broad bean risotto 30, 162
and cauliflower 74
paella with artichoke hearts
192
vegan arancini 144
rocket 49
root fly
and cabbage 71, 72, 76, 86,
96, 99
and carrot 14, 15
root vegetables 12, 19
and storage 24
see also beetroot, carrots,
celeriac, fennel, ginger,
parsnips, potatoes,
swede, turnips
rootstock 63
runner beans 69-70
rye 33

sacrificial plants 15
saffron 38
sage 45
saint's love soup 206
salad leaves 17-18, 22, 47-9
salads
broccoli spring salad 132
parsnip, orange and chestnut
228
sauces
arrabbiata tomato 166
hollandaise 152
mint 44
spitfire 186
tahini 184, 228
tomato 136, 142
sauerkraut 72
savory 45
sclerotina 65
seaweed extract 11, 58
seeds
and edible 36
and herbs 41
and saving 27
and sprouting 52-3
seitan 35

self-sufficiency 21-7
September 60
recipes 191-9
sesame oil 31
sesame seeds 36
shallots
with French beans and
almonds 184
shrubs 19
slow worms 14
slugs 14, 15, 57, 69
snails 14-15, 57, 69
soil
and fertility 7, 8, 10
and rotation 11-12
Soil Association 233
sorbet
rhubarb and orange 148
soups
pumpkin 214
saint's love 206
sowing 22-3, 48
January 55
February 56
March 56
April 57
May 57
June 58
July 58
August 59
September 60
October 60
soy sauce 35
soya beans 35, 107
spelt 33
spices 30, 37-9
spicy greens lettuce 48
spinach 95
and lentil burger 156
and pea gnocchi 164
spitfire sauce 186
split peas
and lentil and tomato
bolognese 114
spreads 30
sprouting 51-3
sprouting broccoli gratin with
homemade vegan parmesan
122
squashes 59, 60, 93
see also butternut squash,

courgettes, pumpkins
stacking 17
staking 60
stevia 32
stews
    caponata 208
    new potato and chickpea 154
    swede, sweet potato and bean goulash 224
stockfree organic growing 7
storage 21, 24, 26-7
    May 57
    August 59
    September 60
    October 60
    November 61
    December 61
    and apples 63
    and apricots 64
    and asparagus 66
    and aubergine 67
    and beetroot 70
    and Brussels sprouts 71
    and cabbage 72, 76
    and carrots 73
    and celeriac 74
    and citrus plants 103
    and garlic 80
    and ginger 103
    and herbs 41
    and melon 84
    and nuts 105
    and onions 85
    and parsnips 86
    and plums 90
    and potatoes 91
    and quinoa 105
    and radish 94
    and squashes 93
    and swede 97
    and sweet potatoes 107
    and turnips 99
    see also drying, freezing, pickling
strawberries 10, 96
    and chocolate cake 168
stuffed aubergine 182
successional sowing 22-3
sugar 31, 32, 33
sunflower oil 30

sunflower seeds 36, 53
supermarkets 29
suppliers 236
sustainability 7
    and palm oil 29
swede 96-7
    and sweet potato and bean goulash 224
sweet corn 97
sweet potatoes 107
shepherd's pie 202
    and swede and bean goulash 224
sweeteners 30, 31-3
sweets
    raspberry truffles 168
Swiss chard see chard
syrups 32

tahini sauce 184, 228
tamarind 39
tarragon 45
tarts
    asparagus quiche 172
    fig and dark chocolate 210
teas 11
tempeh 35
thistles 12
through the year 55-61
    and cooking 109
    see also individual months
thyme 45
toads 13
tofu 35
tomatoes 18, 98-9
    arrabbiata sauce 166
    and pinching out 58
    sauce 136, 142
    and seed saving 27
    sun-dried with lentil and split pea bolognese 114
treacle 32
trees 19
and nuts 104-5
truffles 168
turmeric 39
turnips 99

vanilla 39
veg-box schemes 29
vegan arancini 144

vegan organic agriculture 7
Vegan Organic Network 233
vegan paella with artichoke hearts 192
Vegan Society 4, 5, 233
vegetables see artichokes, asparagus, aubergine, brassicas, celery, chard, cucumber, leeks, legumes, mushrooms, onions, peppers, root vegetables, spinach, squashes, sweet corn, tomatoes
vinegars 41
vitamins: B12 4, 30
VIVA! 233

walnuts 104-5
    oil 31
    pesto 166
websites 233-4
weeds 10, 12
weevils 67
weights, measures and temperatures 109
what to grow 22
wheat 33
    and sprouting 53
Whole Food Plant-Based (WFPB) diets 4
wigwams 57
wildlife 13-14
windowsills 22, 23, 41
winter lettuce 48
world hunger 5
worm composting 9

yeast flakes 39
YouTube 234-5

zoning 17-18

Enjoyed this book?
You might like these

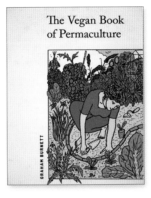

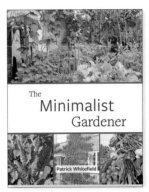

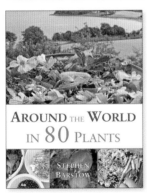

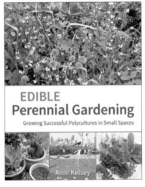

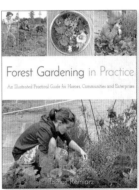

Get 15% off any of our other books above with
discount code: **VEGAN-COOK**
Just visit **www.green-shopping.co.uk**

Our titles cover: permaculture, home & garden, green
building, food & drink, sustainable technology,
woodlands, community, wellbeing and so much more

See our full range of books here:

www.permanentpublications.co.uk

Subscribe to a better world

Each issue of *Permaculture Magazine International* is hand crafted, sharing practical, innovative solutions, money saving ideas and global perspectives from a grassroots movement in over 170 countries

Print subscribers receive FREE digital access to our complete 25 years of back issues plus bonus content

To subscribe call 01730 823 311 or visit:

www.permaculture.co.uk

See our North American specific edition at: **https://permaculturemag.org**